KU-169-980

Aspects of Educational and Training Technology

Volume XXII

Aspects of Educational and Training Technology
Volume XXII

Promoting Learning

Edited for the Association for Educational and Training Technology by

Chris Bell, Jim Davies and Ray Winders

Kogan Page, London
Nichols Publishing Company, New York

© The Association for Educational and Training Technology, 1989

All rights reserved. No reproduction, copy or transmission of this publication may be made without written permission.

No paragraph of this publication may be reproduced, copied or transmitted save with written permission or in accordance with the provisions of the Copyright Act 1956 (as amended), or under the terms of any licence permitting limited copying issued by the Copyright Licensing Agency, 7 Ridgmount Street, London WC1E 7AE.

Any person who does any unauthorised act in relation to this publication may be liable to criminal prosecution and civil claims for damages.

First published in Great Britain in 1989
by Kogan Page Ltd, 120 Pentonville Road, London N1 9JN

First published in the United States of America in 1989
by Nichols Publishing, an imprint of GP Publishing Inc.,
PO Box 96, New York, NY 10024

Typeset by DP Photosetting, Aylesbury, Bucks
Printed and bound in Great Britain by
Billings and Sons Ltd, Worcester

British Library Cataloguing in Publication Data

Aspects of educational and training technology
  Vol. 2
  1. Educational technology
  I. Bell, Chris   II. Davies, Jim   III. Winders, Ray
  IV. Association for Educational and Training Technology
  371.3′07′8

  ISBN 1-85091-775-2 (UK)
  ISBN 0-89397-339-4 (US)
  ISSN 0141-5956

ACC. No.

413963

W4
S/O   SL   £25.00

23 MAY 1989

371.3073 ASP

OXFORD POLYTECHNIC
LIBRARY

Contents

Index of contributors

Section 1:
Issues

1. Living dangerously: educational technology in the eighties

David Hawkridge, *Institute of Educational Technology, Open University, UK.*

Summary: This paper asserts that educational technology is alive and well in the eighties but is living dangerously. It reports on the health of four well-known 'personalities' in the British educational technology community:

- Computers in Schools
- the Council for Educational Technology
- Computers in Company Training
- the Institute of Educational Technology at the Open University.

Finally it offers a few prescriptions to be taken with plenty of water.

INTRODUCTION

My theme this morning is that educational technology is alive and well in the eighties, but living dangerously. Evidence of life is all around us here at this Conference. That we are living dangerously, here in Britain, is less obvious. I believe we are living dangerously because of what Malcolm Bradbury, the well-known professor, has called the Sado-Monetarism of the present Government. The Government's ideology leads it to take up attitudes towards education and training and indeed towards educational technology that make life dangerous for us.

This Government demands excellence but drives us towards expediency. It calls for accountability but obliges us to sacrifice long-term thinking for the sake of short-term action. It seeks value for money but ignores the need for social equity. In commanding and controlling it neglects to clarify its own policy and avoids the traditional channels of consultation.

Perhaps you are saying to yourself that you did not come to ETIC88 to listen to a political diatribe. You will not hear one. But I make no apology for bringing national politics into a keynote speech. If we educational technologists accept the systems approach we cannot ignore our political surroundings.

I want to be specific, however, rather than continue to make broad accusations. The evidence I shall put before you concerns the health of four well-known 'personalities' in the British educational technology community.

COMPUTERS IN SCHOOLS

Few would deny that educational technology (that is, the study of the systems, techniques and tools of education) received a huge fillip with the arrival of microcomputers in schools.

Almost from the beginning of the eighties, excitement ran high among us as we saw the possibilities. Computer-assisted learning always seemed in the seventies to be the province of researchers and mainframe computer boffins, not of teachers. The worthy National Development Programme for Computer Assisted Learning never set the Thames on fire. Suddenly in 1980 the prospect of living well, if dangerously, with the backing of the Government and big industry, seemed very attractive. Little did we realize how much the political and economic environment would become polluted.

The DES launched the Microelectronics in Education Programme (MEP), for England, Wales and Northern Ireland with benevolence and patronage; and cash for British-made microcomputers from the Department of Trade and Industry. There were smiles all round from its Minister of Information Technology, Kenneth Baker. In Scotland, the Scottish Microelectronics Development Programme (SMDP), under David Walker, was launched. Both MEP and SMDP were intended to cover teaching about microelectronics in schools and the introduction of microcomputers into teaching. Nobody knew exactly how long they would last but in 1980 we had not realized the Government's capacity to find cheap projects that yielded high political returns for a few years. And the battle was not yet joined between the Department of Education and Science, accustomed to longer-term funding, and the Manpower Services Commission, with its short sharp shocks and so-called commercial approach.

The MEP's plans were ambitious under its Director Richard Fothergill. The aim of the programme was to help schools prepare children for life in a society in which devices and systems based on microelectronics were commonplace and pervasive. Curriculum development, teacher training and resource organization and support were its three chosen areas of work (Fothergill, Anderson et al, 1983). In early 1985 the MEP was alive and well with a staff of 320 and had no less than 5 million a year to dispense. But it was living dangerously.

A year later the MEP was closed down. There was an awkward and damaging gap before its successor, the Microelectronics Education Support Unit (MESU), was established with a much smaller budget and fewer staff. Fothergill said afterwards, 'The gap had been very unfortunate, creating much uncertainty among the staff and in the teaching community and a loss of impetus from the original initiatives' (CET, 1987). I understand that MESU is still trying to recover from that hiatus, but more about MESU in a moment. The smaller Scottish programme, SMDP, with only a tenth of the budget of the MEP and a much smaller population to serve, fared better. It received continuous funding and became part of the Scottish Council for Educational Technology.

To summarize, we can say that micros in schools are alive and well, but surprisingly so considering the stop-go funding from the Government for hardware, software and teacher training. It seems inconceivable that micros in schools could die, but the programme lives dangerously with its future by no means guaranteed.

THE COUNCIL FOR EDUCATIONAL TECHNOLOGY

The Council for Educational Technology (CET) has been a feature of the landscape for a long time, so long that some people may think of it as not living dangerously at all! Under Geoffrey Hubbard it pursued quite healthily for about 15 years its functions of promoting and developing applications of educational technology. Only towards the end of Hubbard's reign did real danger loom: the Education Departments which support CET cut its grant by one-third in the early 1980s then appointed Terrence Price, from the Nuclear Energy Inspectorate, as a one-person review commission. Price noted that CET was 'no longer the sole occupant of its professional territory' and that 'substantial initiatives, involving resources considerably larger than those available to CET' had been launched 'with no more than CET's peripheral involvement' (Price, 1985). Apprehension followed about fallout from his surprisingly expansionist findings which were delivered to the Government and CET in June 1985. A long period of deliberation and reorientation began during which the health of CET can probably be described as shaky. Hubbard retired in January 1986 to be succeeded by Richard Fothergill, of former MEP fame.

A change in the Chairmanship of the Council also occurred in 1986, when John West, a Vice-Chancellor, stood down after five years and Donald Grattan took it on, for only a year in the first instance. He had recently retired as Controller of Educational Broadcasting at the BBC.

Grattan began the process of reorganization envisaged in the Price Report. The benign old Council and its big committees disappeared and a smaller Council arrived, more like board of management, with committees attached. In real terms the grant from the Education Departments declined although the total funds under the CET umbrella rose through increased contract work.

With the appointment of Richard Fothergill perhaps the dangers seemed past: it was unlikely that the DES would close down CET just after making such an appointment. But after only 21 months in office he resigned.

The DES continued to consider CET's national role and, in parallel, was looking at the short-term future of MESU. In January this year it announced that MESU would become part of a new National CET (NCET) though retaining a separate identity and a measure of autonomy. The formal merger was on April 1st, 1988. The Secretary of State expects economies from merging the two units and proposes that NCET should do the bulk of its work in Coventry. At the time of the merger CET had about 35 permanent staff and 55 employed on a contract basis on specific projects. MESU had a staff of about 60, all temporary. You may have seen the advertisements in *The Times* last February for NCET's new Chief Executive whose Grade 4 Civil Service salary of 35,000 or so presumably reflects the heavy load he or she will carry during the integration period and beyond. The title reflects the Government's new style management of quangos. Apparently the NCET requires a Chief Executive who may or may not have professional standing in educational technology which features as only seventh in the list of twelve attributes required of this god or goddess.

The NCET budget for 1988 is about 2 million, of which 800,000 is DES grant, the rest being contracts of limited life. The MESU budget this year is an apparently healthy 3 million but MESU is due to be reviewed next year and its remit runs only as far as 1991. The Special Education Microelectronics Resource Centres (SEMERCs), which were left over from the MEP, lose their Government funding in 1989. Once again NCET is living dangerously.

COMPUTERS IN COMPANY TRAINING

Computers were scarcely alive in company training in the seventies, with a few notable exceptions. As elsewhere, educational technology gained a new lease of life in the training field as microcomputers arrived. Interactive video systems are another dose of tonic. Computer-based training in this country is expanding fast especially in large companies, as I found in a recent study (Hawridge, Newton and Hall, 1988), which is discussed elsewhere in this volume.

Educational technologists working in this field are certainly alive and well but thanks to Government policy on computer-based training they too are living dangerously. Although the Government's main training agency, the Manpower Services Commission, took some very useful steps to promote computer-based training, it did so through dozens of short contracts awarded to private and public institutions. To obtain a three-year contract was remarkable. More often the delivery dates were a year or so from start-up. Again, short-term gains were the order of the day, to be presented with as much razzamatazz as possible at the annual conferences sponsored by the MSC. The contracts were awarded against a background of changing policies towards training with repeated calls being made to employers to accept the costs of development, including computer-based training.

I would like to mention a particular group that lived very dangerously for a few years but now seems to lead a more stable and very active existence. I refer to the National Interactive Video Centre in London, led by Angus Doulton. The Centre started life with financial support from several companies and the Department of Trade and Industry, under an administrative umbrella provided by CET. Company training was one important focus for its activities, and another was its demonstrations for local education authorities. The Centre was eventually such a success that it is now an independent body supported partly by companies and partly by income it earns in a competitive commercial environment.

Yet this is what Angus Doulton had to say in his final report (Doulton, 1986):

'In ... training ... the Centre is dealing with committed individuals, often working very hard to crack entrenched attitudes in their organizations, rather than with coherent groups intent on a major improvement programme. Not enough organizations have seen the need for a long-term strategy that is owned and driven at a very senior level and which considers, from the outset, future goals and requirements.'

THE OPEN UNIVERSITY'S INSTITUTE OF EDUCATIONAL TECHNOLOGY

I speak with some feeling about living dangerously in the Open University (OU). Governments have given the OU a roller-coaster ride since its genesis in 1969. It has been feast or famine. Famine loomed in 1984 when the present Government announced cuts of 20 million in the OU budget. The Institute was not exempt and never has been. Let me give you a few statistics, covering 1980-87. We lost 30 staff in that period. Some took early retirement or voluntary redundancy, others left as their contracts or secondments ended and a few resigned to take up jobs elsewhere. Had it not been for the fact that the Institute grew steadily during the 1970s we would not have been able to withstand such a drain of talent. Its academic staff in 1980 consisted of four professors, 12 readers and senior lecturers, 24 lecturers, 19 research fellows and research assistants and about 30 other staff.

During the eighties the Institute's established staff has become smaller, but those who left have been replaced by an increased number of contract staff, many of them well qualified. The University, like others under pressure from the Government, has adopted a policy of seeking several million pounds a year for contract work from a variety of clients. Institute staff have been quite successful in bringing in these funds and have also obtained grants from the Research Councils and several foundations. Here again, however, we are living dangerously. Take, for example, the occasion a few years ago when I was approached by a senior official in a Government department and asked to bid for a high-risk evaluation project worth about a million pounds over three years. To do the project we would have had to pull at least three excellent people off the vital work they were doing for the University. In the end we declined to bid and earned no thanks of course. Or, conversely, take the example where we were kept waiting for over a year for the award of a contract, again worth a million pounds, from a different Government department. Again some of our best staff were required so we had to ask them to do a succession of short jobs and to take no long study leave while we waited, week by week, for an answer. No award was made to us or anyone else.

This new climate has made life more dangerous for our academic staff. The efforts they put into satisfying paying clients can be prodigious, yet earn little recognition for them when they are up for promotion. At the OU, promotion prospects are brightest for academic staff who have made exceptional contributions to teaching and research. Working on externally funded contracts counts for little and can actually detract from an individual's case. Should the criteria change? If they did would universities be in danger of becoming more like businesses aiming at profit?

As from last November no new academic staff in the Institute will have tenure and those existing staff who get promoted will lose the tenure they have. Life will be more dangerous for them in that in future they could face dismissal if the University budgets are cut again. Should they become grossly entrepreneurial to safeguard their salaries? The Government certainly encourages that but in the present murky political and economic atmosphere doing so carries serious risks.

A FEW PRESCRIPTIONS

I hope I have said enough to convince you that educational technologists have been and are living dangerously in the eighties. Allow me to suggest a few prescriptions that may extend our life expectancy.

First, we need fresh air. Educational technologists need an atmosphere free of the corroding influence of short-term goals, short-term contracts and short-term, politically expedient results. The Government will argue that it needs to retain political control. It can do so, indeed it has a duty to do so, within a framework of longer-term policy in our field. The NCET would do all of us in Britain a great service by advising the Government on such a framework.

Second, we need better intellectual nourishment and time to digest that food properly. Again, the NCET could well combine with those of us in universities and research institutions in advising the Government that more effort needs to go into developing the knowledge base on which our technology rests and that less should go into rushing forward new, hastily invented applications of that technology.

Third, we need exercise. Educational technologists should be working on aerobic tasks that send the oxygen of critical analysis flowing through their minds. Evaluation, in particular, provides this exercise and is central to NCET's national mission but we should not neglect the vital work of design and development. It is better to get the design nearly right first time and then correct it through evaluation than to evaluate repeatedly an initially poor design. For example, cost-effectiveness studies, much favoured by this Government, are worthless if the educational technology being studied has been poorly designed and weakly developed.

Finally, we need to take these remedies with plenty of water. Without steady and assured funding we educational technologists will be unable to serve the nation as we should. Science and technology in this country suffers frequent thirst. Educational technology needs every year those refreshing liquid assets that only the Government can guarantee. The NCET, indeed all of us, must urge it to provide these funds because we believe strongly that to do so is in the national interest.

Living dangerously is what we are obliged to do in the eighties under this Government. Yes it can be very exhilarating and it can cause disablement and even death. Let me end by quoting Jack Nicholson, who, in the film *Easy Rider*, said: 'It's real hard to be free when you're bought and sold in the market place.'

REFERENCES

Council for Educational Technology (1987) *Annual report for the period October 1985 – December 1986.* CET, London.

Doulton, A. (1986) *National Interactive Video Centre: Final Report.* NIVC, London.

Fothergill, R., Anderson, J.S.A. and others (1983) *Microelectronics Education Programme Policy and Guidelines.* Council for Educational Technology, London.

Hawkridge, D., Newton,W. and Hall,C. (1988) *Computers in Company Training.* Croom Helm and Methuen, Beckenham and New York.

Price, T. (1985) *A Review of the Council for Educational Technology.* Department of Education and Science, London.

2. Software evaluation: who cares?

Richard N Tucker, *Director, Educational and Information Technology, Netherlands Institute for Audio-Visual Media, Netherlands*

Summary: The paper presents a summary of a comparative study on criteria and procedures for the evaluation of educational software which was undertaken for UNESCO.

TERMS OF REFERENCE

Under the UNESCO programme on enhancing the quality of educational software, the International Council of Educational Media (ICEM) was asked to conduct a study based on reports from a selected number of the ICEM member countries. This selection was to represent different styles of educational organization from the centralized to the decentralized, and the different organizational methods for the production of educational software from governmental to commercial. The countries were also to be selected to represent different levels of integration of the computer into education. On this last point it was reasonable to select countries with a relatively high integration in order to find enough evidence of the evaluation of software.

TYPES OF PROGRAM

Three types of program can be identified:

- Professional programs. These are programs produced initially for the professional or business community and which may later be used for education (eg wordprocessors, databases, spreadsheets, graphics and CAD/CAM etc).
- Open or applications programs. These are sometimes called 'content-free' programs, although some are in fact built around specific content which can be added to or altered by the user. Some are simplified versions of commercial professional programs. The adaptations to the educational market often rest on the provision of different documentation and some in-built examples.
- Didactic programs. These are programs with specific content and usually with stated learning objectives or goals. Here can be found the bulk of the 'educational' software, including drill-and-practice, tutorial, simulation etc.

EVALUATION

Evaluation may take place during at least three phases. Although there can never be fixed boundaries between the categories, these may be regarded as:

- Development. The producers of programs must have criteria on which they base the

decision to produce a program, technical and methodological criteria for the
development and user criteria against which they test the product.
- Selection for translation and conversion. The needs of the converters are seen mainly
  in the smaller countries which, because of market sizes, are more concerned with the
  purchase and conversion of existing software than developing their own.
- Selection by authorities and schools. The eventual users of programs must have
  criteria by which they determine which programs are bought to meet their
  educational needs. This is perhaps the most widely known form of software
  evaluation, particularly because of the publicity which it has received from the USA
  and Canada.

The questionnaire

A detailed questionnaire was developed and given to each of the correspondents. This
asked for background on the educational context since this is seen as major conditioning
factor. The nature of software development, whether Government-subsidized or
commercial, was covered together with supply and how the decisions about content are
made. The criteria for any field testing were requested. Production criteria followed in
order to examine the economic factors which influence decision making. Where software is
bought in from other countries and converted in any way the study sought the criteria by
which this was done.

From experience, it was obvious that the majority of evaluation is related to the selection
of commercially produced software. This needed to be examined to determine if there were
common criteria. It was also important to discover whether the evaluation for selection
which we have come to know from the USA and Canada operated in other countries.

Finally, the questionnaire asked for criteria used to evaluate the use of programs in the
classroom.

The questionnaire attempted to provide a matrix within which the commissioned
authors would write the national studies (see Figure 1). It was recognized that not all the
elements on the matrix would be applicable in every country.

THE COUNTRIES

Contributions to this study came from Canada (Alberta, Ontario and Quebec), England,
Hungary, Italy, Japan, the Netherlands, Scotland and the USA.

Evaluator \ Software	Software	Professional	Applications	Didactic
Developers				
Converters				
Users				

Figure 1. *Matrix within which national studies to be written*

SUMMARY OF FINDINGS

The contexts

Though evaluations, one might even say the evaluation industry, to be found in the USA are frequently cited in reports on the use of microcomputers, a number of specific aspects are clear:

- many people outside the USA seem to feel that they should also have evaluation services such as EPIE;
- very few people outside the USA do anything about American reviews in that they buy and convert very little foreign material; and
- the contexts in which non-USA viewers stand is often radically different from that of the USA.

America, with its system of devolved school control, operates with a large body of commercial production originating outside the education structure. Thus the market-place imposes a demand on education to produce a 'best buy' list. Canada, also a federation, presents a wide range of provincial organizations. Though there is a national software review system based in Alberta, not all provinces base their software selection so strongly on reviews of commercial products. For example, Ontario chooses projects for development based on submitted proposals and then ensures widespread distribution of the finished products.

When one considers Europe other patterns emerge. The UK development projects have ensured a high degree of hardware penetration into the schools. The software development is not so consistent. In Scotland such production is largely centralized whereas in the rest of the UK the products of the projects are sold off to commercial publishers. Another factor which must be taken into account when considering the UK schools is that not only is there a largely unified school system but also that these schools have been working in a context of resource-based, project-based, and even interdisciplinary education for the past 15 years at least. This has undoubted advantages for the integration of computers into education.

The Dutch, Italian and Hungarian examples run the gamut of a highly complex system of schools: in the Netherlands there is an in-built freedom of choice, through the Italian situation where the school system is not complex but there is apparently a lack of central guidance for the provision of hardware or software, to the Hungarian state system where the decision making is perhaps the most centralized.

Japan, despite its thrusting image in the world of computers, is currently taking the most cautious stance of all the countries surveyed. The penetration of information technology into the Japanese schools is less well advanced. The traditional nature of many of the attitudes in Japanese education provides a resistance to innovation which is also to be found in many other countries. It is, however, encouraging to read the report in the latest edition of *Audio-visual Education in Japan*, produced by the Ministry of Education, which presents a more positive picture than that which was available to the correspondent through the 1984 and 1986 figures.

What can be drawn from these descriptions is that it is not easy to separate software and the criteria for its evaluation from the context and history from which it has grown.

Development of software

Wherever software is being developed it is with an eye on the market. Apart from a small amount of development for personal satisfaction or to solve a very local problem, software developers want others to use their programs. That market may range from a small group of teachers to whom a particular program is freely given and who pay with their gratitude and accolades, to a potential pool of many millions of people (eg the major language groupings of the world).

What can be deduced from these reports and others which were previously available is that criteria for the evaluation of programs during design and development are most likely to be found where educational institutions play a central role. The Scottish SMDP and the French software development linked to 'L'Informatique pour Tous' both show clearly the way in which proposals from teachers can be formulated within guidelines and against sets of standards. This ensures at least some of the aspects of the quality of the program before it is finally produced. Toronto, for those programs which fall within the provincial programme, has equally stringent criteria.

Because the criteria and procedures for these projects have been widely published, we have become sensitized to the fact that we frequently know very little of how other programs are produced or evaluated. One has reason to believe that much of it, even the very best programs, is written by the sort of educationalist who previously wrote excellent text books out of personal and professional experience but without much field-testing, and rarely against lists of educational criteria.

Production

The same sort of range of experience can be seen in the production stages of a program from countries which are mainly commercially based to those in which central government or large institutions have a major role to play. In both cases economic factors have a higher priority than educational criteria. One has to assume that these educational criteria had full operation in the early stages of planning and development. Where national projects such as those to be found in the Netherlands or Hungary arise, decisions can be taken to make large-scale provision of particular programs which negates the normal market criteria. One has also to assume that these programs have been selected for sound educational reasons.

When producing for an open market, the normal criteria for deciding on any product must operate. Is the market sufficiently large? Will somebody (and not necessarily the customer) pay for the product? Large language markets such as the English-speaking world provide a good test of the quality of a product. For many other countries such criteria cannot be applied. If the maximum potential market in a particular language area is insufficient to cover the development and production costs then either those costs have to be lowered, the selling price increased or a cost-covering subsidy has to be found.

One of the results of these pressures to cut costs has been the selection of cheaper systems which later fail to match up to the needs of the users, and the marketing of programs which may create negative reactions to the computer over a period. One can cite here the underuse bordering on rejection of the computer which has been reported from the USA and attributed by some writers to the plethora of dull, boring (but cheap!) drill-and-practice programs. In this sort of situation the publishers with their large overhead costs may be reluctant to enter the market and the future may lie with the small unit which can manage to produce high-quality software.

Conversion

Of all the contributing countries only the Netherlands has made any consistent effort in converting software originally produced in other countries. It is therefore not justifiable to attempt to draw conclusions about criteria in this field.

While not underestimating the problems of converting programs from one computer system to another, from one language to another and from one cultural context to another, the Dutch have shown that there can be considerable benefits and cost savings if programs are selected carefully. The process is similar to the normal selection of software with the added dimensions of being able to determine if the way in which a program has been constructed makes it relatively east to convert to another system. Netherlands Institute for Audiovisual Media (NIAM) has discovered the value of having a few people who can build up their experience with specific systems. A further dimension is the ability to recognize which parts of a given program will need to be rewritten or replaced entirely with new examples in order to make the program acceptable culturally to the intended users. Underlying these questions are the essential elements to be found in the criteria for selection.

One must ask how much good material is not finding its way into other countries because it is written for one system which is not predominant in the other country. Equally one has to raise questions about instances where software is brought, say, from the USA into the UK. How much consideration is given in that selection to items which are specifically American (context, terms of reference, even differences between the two types of English) which really ought to be converted if the program is to be used effectively. One suspects on the basis of these reports that the problem is not recognized. Conversion is something that is necessary for 'foreign' programs. It would appear that smaller countries could do well to consider the criteria and processes of conversion.

Selection

Criteria for the selection of existing materials are perhaps the best known and most developed. They are most readily to be found where there are large amounts of software and the problems for the purchasers are those of knowledge of what is on the market and discrimination between the programs offered. It is not surprising, therefore, to find that in the USA there is a number of evaluation services. At a national level these may be published in journals, available to subscribers by post or even on-line. Some states have their own evaluation services and there are many more local and district services.

The selection of software is made in some cases by state bodies who then bulk purchase on behalf of the schools, and in the majority of situations the selection is made by the individual teacher. In all cases it is important to the software producers that their products get evaluated. Without this sort of publicity (even with the risk of bad reviews), making such a large audience aware of your products can be very expensive. The provision of information about what is on the market is obviously of major importance in a market such as the USA. Without this knowledge, teachers will be hampered in their choice. Therefore many people demand, subscribe to and actively support evaluation services such as EPIE and MicroSIFT.

However some critical points emerge from the report. It seems that despite all these reviews the selection of media is more likely to result from having seen a demonstration than from reading a review, and that even where a review is read the general description carries more weight than the apparently more scientific evaluation. Despite their inaccuracies and variable terminology, publishers' catalogues still function as one of the main sources of guidance for the selection of software.

There are also some problems with the instruments which have been devised for the evaluation services. They purport to be scientific and present their evidence as though it were objective. Yet most of these evaluation forms were evolved for the recording of both fact and personal judgement about drill and practice programs. It is not certain that they function as well when applied to the more sophisticated applications programs. If, for the sake of argument, considerable importance is given to the criterion which checks whether a program gives a cumulative score for the user, then this will have little relevance to a program such as a database. A largely graphic program may not match the criteria which were established when most programs were textual.

It is not simply a question of having a more flexible set of criteria. One has also to recognize that these reviews are of necessity applying generalized criteria to specific programs which may be used in educational contexts which are very different from each other. Where these reports do seem to score highly is in their informative function and in the general description of the programs. Research has shown that it is the descriptive element of these reviews and journal articles which have a major influence on the way in which teachers select software.

The Canadian reviews are also based on what look like objective reports. Yet when one considers the forms it is easy to see that apart from details like size of the disc, the type of computer system, the language and memory requirement, most of the answers required are a matter of judgement on the part of the reviewer. There are general checks as to whether it matches the curriculum, but against which curriculum is the program to be matched when there are so many to be found in a country as diverse as the USA or Canada? Local or state reviews may have less of a problem in this regard where curricular decisions may make it easier to match programs to lesson requirements.

What one ends up with are generalized criteria which require subjective judgements (often on a one-to-five scale) from the reviewer. These are then presented in tabular form as though they are definite values. Such presentations have to be suspect. However, both the US and Canadian experiences seem to point to a heavy reliance on the part of readers on the descriptive reviews. For these to have currency there has to be an agreed basis for comparison.

The Dutch review instrument relies heavily on subjective responses from the reviewers but recognizes that these should be based on professional experience of the educational level and subject in question. It also provides quite clear guidance in its questioning. The resulting reports are written like literary reviews. Readers can begin to get a feel for the way in which a particular journal reviews just as they have their personal preference for reviewers of football or theatre.

The strength and value of the descriptive review, particularly reviews of the application of a program (ie how it functions in a classroom) is strongly reinforced by the English report.

Research

Given that so much attention is being paid to evaluation around the world it seemed only right to ask whether it was of any value. Does it improve the choice of programs? Is a program which receives good reviews going to make a greater impact in the classroom? Given the vast range of questions that are asked, if one bothered to put all the evaluation forms together one would have expected to have found some research to back up all this effort. Sadly, but perhaps not surprisingly, there is very little evidence of research. Some academic research is reported from the USA. What is of interest and value is the comment which is made, explicitly or implicitly, by the American, Canadian, Dutch and English correspondents that out of all this reporting and evaluation what has proved to be the most valuable has been the illuminative style work. This is, by its very nature, more an evaluation of the software in use in a learning situation than an evaluation of the software as a 'thing'. The most valued evaluations are of the process rather than of the product.

CONCLUSIONS

Development

There is considerable value in having guidelines and principles for the development of software. These should be evolved with a strict relation to the existing curriculum and methods of learning. At the same time they should be designed in such a way as to guide program developers towards those methods and subjects which are desired for the near future. Where programs are developed within the educational structures, such guidelines should be applied as widely as the organization of education permits. The only proviso is that those administering these standards should recognize that they are guidelines and not apply them so rigidly as to crush innovation. Where development takes place outside the

educational system one can do little more than offer the guidelines. In smaller countries
and language areas government support may have to be greater.

Production

After years of program production of very variable quality, it ought to be possible within
education to limit some of the idiosyncrasies. It ought to be possible to agree to a limited
number of computer languages (if not a single language). It ought to be possible to agree to
a small number of processes, such as always keeping text in separate files so that
translations or versions of a program can be made more easily. It ought to be possible to
operate with a limited number of common commands. It ought to be possible to agree
within any one system to a range of basic standards of screen presentation (eg number of
lines of text on a screen, the design and spacing of questions, the use of colour and colour
contrasts, and so forth). This should make it easier for users to work with new software.
There could even be agreement about the basic principles of putting menu bars and pull-
down menus into programs. It ought to be possible!

Selection

The conclusion has to be drawn from these reports that where the schools have a choice of
software there is an important role for what are now termed 'evaluations'. It also has to be
recognized that the majority of what are put forward as 'evaluation forms' are very flawed
and when applied rigorously across the range of software, largely inappropriate. Where
evaluation forms do score highly is when they give the reviewer guidance on the aspects to
look for and how to make judgements in the broad sense. They also act as a checklist to
reduce the risk that a reviewer might forget aspects which may be crucial to other
potential buyers.

If we recognize that the apparent objectivity of most of the published evaluations is an
unsupportable pretense and that they are subjective but written on the basis of agreed
standards, then we can give that subjectivity its true value and start treating them as
reviews of products. What we then need to do is extend this practice of reviewing to
equally 'guided' reviews of the programs in use, the process for which the software was
originally written. Let us recognize that this illuminative evaluation of the process is the
most valuable guidance that we can provide for education.

Conversion

Without labouring the argument that there are good reasons for converting software,
criteria can be established by which the value of a program for possible conversion can be
established. First of all use the criteria for selection with a special emphasis on the
'curricular-fit'.

If a program fits the curriculum, has a good track-record in its country of origin and
does not have effective competitors in the market into which it is being brought, then it is
worth looking further at the program itself. If this conforms to the ideal production criteria
then there will be few difficulties. Judgements will have to be made on the degree of
difficulty involved in taking a program from one system to another.

The greatest thought and effort will have to be given to the cultural conversion for
which there can be few standard criteria.

Research

It appears doubtful if there is much valuable research to be done into the effectiveness of
the present method of reviewing. With better review procedures there would be much to
be gained from action research which supported the illuminative character of the reviews.
The use of the software in classes is far better and more valuable than comparative

researches about the products, and certainly better than researches about how people fill in forms. Those searching for absolute answers with regard to any learning materials should be cautioned that no matter how carefully prepared a resource might be, teachers and learners will use it in wholly different ways. Some of these will be better than that originally intended, some will be worse.

General Remarks

In concluding this report one is forced back to the consideration of why we want educational software to conform to a level of objective evaluation which we don't apply to any other medium. It is tempting to assume that the nature of the programs can be captured in tables of figures or circles in a matrix. Educational software at its best is powerful enough to resist being so caged. It comes to life in its use and the learning process often occurs between individuals in a small group of users of a program who are stimulated by the program rather than by one-to-one interaction with the program. We need to have more and better descriptions of the process of use in order to spread as many of the alternative practices and advantages throughout education.

FURTHER READING

The following works were cited in the complete report:

Becker, H.J. (1986) *Instructional Uses of School Computers: Reports from the 1985 National Survey*. Center for Social Organization of Schools.

Cooperative Committee on Elementary and Secondary Education and the Information Society (1985) *First Report*. Tokyo.

EPIE Institute (1986) *TESS: The Educational Software Selector*. Water Mill, NY.

Fisher, G. (1983) Where to find good reviews of educational software. *Electronic Learning*, October, pp86-7.

Hills, P.J. (ed) (1982) *A Dictionary of Education*. Routledge & Kegan Paul, London.

Kanselaar, G. (1985) *Courseware nader bekeken*. Rijksuniversiteit Utrecht Vakgroep Onderwijskunde Huisdrukkerij IPAW.

Mattas, L.L. (1986) *Only The Best; The Discriminating Software Guide for Preschool - Grade 12*. Education News Service, Sacramento.

Moonen, J. and Plomp, T. (1987) *EURIT 86. Developments in Educational Software and Courseware*. Pergamon Press, Oxford.

NEA Educational Computer Service (1985) *The Yellow Book: A parents guide to educationally sound courseware*. National Education Association, Washington DC.

Percival, F. and Ellington, H. (1984) *A Handbook of Educational Technology*. Kogan Page, London.

Perkins, W. and Bass, G.M. (1984) Teaching critical thinking skills with CAI. *Electronic Learning*, **94**, pp 32-34.

Plomp, T., Van Deursen, K. and Moonen, J. (1987) *CAL for Europe*. Proceedings of a conference of the European Commission on the Development of Educational Software. North Holland, Amsterdam.

Social Education Council: Subcommittee on Educational Media (1985) *A Manual for Development of Educational Software*. Tokyo.

Social Education Council: Subcommittee on Educational Media (1985) *Utilization of Micro-computers in Education*. Tokyo.

Sturdivant, P. (1984) Courseware for schools; Present problems and future needs. *AEDS Monitor*, **22**, 7-8 pp 25-27.

Taylor, R. (1985) *Microcomputer Coursework Evaluation Sources*. ERIC Clearing House on Information Resources, Syracuse, NY.

Truett, C. (1984) Field testing educational software: are publishers making the effort? *Educational Technology*, **24**, 5 pp 7-12.

Unwin, D. and MacAleese, R. (1978) *Encyclopaedia of Educational Media, Communications and Technology*. MacMillan, London.

Wighton, D. (1984) Alberta Education's Clearinghouse: functions and findings. *Computers & Education,* **8**, pp 449-453.

Evaluation forms used in this study came from:

- The School Board of Broward County, Florida, USA
- The Educational Software Evaluation System from MCKB, Brigham Young University, Utah, USA
- National Science Teachers Association, Washington DC, USA
- Florida Centre of Instructional Computing, Tampa, Florida, USA
- MicroSIFT, Northwest Regional Educational Laboratory, USA
- Software Selection Criteria
- Educational Software Description/Evaluation Forms, TECOM, Italy
- Scottish Microelectronics Development Programme, SCET, Scotland
- MEP (form from Open University study course) England
- GQTM, Quebec, Canada
- SCEN, Enschede, Netherlands.

Grateful thanks are given to the authors who contributed to this study:

Hans Kratz	*Alberta Education, Canada*
Richard Fothergill	*CET, England*
Ferenc Genzwein	*OOK, Hungary*
Marcello Giacomantonio	*TECOM, Italy*
Haruo Nishinosono	*Kyoto University of Education, Japan*
Pieter Burghard	*NIAM, Netherlands*
Alistair Thomson	*SCET, Scotland*
Dr Robin Taylor	*University of Maryland, USA*

3. A strategy for training trainers: a two-pronged approach

Squadron Leaders H M Brown and S W Tofts, *Royal Air Force, UK*

Summary: Trainers in the armed services are fortunate that military leaders have long recognized that it is the poorly trained army which loses the war. Consequently training in the services, unlike some other large organizations, is taken seriously and is relatively well funded. This fortunate position in terms of recognition and resources has, on occasions, led to the development of an inward-looking, even complacent, attitude. The two papers which follow describe ways in which we, in the RAF, are currently developing training for two very different groups of trainer in response to rapidly developing technology. In doing so we hope to show that we are willing to listen to and learn from some of the developments which are currently taking place in the field of human resource development. We also hope that our experiences in developing training for our trainers will be of interest to other organizations facing similar problems.

PART 1: TRAINING THE PROFESSIONAL EDUCATION AND TRAINING OFFICER

Squadron Leader H M Brown, *Department of Education Officer Training, RAF School of Education and Training Support (SOETS), UK*

INTRODUCTION

Teams in the RAF's major ground training schools are currently designing the courses which will train our engineering tradesmen for the 1990s and beyond. This paper outlines those areas which we have had to consider in order to provide trainer training in anticipation of the likely changes. In particular, it focuses on how a highly structured organization is coming to terms with the need to provide both trainers and trainees with a wider range of skills, often in less formalized methods, than in the past. These are issues which are of relevance to all those involved with solving the UK's perceived difficulties with training. The views expressed are personal and do not represent official policy, particularly when forward projections are suggested.

IMPETUS FOR CHANGE

Technology

By its very nature, aircraft engineering in the RAF is at the forefront of technology and in recent years there has been a variety of surveys and working parties which have attempted to predict the 'way ahead'. Their reports have usually made some comment on the type of training required for new technology and since some 40 per cent of our 93,000 strength comes under the broad heading of 'engineering' such comment must affect our evaluation of the training involved. The bulk of our 400 education officers are employed in this training, either as instructors or training managers in the formal schools or in providing support to the less formalized training on our operational stations. The use of systems-based evaluation suggests that the training of these trainers should take into account likely developments in their employment. The first stage in this process is to consider the possible impact of technology on our tradesman training, bearing in mind that this impact will be on both the workplace and the training environment.

Technological change is of concern both because of the rapidity with which it occurs and the operational environment which it creates. Black box systems with long periods between servicing and increased reliance on replacement rather than repair have generally been accepted as leading to a reduction in the skills required by tradesmen, including technicians. However, there is also a need for a few very highly skilled core workers, often with some supervisory function. Such developments affect the military as well as our civilian counterparts. The investment costs of formal training make it easy to understand the concern for both effectiveness and efficiency. Contractual lengths of service do mean that, unlike civilian organizations, we can at least amortize the return on the investment.

Thus we may move towards providing the skills necessary only for initial employment rather than attempting to provide a fuller range for the whole of a tradesman's career. The rate of technological change would be a strong argument for adopting such a strategy (eg through reducing the length of basic training and concentrating on pre-employment and further training). Similar pressures are likely to lead to greater reliance on on-job training (OJT). Such changes in the level of skills taught in formal training may affect both the amount of associated theory needed and the methodology used to teach it. However, there may also be pressures for a broadening of skill mixes.

Modern aircraft such as the Tornado operate from hardened shelters supported by small teams of tradesmen providing a rapid turnaround service that maximizes the utilization of these scarce assets. Hence our tradesmen may well require a broader range of skills enabling them to work in teams where roles are less clearly assigned to specific individuals. These skills include those interpersonal ones which are often crucial for success. There are similarities with our much greater reliance on self- discipline rather than traditional methods of enforced discipline.

Course development

The systems approach which we use is firmly based on end-user analysis of the job and task requirements. However, specification of behavioural objectives has not radically altered the methods used to achieve them. Indeed, in some cases the introduction of a 'systems approach' seems to have focused on the specification of behavioural objectives which were entirely content-related with insufficient regard for process. The problems, for example, of training based on the use of multiple-choice objective questions, whether computer-delivered or not, can be well understood when thought is given to modern theories of learning (Entwistle, 1987).

Currently an initial input of theory taught in basic studies squadrons is followed sequentially by skills training. The majority of our professional trainers are employed teaching this theory using traditional methods, broadly in line with the BTEC strategies of civilian colleges. We are investigating whether new approaches can meet the challenges outlined. For example, competency-based training with much closer links between theory and skills could influence both the organization of our training and the methods used (eg CBT and individualized learning). Additionally, our major course-design teams are using approaches based on integrated job performance training which are likely to confirm these possible changes.

One possible solution to the management of such courses would be single-trade training squadrons using team teaching to increase the links between theory and skills. The aim would be to create both a methodology and a structure which was closer to that of the operational environment while maintaining the cost-effectiveness of formalized off-job training. The skills required of our professional trainers would change accordingly. For example, they would need to amalgamate their content much more closely with the skills taught by our NCO trade instructors.

TRAINER TRAINING

The trainers

We thus have had to consider most carefully the training of our trainers and of course their recruitment and selection. In the past year we have trained some 50 of these professional trainers. While young ex-teachers are still our main source they are not the majority, indeed previous teaching experience will be of less concern to us if we move further away from purely academic methods. Our main interest is to attract those with an appropriate technical or scientific background, the minimum qualification being HNC in an appropriate subject area. While their backgrounds and ages may differ, they will all have undergone the 18 weeks of Initial Officer Training.

Of the 50 likely to be trained in any one year, some 35 will go to initial appointments as instructors while the remainder, usually those with arts or language backgrounds, will go to jobs requiring a large element of support to training on our operational stations. Hence we are concerned with identifying a common core of competencies which will be required by all these professional trainers.

EdOTC common core

In April 1987 we introduced the new Education Officers' Training Course, consisting of a five week common core followed by separate job-specific training. Throughout, the emphasis is on practical skills and maximum student involvement. The course framework is similar to those which we anticipate our future trainers will themselves be working within. The systems view has also caused us to be concerned with the process and interaction which occurs during the course. Hence we have moved away from formal classroom inputs towards greater reliance on working in small groups (Smith, 1980).

The crucial section is that concerned with instructional techniques where we use progressive microteaching to develop practical skills. While maintaining our bedrock of traditional methods such as the theory lesson, we are developing other areas (eg presentational and interpersonal skills and brief, monitor, debrief (BMD) techniques). The students undertake a series of sessions (eg practice lessons on one another) which are normally videotaped. Individual appraisal forms are then used to debrief and develop learning.

In recent years the RAF has developed BMD as a sound method for skills training on a one-to-one or one-to-small-group basis. Using various card and computer games, together with wordprocessing, we train our trainers in this method for later use in both formal training and OJT.

Appraisal

We award an overall course grade based on student performance in the various competencies, with particular reference to instructional techniques. As with other initial specialist training, we expect a minimum training performance standard, in this case as a capable instructor which we classify as a B1. This appraisal provides management with information about the individual trainer, a necessity for career development in an organization as large as ours. In particular, we are concerned with developing a trainer who is able to facilitate and support learning using a wide range of methods.

Like many of those involved with appraisal systems we are concerned with possible problems of validity and reliability, particularly when appraising instruction (Elton, 1987). We have a major advantage in that our organizational culture is founded on a climate of excellence and trust. In some ways the lessons of Japanese management do not come as a shock to us. The RAF has always had a concern for human resource development because of its critical reliance on suitably motivated manpower.

The validity of our appraisal rests on a selection process which seeks to place those with proven experience of instruction in appropriate posts. Additionally, career development, which sees a continual movement of personnel between jobs, enhances the relationship between trainers and trainers of trainers! Nevertheless we are aware of the possibility of becoming too inward-looking and therefore seek to maintain awareness of ideas, such as modern theories of learning, which may be of value to us. Thus the modifications have been primarily concerned with the process and structure of the course rather than the content.

Appraisal reliability rests on a categorization system which has its roots in flying and flying training. This system is clearly defined and generally understood and accepted throughout the RAF. The grades used are backed up by the use of checklists and staff training to achieve an element of standardization without compromising the validity of particular instructional sessions.

When appraising instructional techniques we rely primarily on the debrief as a means of development. To continue in an earlier vein, our approach is similar to that of Eastern philosophy in that we focus on strengths (ie original virtue rather than original sin). During training we also give the student an indication of how an individual session would have been graded. This provides a basis for development, knowledge of the overall grading system and the foundation of their own appraisal skills.

Further training

Following the common core, those going to instructional posts undertake a one week Engineering Practices section. This includes a presentation on the day-to-day working of an RAF Engineering Wing followed by a four day visit to a station. During the visit our prospective trainers work alongside tradesmen to gain an understanding of the life of their future trainees. Initial evaluation shows this to have been a most welcome addition to the course.

Meanwhile, those trainers going to posts in station education and training undergo two weeks of practical training in the office simulator. The general approach is to issue reading material, discuss possible problems in a tutor-led session and then run an exercise in the simulator with individual and group debriefing as necessary. There is a strong focus on providing support to OJT.

On completion of the formal course our trainers themselves undertake a period of structured OJT. This takes place with their superior acting as a mentor and RAF SOETS providing advice and consultancy. The OJT is based on objectives which include the requirement to achieve an A2 grade as an able and skilful instructor within 6 to 12 months. This ensures that our trainers have the necessary level of skills to provide assistance to those who may have a training commitment which is not full time and hence may not warrant their being formally trained in instructional techniques.

CONCLUSION

Increased focus, using internal and external validation, has given the military a systematic view of the efficiency and effectiveness of its training. The increased use of the term evaluation has focused our awareness on the wider impact and worth of training. The rate and impact of technological change has heightened this awareness, with it has come an increased concern for process and structure in addition to content. Developments in engineering training must be anticipated by appropriate training of the trainers. The use of a true systems approach which brings in these wider issues should, we believe, enable us to meet the challenges of the 1990s and beyond.

REFERENCES

Elton, L. (1987) *Teaching in Higher Education: Appraisal and Training.* Kogan Page, London.
Entwistle, N. (1987) *Styles of Learning and Teaching.* Wiley & Sons, Chicester.
Smith, P.B. (1980) *Small Groups and Personal Change.* Methuen, New York.

PART 2: TRAINING THE PART-TIME TRAINER

Squadron Leader S W Tofts, *Educational and Training Technology Development Unit, RAF School of Education and Training Support (SOETS), UK*

INTRODUCTION

For several years the RAF has been aware of the need to provide two broad but distinct types of training which it has labelled 'formal' and 'continuation' training.

Formal training is established through a syllabus approved and issued by the Ministry of Defence. Examples include recruit training, basic trade training and a wide range of job-related pre-employment courses. It is carried out at a training school or unit established and resourced specifically for that purpose. In particular, the staff of such a school are involved in training on a full-time basis and are trained in instructional techniques.

Continuation training is the training carried out on operational RAF units from within each unit's resources. It includes the training which is needed to help individual servicemen and women to develop their careers through promotion examinations and civilian qualifications, but its main aim is to enable personnel to achieve and maintain a state of operational effectiveness.

Despite the work which has gone into identifying and defining continuation training, it remains a relatively neglected area within the RAF and, I suspect, within other organizations which are faced with a large and diverse training task. It exists for several reasons but primarily because formal training courses, with very few exceptions, do not produce trainees who can perform to the standard required in the operational environment. Sometimes this is because the real equipment (particularly if it is new, complex or expensive) is not available in the training school. In most cases however, continuation training is needed because tradesmen require both training and experience to be able to perform at an operational level. Despite the use of rigorous competency based training design models, much of our formal training remains knowledge-based and only partly prepares a trainee to carry out his operational job.

Because continuation training is carried out from within an operational unit's resources, those who provide the training must do so on top of, or as part of, their own job. Consequently a training strategy which is perceived as not requiring sophisticated or highly trained instructors is used to provide continuation training. The method that is most commonly used is one-to-one on-job training (OJT).

ON-JOB TRAINING

OJT is often regarded, especially by professional trainers, as an inefficient and haphazard way of providing training. Sadly this view is often well founded, but not because the method is inherently weak. In fact, training on the real equipment in the real environment provides the learner with context and motivation which are often missing in a formal training school. Where OJT is carried out badly it is usually because the instructors, through no fault of their own, lack the basic skills of training.

Like any other form of training, OJT is concerned with developing knowledge, skills and attitudes so that the trainee is able to do his job effectively. It differs from any other type of training in that it is usually practical training given on the *real* equipment in the *real* place of work. Consequently OJT lends itself to techniques which might not be considered appropriate in formal training. In particular, effective OJT depends heavily on the monitoring and debriefing of a practical performance. These are skills which an instructor can, and needs, to develop like any of the other skills involved in conducting training.

Although the RAF runs courses in instructional techniques for tradesmen employed in formal training we have, until very recently, provided little practical help for those involved in continuation training. Indeed, because continuation training was not established through a syllabus it had been difficult even to estimate the number of tradesmen involved and the amount of time that they are required to spend on OJT. The only thing that was clear at this stage was that any training for OJT trainers had to be provided at minimum cost.

OJT WORKSHOPS

In response to a clear but as yet unquantified need, the Department of Instructional Techniques at the RAF School of Education and Training Support (RAF SOETS) had developed a travelling, two-day workshop on OJT techniques which it offered to stations on a limited, first-come first-served basis. It was the response to this workshop which prompted us to investigate the provision of OJT in greater depth.

Each of the stations which had hosted a workshop had rated it as a great success and had asked for more. However, providing more workshops placed a strain on the Department's limited manpower as their primary task remained the provision of formal instructional techniques courses. Before we could consider extending the workshop programme we needed to obtain a clear idea of the size and nature of the potential audience.

Identifying the potential audience

We asked the education officers on a sample of operational units to estimate the number of tradesmen, by rank, who were involved in the conduct of OJT on the station. The returns were remarkably consistent and highlighted two significant factors. First, it appeared that the numbers involved were large, approximately 10 per cent of each station's total manpower. Secondly, there were two distinct levels of involvement. On most stations junior NCOs (corporals and junior technicians) were responsible for carrying out OJT. A roughly equal number of senior NCOs (sergeants and chief technicians) played a more supervisory role, organizing and managing the training.

Clearly the very large potential audience was beyond the reach of an *ad hoc* programme of workshops which were able to train only between 12 and 18 students at a time. However, the response to the workshop had shown that its aims and objectives were correct and were pitched at the right level. The problem lay in the cost and expert manpower involved in providing the workshops for all the tradesmen who required them.

AN OPEN LEARNING SOLUTION?

The solution to the problem appeared to lie in the concept of open learning. If we could make the workshop format more flexible by packaging it in a form which depended less on the presence of expert tutors the material could be made available to many more tradesmen. However, we quickly encountered one of the fundamental problems of open learning, one that is often ignored, namely that not all training can be neatly packaged as text, video or audio. When we examined the workshop closely we identified about 25 per cent of the material as dealing with the cognitive elements of instructional technique (for example, 'analysing skills' and 'structuring the learning situation'). This material did not appear to be totally dependent on the presence of a skilled tutor and could be delivered effectively using other media. The remaining 75 per cent of the workshop programme involved the tutors in intensive coaching of the students as they worked through a number of practice instructional sessions. This phase of the workshop was highly dependent on the presence of tutors who not only exemplified the techniques they advocated but who, as tradesmen themselves, had the ability to understand the students' working environment.

The senior NCO supervisors, whom we had earlier identified as having a mainly organizational role in OJT, fulfilled this latter criterion although their grasp of the theory of instructional technique might be somewhat shaky. Our final solution was to adopt the cascade system shown in Figure 1.

The senior NCOs would receive a modified workshop backed up by a distance learning text and video package. They in turn would run a series of practical exercises for the Junior NCOs who would also have completed the distance learning package. Additional tutorial support would be provided on each station by the education officer. The distance learning package, which provides about eight hours of study material, and the modified workshop are approaching completion and will be evaluated by sample of operational units in the summer of 1988.

DEVELOPING OPEN LEARNING MATERIAL

The development of the distance learning package was our first real attempt, on an RAF-wide basis, to package training using the principles of open rather than programmed

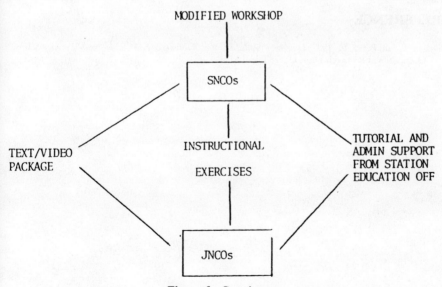

Figure 1. *Cascade system*

learning. In doing so we learned a number of lessons which may be of interest to other organizations which are considering packaging their own material.

Communication level

RAF tradesmen, in general, are not easily impressed by educational or training theory. The cognitive element of the workshop had been successful mainly because of the rapport the tutors had been able to establish with their students. The distance learning material would need to emulate the quality of the conversation which the tutors had achieved without being patronizing and, above all, without recourse to educational jargon.

Developing skilled learners

The fact that we were using an open learning strategy primarily to benefit the organization did not mean that we should ignore the needs of the individual learner. Wherever possible the principles for developing skilled learners put forward by Downs (1987) were incorporated into the material. We felt that it was particularly important to provide students with an appropriate context and to encourage an active approach to the material. We tried to achieve this by including a number of practical examples and exercises in the package. The main problem here lay in how specific the exercises should be. They needed to be relevant to the RAF, or at least to a military environment, which meant that we were unable to buy a package off the shelf. At the same time the exercises had to be sufficiently general to be of use across the range of RAF trades from aircraft technician to kennel maid.

Quality

Finally we maintained an emphasis on quality throughout the development of the package, both in terms of content and presentation – a consideration which often appears to be lacking in the production of OL material. Perhaps the most important lesson we have learned from this project is that there is far more to open learning than glossy packaging and the use of the latest hi-tech hardware!

REFERENCE

Downs, S. and Perry, P. (1987) *Developing Skilled Learners: Learning to Learn in the Youth Training Scheme.* Occupational Research Unit, UWIST and MSC.

4. Courseware design metholdogy: the message from software engineering

T R Black and T Hinton, *Computer Assisted Learning Group, University of Surrey, UK*

Summary: Many software tools are now available to facilitate the design and development of new software. These are based upon established principles of software engineering and not only facilitate the design process ensuring well-structured programs, but are also self-documenting to enhance debugging the prototypes and maintaining the final products. With recent developments the field of software engineering is expanding its repertoire of skills and tools. Many of these are of considerable value to courseware development teams, and with time others should be developed to meet the idiosyncratic needs of courseware design teams in industry, commerce and education. This paper highlights developments in software engineering that are relevant and indicate the areas of potential research in design methodology and development of new courseware design tools.

INTRODUCTION

With an increased interest in computer-based learning there has been a growing number of authoring languages and systems on the commercial market. The designers tend to make claims that such software will facilitate the production of computer-based learning materials. For some objectives these claims are well justified and such tools are invaluable, but many authoring languages and systems tend to be better suited than others to certain objectives and/or design situations. One consequence is that design methodology needs to accommodate limitations of the specific languages/systems available and include the possibility of changing from one language to another within a courseware package.

Demands on languages by design teams are most often related to such factors as planning and coding times, routeing and decision schemes deriving from the cognitive emphasis of aims/objectives of the proposed courseware (see Black, 1987a). Commercial CAL software houses must be efficient as well as effective in the production of high-quality bespoke courseware, although this has not always been of apparent importance in the production of courseware for schools. In this paper consideration is given to development models ranging from the 'cottage industry' to full design/production teams.

THE DESIGN TEAM STRUCTURE

Numerous models for delegating tasks in design teams have been employed by various organizations. The simplest is the 'cottage industry' consisting of the individual working alone, being both the subject expert and computer programmer. Early school software was developed by teachers and distributed through teachers' centres or organizations (eg MUSE, RML, BeBug). Some publishers attempted to exploit the cottage industry model by buying and distributing such courseware. Even some courseware houses tend to work on this principle: the contract is taken on and the courseware development (design and implementation) is assigned wholly to one person – a programmer/subject expert.

The second model involves a limited team consisting of a teacher(s) or subject expert(s) (non-programmers) who design the content and structure of the courseware and a programmer who implements the courseware often in BASIC or a simple language like Microtext. Numerous problems can arise in such situations, particularly the one of communicating educational ideas to programmers through paper and pencil designs (see Crossfield et al, 1984).

The third, and preferred, model involves an integrated team of experts led by the educational systems analyst (Hinton 1984). Quality commercial software is not commonly written by individuals working in isolation but by teams; there is no reason to believe that educational or training courseware is any different. Considering the complexity of the task and diversity of skills required, a model maximizing the contribution of each member is preferable. The team would consist of people whose inter-relationships are as shown in Figure 1 and individual members would have a range of skills and responsibilities (Black, 1988).

The *educational systems analyst* is the team leader, with a background in teaching/training, educational technology and software engineering. He or she coordinates the efforts of the other team members, serving as consultant and trainer for new skills required by members. The role is parallel to that of computing systems analysis with the added requirement of educational and training expertise needed to develop interactive multimedia training systems.

The *subject matter expert(s)* are the teachers or practitioners in the industrial or commercial environment. It is possible that such persons may have little experience in computing though they may use information technology daily. What these persons do have is academic, technical or commercial knowledge and expertise that others need to acquire. One challenge for the educational systems analyst is to facilitate the transmission of specific skills and knowledge by these experts through the medium of CAl courseware to the untrained.

The *computer programmer* has immensely valuable and hard-to-acquire skills but does not tend to be a subject or educational expert as well. The materials produced by the subject expert in consultation with the educational systems analyst must be clear and have no ambiguities. The programmer's task is programming: implementing the design, routeing, models behind the simulations, etc.

The *audiovisual aids technical advisors* will advise and assist on graphics, hardware and other technical problems associated with the design and implementation of courseware (eg interactive video). Visually conveying information requires skills most people lack but can well appreciate. The educational systems analyst provides the educational insight to help the subject expert and AVA advisor to present ideas visually in the best way possible and to encourage appropriate responses in the interactive environment.   With reference to software design, to enhance project management Enos and Van Tilburg (1979) have noted the necessity to identify tasks with personnel where there is overlap of activities in such a problem-solving process as software engineering. A systems approach is employed by the educational analyst to achieve such ends in the design and development of courseware. While a number of these exist, the one in Figure 2 (on p 28) has been designed to highlight all the skills required in this complex process. It is intended primarily as a teaching structure for a postgraduate course for aspiring educational systems analysts. Consequently it is as much a job analysis as it is an idealized guide to design and development.

Any team will need a system, if for no other reason than to have a checklist of tasks or a starting point for project management techniques such as critical path analysis. All of these strategies should make the process more effective and efficient by facilitating the achievement of goals like reducing development time, directing courseware at the most appropriate cognitive level and enhancing the input of the subject expert.

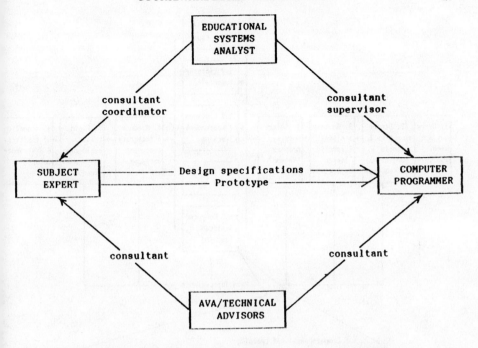

Figure 1. *Inter-relationships among design team members (Black, 1988)*

SOFTWARE ENGINEERING

Included in the systems approach of Figure 2 are many of the analysis and design stages that are a part of any systems or problem-solving approach. There are numerous underlying principles with parallels to those advocated in software engineering texts (eg Jensen, 1979; Tonies, 1979). For example, the need for quality assurance through continual verification and validation is reflected in formative evaluation with iterations at numerous stages in the courseware design system.

A typical scheme (Enos and Van Tilburg, 1979) has four major stages:

- requirements definition;
- system design;
- software design; and
- software implementation.

The parallels in analysis and design are best illustrated through two summary listings of major headings which are given in Figure 3. Both approaches include determining the exact need of the end user by defining the objectives and constraints, breaking down the task into simpler components to enhance comprehension, specifying in detail what the final product should be and implementation (including trials and evaluation).

However, in the design of CAL courseware the processes that need to be planned are somewhat different. First the overall system needs to be planned from the learner's point of view because it is the interaction with the computer that makes CAL intrinsically different

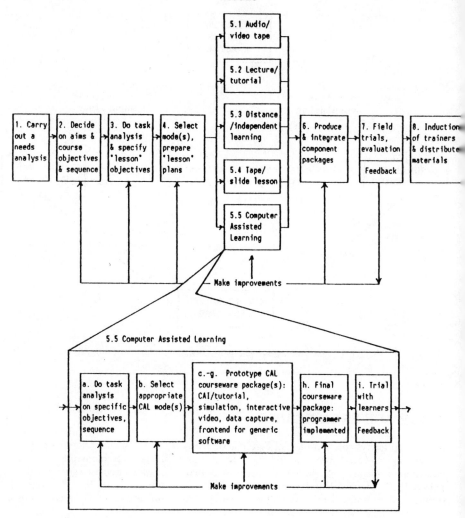

Figure 2. *Systems approach for developing CAL courseware as part of the overall design of a training course (Black, 1988)*

from other learning media. The essential elements of CAL coursework can be considered to be:

- screen text and graphics images, including overlays;
- special purpose graphics (dynamic images and animation);
- simulation, requiring a full range of computational facilities involving complex mathematical computation techniques for technical or logical computation for non-technical applications;
- analysis of user response or input (input analysis), requiring a full range of computational facilities including file access and complex numerical and string processing; and

SOFTWARE ENGINEERING (from Enos & Van Tilburg 1979)	COURSEWARE DESIGN (numbers refer to Figure 2 stages)
Requirements definition statement of user's problem: define problem, collect information about it, identify performance requirements, standards for development, and any design constraints and systems dynamics.	Needs Analysis determining training needs (1)
	Identify Aims/Objectives of course and lessons (2,3)
	Select Teaching/Learning Mode and determine context of CAL courseware (4)
System Design Top down: decomposition from a high level abstract definition of a problem to a more detailed level.	Task Analysis, select CAL modes (5a, b)
	Elicit skills, teaching/learning style from subject expert, encapsulate it in
Software Design using a) data flow charts, structure charts, etc., and b) possibly "modeling/simulation" of final package	a) documentation including routing charts, and b) a prototype with screen designs (5c-5g)
Software Implementation coding of the final package, trials, debugging, with continual verification and validation.	Programmer Implements courseware package (5h)
	Trial with learners (5i)
	Integrate courseware into programme, field trials and evaluation (6, 7)
	Induction of trainers (8)

Figure 3. *Parallels between software engineering and CAL courseware (Figure 2) development models*

- flow of control depending primarily upon the learner's response because of the emphasis on interaction.

Prototyping of software, sometimes referred to as 'simulation/modelling' of the software product (eg Enos and Van Tilburg, 1979), involves developing a limited working version, not necessarily in the same computer language as the final product. In the case of CAL courseware the prototype would demonstrate, for example, the screen designs and routeing scheme for tutorials (Black, 1987b) or the solicitation of information and resulting output to the learner for a simulation. Even if it necessitated extra keyboard input, the aim is to show the nature of the interactivity to the design team in order to evaluate the validity of the program. This avoids the problem of ambiguities filled in by programmers who lack the subject matter and educational knowledge necessary to make such decisions.

Most of the input for the prototype should come from the subject expert. With the various text and graphics editors available (PC Paint, those in MENTOR, etc) the direct input by non-programmer subject experts becomes possible. This has the distinct value of making possible the inclusion of more specialist-oriented content rather than just the elementary and sometimes trivial material created by the subject expert cum programmer working alone. The use of some authoring systems (eg MENTOR) may mean that some subject experts may be able to create their own prototypes with only limited assistance (Black, 1987b).

If the design time includes using the prototype as a means of eliciting content and teaching/presentation style, then the suggestion that design time is 40 per cent, coding time by the programmer is 20 per cent, and testing and integration time is 40 per cent of the total (Tonies, 1979) will not be far off. As with any software development project team, there is a need to establish a 'house style' which will include such aspects as documentation, coding style (for structuring and comments) and learner's guides. Communication within a team, flexibility for team member changes, courseware debugging (both software and educational bugs) and long-term maintenance will all benefit. Project management may appear to involve trivia but with such a complex process it is a necessity.

STRUCTURED PROGRAMMING

Regardless of which authoring language/system is employed and which design model adopted, the planning of the courseware routeing at some stage should become highly detailed prior to coding. It is at this point that the design team could benefit from developments in the self-discipline associated with structured programming, especially when employing highly unstructured authoring languages.

Defining structured programming is not easy since not everyone agrees what it is. For the purposes of this paper Jensen's (1979) description will suffice:-'... the formulation of programs by stepwise refinement resulting in hierarchical, nested structures ...'. A well-formed program consists of these control structures. A set of nine covering what most procedural languages can do are described by Jensen (1979) as:

- Sequence
- Selection: if-else
                 if-or if-else
                 case of
                 posit
- Iteration: while
                 until
- Exit: escape
                 cycle

The details of these will not be elaborated on in this paper but let it suffice to say that while programming in PASCAL encourages one to use most of these, others, including most authoring languages, lack any facilities that encourage well-structured programs. The key rule is that one rarely (possibly never) uses the GOTO statement except to emulate the above structures. The indiscriminate use of the GOTO results in 'spaghetti' programming which is so common a definition is not considered necessary.

The second proviso associated with the use of the control structure is the rule about blocking: for any structure, there is only one way in and one way out. Nesting is positively encouraged but using a GOTO to jump out of one structure into another is forbidden.

Authoring languages are sometimes promoted as 'easy to use' by non-computer programmers who are going to be courseware developers. While there is no doubt the syntax of many of these languages facilitates development, one still needs to have the skills of professional programming to exploit them fully. In some cases the syntax loses high-level, general-purpose facilities or they become difficult to access (eg setting flags, using arrays, subroutines). Authoring languages tend to be like BASIC in that they are easy to use on an elementary level but no easier than any other language to implement complex algorithms needed to carry out even slightly sophisticated routeing in courseware. Not separating data from program control can also impede the implementation of algorithms. They can also tempt one into unstructured practices which result in courseware that is difficult to debug and maintain.

In the experience of the authors of this paper, it takes minimal effort, though considerable self-control initially, to follow principles of structured programming. It is not difficult to emulate structures not included by the natural syntax of the language and this has been consistently implemented in BASIC, FORTRAN, MENTOR and TOPCLASS, as well as PASCAL, in projects. The code tends to be slightly longer but the programs (liberally laced with comments) when combined with their respective flow- or structure charts, are relatively easy to test, debug, alter, and maintain.

A structured programming approach will also facilitate communication between subject expert and programmer: if the subject expert's prototype has been designed in a structured manner with the assistance of the educational systems analyst, not only will making alterations be easier but assistance from other team members will be enhanced and the programmer's implementation of a final version less prone to misinterpretation.

Yet with all this possible programming power there is one cautionary note: since the potential of programming complexity is now so great, there is a need for restraint. The danger exists that courseware will become so complex and convoluted that the learner will become lost as in a maze, detracting from the achievement of learning goals. We must always remember the 'customer'.

SOFTWARE DESIGN TOOLS

A number of software design tools exist on the market to facilitate the design and documentation of new software. However, no tools have been developed specifically for the CAL courseware environment. Existing ones will assist with components such as a technical simulation, but in practice when designing educational or training materials the difficulty lies within integration of the whole to produce a robust error-free system. This requires a tool that ensures a valid design and produces a documentation that is usable by typical members of a team.

There are a number of tools of the programming trade, some of which are more appropriate for CAL courseware development than others. Flowcharts have the advantage of being simple and relatively easy to use like a map but they can grow and become unwieldy. This tends to discourage designers and developers from properly documenting their work. Another system is structure charts (schematic logic) which are slightly more abstract, with a tree-like form. This scheme is much neater to use but can still be cumbersome when carried out with paper and pencil. Pseudo code tends to be very abstract but provides a bridge between the various charts and the source code of the implementation language.

Routeing charts can be imagined as simple flowcharts or high- level structure charts at an early stage of the stepwise refinement. They convey the possible routes the learner could take through the learning experience (tutorial, simulation etc). A modified version of these could be used as a courseware map for the learner.

The production of a valid, documented design can be achieved in part by the use of a software system that generates validated flow or structure charts. The use of these to model the learner's interaction with the courseware ensures that every possible state has a correspondence in the documentation and all possible routeings are clearly seen. What is not visible at the top level are the processes by which the detailed analysis of such input as answers and data will be carried out to control the routeing and meet the design specifications.

Such documentation and design facilities are useful at the high level at which a team is likely to work because, in general, they are not concerned with the computational details of how their design is to be implemented. However, it should be noted that when specifying a complex condition involving, for example, 'input analysis' and possibly considering previous inputs and data, a detailed specification must be provided by the team. If this is not done and the high level design is only annotated, then difficulties are likely to arise. The high-level charts can be expanded down to any level of detail and a complex routeing criteria can be readily specified and documented (stepwise refinement).

Free exchange of ideas is more likely with the availability of computer-based documentation tools in which designs can readily be changed and updated without a major manual drafting effort. However, it should be noted that the use of any of these charts only helps to specify the structure and internal links. They provide no task-specific tools that would be of benefit to the CAL team. For example, the importance of screen design which includes the possible use of dynamic effects, overlays and partial screen clearing is not supported by any specific design tool. Those that currently are available within many authoring systems are usually limited to a set of basic tasks involved in screen display and answer analysis but with no design-level documentation facility.

THE FUTURE

Future developments should provide design teams with software tools that will automatically carry out many structuring tasks and be self-documenting in the process. The flexibility of such systems as graphic courseware map generators and compilers would enhance the creative endeavours of teams and increase the effectiveness of the product as well as the efficiency of production.

REFERENCES

Black, T.R. (1987a) CAL delivery selection criteria and authoring systems. *Journal of Computer Assisted Learning*, **3**, 204-213.
Black, T.R. (1987b) Prototyping CAL courseware: A role for computer-shy subject experts. In Mathias, H., Rushby, N. and Budgett, R. (eds) *Aspects of Educational Technology XXI*. Kogan Page, London.
Black, T.R. (1988) Courseware design methodology: an overview. Unit 1 in *Courseware Design Methodology: Study Guide*. University of Surrey, mimeograph.
Crossfield, L., Hinton, T., Laubli, M. and Pope, M. (1984) *Final Report on an Evaluation of the Coventry PLATO Project*. Manpower Services Commission, Sheffield.
Enos, J.C. and Van Tilburg, R.L. (1979) Software design. In Jensen, R.W. and Tonies, C.C. (eds) *Software Engineering*. Prentice Hall.
Hinton, T. (1984) Authoring systems in computer-based training. Paper presented at a conference on computer-based training, Danish Postgraduate Engineering Society, Copenhagen, 3 May.
Jensen, R.W. (1979) Structured programming. In Jensen, R.W. and Tonies,C.C. (eds) *Software Engineering*. Prentice Hall.
Laubli, M.M. and Hinton, T. (1988) Implementing problems of computer based training within the UK governments Youth Training Scheme. *Computer Education*, **12**, 179-183.
Tonies, C.C. (1979) Project management fundamentals. In Jensen, R.W. and Tonies, C.C. (eds) *Software Engineering*. Prentice Hall.

5. Computing support services in further and higher education: managing mindstorms at maturity

Roger K Greenhalgh, *Harpter Adams Agricultural College, Newport, UK*

Summary: The role of a computing department and of a support service are fundamentally different though mutually supportive. The development and maintenance of cross-curricular initiatives utilizing information technology needs a special type of support, not necessarily originating from traditional computing specialists. Development of such support services often generates paradoxes that are difficult to resolve within traditional educational infrastructures. The evolution of novel learning micro-climates utilizing information technology resources relies upon exploratory and innovative changes requiring coordination and support. The further and higher education sectors could benefit from reflection upon some of the primary and secondary sector initiatives in this respect.

INTRODUCTION

Providing a computing support service to institutions in the further and higher education sectors presents a continuing problem in that the market forces acting upon this provision are undergoing considerable change. Traditionally computing provision has often been developed within the remit of a specialist computing department whose primary aim has been the servicing of specific computing-oriented disciplines of study and development or the processing of research-generated numerical data (Van Houwelling, 1987). As the potential for computing as a support medium for a wide range of courses of study has become apparent, the proportion of users requiring educational computing support continues to increase. In short, the profile of the typical institution computer user is changing. This paper addresses the paradoxes and opportunities which such a change precipitates.

In response to the historical and general intention of UK Central Government to stimulate the application of information technology within education, a variety of groups have been initiated within education, either directly or indirectly supported, with varied yet specific stimulation and support remits. The activities of groups such as these (Figure 1) have led to the production, stimulation or dissemination of tools, techniques and curriculum developments to the educational user. An onus has consequently been placed upon institutions themselves to evolve infrastructures which support the new computer-orientated organelles and processes so generated.

As initiatives utilizing computing tools and techniques have been implemented it has become evident that the learning environment itself is altered. For effective use of this new technology new facets to existing educational methodology became possible or even co-requisite (eg Chandler, 1984; Croucher, 1987, 1988b; Maddison, 1983). Thus a need for support with regard to both computing operations and to the induced modification of methodology is now recognized (eg Greenhalgh, 1987; Hart and Lesquereux, 1988; Murphy, 1986). The convergence and coalescence of communications and computing

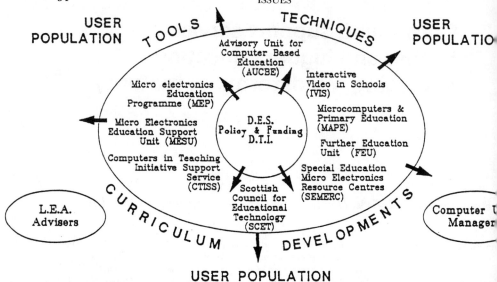

Exemplary Supporting Services of Educational Information Technology

Figure 1. *Exemplary supporting services of educational information technology*

technologies during the same era as large-scale computer integration into education extends this support requirement to the wider field of information technology (IT).

INFORMATION TECHNOLOGY SUPPORT

The evolution of any developing IT support infrastructure is influenced by the framework from which it was first drawn and the ethos of the establishment which it serves. In the last decade two existing extremes of institutional arrangement were clearly recognizable (Figures 2a and 2b) as either 'central' or 'diffuse' in their provision of computer service. Such differentiation was often a functional consequence of the computer systems adopted. Larger multi-user systems are more readily supported and maintained by a central computer unit. For the smaller minicomputer or microcomputer-based systems this requirement is immaterial; the systems may be supported entirely by the user departments.

As general user awareness and requirement for use of a wider range of software and hardware tools have increased, overall provision has often evolved in a piecemeal fashion. The result is often a 'complex' state (Figure 2c on p 36) in which the array of interactions between user groups on a site requires a significant coordinating input if efficient, functional and flexible modes of operation are to be maintained (eg Foote, 1987).

WHAT ARE THE ORGANIZATIONAL CHARACTERISTICS OF THE INSTITUTION'S TOTAL IT SERVICE?

Should IT development be coordinated hierarchically and driven paternistically, or should an organic, user-group driven structure be adopted?

In allocating responsibilities for coordinating IT resourcing, it is useful to identify spheres of influence for key personnel. It is not uncommon for further education colleges to operate

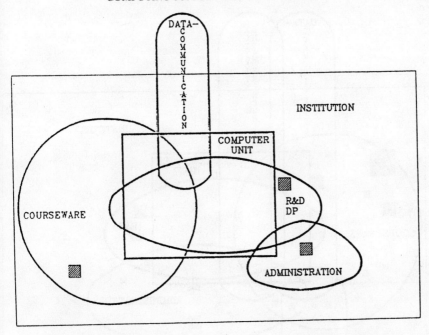

Figure 2a. *Computing provision in FE/HE institutions – Option A – 'central'*
– earlier days

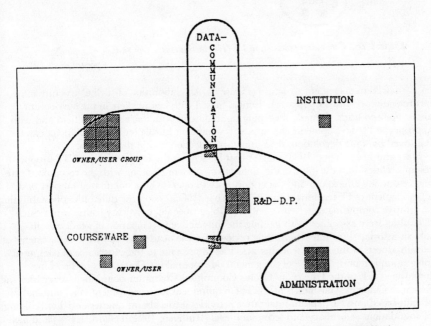

Figure 2b. *Computing provision in FE/HE institutions – Option B – 'Diffuse'*
– earlier days

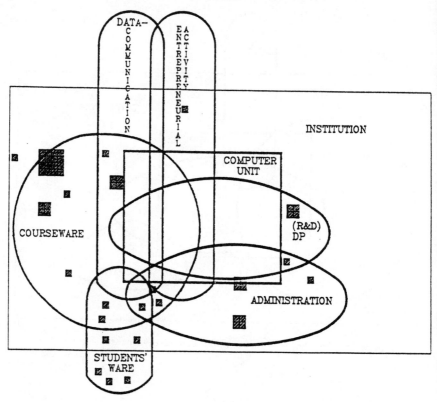

Figure 2c. *Computing provision in FE/HE institutions – Option C – 'Complex'*
– present needs 1988

on a 'matrix' management structure (Figure 3). An elaboration of such a structure may incorporate specialist IT support personnel linked with key workers in the curriculum areas. For end-users, the task of keeping up to date in both one's specialist field and with appropriate IT developments can appear a significant hurdle (eg Ford, 1988) yet can be improved by some devolution, delegation and selection within the IT area.

Hart and Lesquereux (1988) suggest that for schools the incorporation of 'IT support responsibilities' into the job specifications of key personnel, along with the recognized time and resourcing allocations and the opportunity to operate on a one-to-one support basis, is a key element of IT teaching support. Croucher (1988a) notes the difficulties of establishing integrative computing experiences within 'subject specific' university course areas. Such difficulties were associated with gaining the fully active participation of academics in subject-associated team teaching. The review by some academics and their departments of certain aspects of their own teaching activities in response to the experience of computer integration is reported as one of the general outcomes of the Computers in Teaching Initiative (CTI) of the University Grants Committee/Computer Board for Universities and Research Councils (Gardner, 1987a). The requirement for development of a combination of skills-based and curriculum-integrative activities seems almost quintessential to building IT foundations at primary and secondary level (Ruthven, 1984; Telford, 1988a) and has been adopted as a strategy in some higher education initiatives (eg Croucher, 1988a; Littler and Williams, 1988; McDonough, 1986; Trainor, 1986).

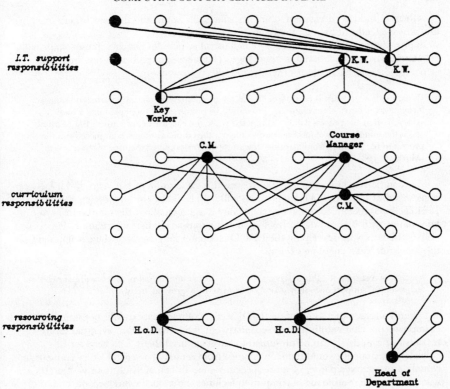

Figure 3. *LT support personnel in education line-management*

This type of approach necessitates the coordination of teaching teams often drawn from across traditional subject boundaries. Gardner (1987a,b) emphasizes the challenges to the academic community of dissemination of its educational computing products and experiences and of organizational issues for project management. Several CTI project managers also identify this need for close coordination and regular evaluation at all levels of educational computing project development (eg Jones, 1986; Waddicor, 1986).

The ambivalence of academic commitment to university educational computing projects is associated with the current emphasis on research rather than teaching as an assessment of performance (Waddicor, 1986). The concept of 'bridge-building' posts between academia and computing (Hirschheim et al, 1988) seems to provide at least one means of addressing the organizational challenges outlined above.

DOES THE INSTITUTION PERCEIVE A NEED FOR THE PROVISION OF INTRODUCTORY OR REMEDIAL IT EDUCATION FOR ITS MEMBERS AND HOW IS SUCH NEED EXPECTED TO CHANGE OVER TIME?

What are the perceived skills in IT applications widely evidenced in the pool of recruits to the institution and how readily are any such skills transferable to the institution's environment?

What are the expected changes in the institution's IT resource environment?

Is there a 'hidden curriculum' of information skills implicit in the institution's teaching and which IT education might enhance?

In providing an IT support structure it is useful to plan for changes in user skills, skill requirements and educational methodology. The following has been a not untypical criticism of recent curriculum structure and interpretation:

> 'Learning how to learn is rarely specified as a curriculum aim, nor are information skills a formal part of curriculum planning. It seems to be presumed by those planning school syllabuses that the process will be assimilated while subjects are being studied. But as pupils reach the middle years of secondary schooling ... the emphasis moves even more from the process to the product, from learning to learn to a short-circuited learning of the answers.' (Marland, 1981)

Many initiatives have attempted to redress this criticism in recent years and it has been suggested that integrative IT applications will help facilitate this process (eg Ruthven, 1984; Telford, 1988a). Information technology is as much about the management of information as it is about the technology helping to manage that information. Papert's (1980) philosophy in developing the LOGO computer language was the development of the computer as an enabling device:

> '... that of a carrier of cultural 'germs' or 'seeds' whose intellectual products will not need technological support once they take root in an actively growing mind ... '

It seems a reasonable assumption that one effect of information skills becoming accepted as implicit core curriculum skills in secondary education will be that eventual future recruits to FE and HE can be presumed to have acquired them. The need for IT education in students would therefore change from remedial or introductory contexts to consolidatory, emancipatory or more specialist ones. In lieu of institutions wishing their students to make routine use of computing facilities the scenario may become one of students wishing for more computing facilities to make routine use of.

In a 1987 census of microcomputer use in the county's primary schools, the generic software package availability for pupil use was recorded (Telford, 1988a). The percentage uptake of packages for pupil use is not evenly distributed (Figure 4). A tempting conclusion is that the types of package which are easiest to use (or require least support) are those most readily adopted. This trend seems also to be supported in a repeat of this census in the first quarter of 1988 (Telford, 1988b) in which the uptake is greater, yet the trend remains the same. Evidently there is some aspect of 'information retrieval' with which staff find (or anticipate finding) particular difficulty in a classroom context.

CONCLUSION

There is a growing body of practitioners in education who are making use of computing and information technology tools and techniques as media for learning. In evaluating the success of the applications of this medium, several facets are open to examination. The capabilities of the users and of the instructors in the use of these tools together with the quality and suitability of the materials themselves, form only a starting point. The context and techniques of their application are also open to experiment and enquiry and through such enquiry and evaluation teaching methodology, including the use of this medium, may undergo change.

The literature provides ample indication of the continued 'reinvention of the wheel' as practitioners develop their own IT inclusive methodologies. There is arguably a new role for support-staffing to aid this development and its dissemination. The breadth of applications and variety of tools and techniques required or available throughout an

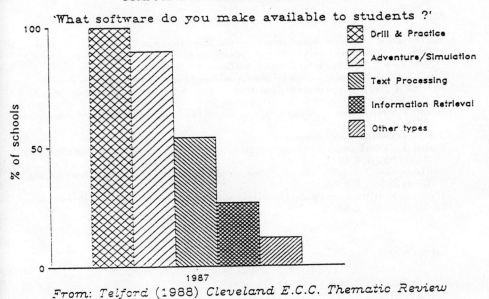

Figure 4. *Software usage in primary schools* (From: telford (1988) *Cleveland ECC Thematic Review*)

institution, particularly regarding its high capital cost, suggest an additional requirement for a coordinating role to be assumed by such a support team. The nature of the developments suggests that support staff would need some depth of appreciation of computational, educational and subject elements of their support areas. Their posts would be recognizably incorporated into the institutional staffing structure with aims specified by an institutional IT support strategy.

REFERENCES

Chandler, D. (1984) *Young Learners and the Microcomputer.* Open University Press, Milton Keynes.

Croucher, A. (1987) Teaching introduction to computing courses at Exeter. *The CTISS File*, **3**, 24-26.

Croucher, A. (1988a) Learning computer lessons at Exeter, *Computer Education*, **56**, 19-20.

Croucher, A. (1988b) CTI project report: teaching subject specific courses at Exeter. *The CTISS File*, **5**, 17-21.

Foote, K.E. (1987) Project Quest at the University of Texas. *The CTISS File*, **5**, 40-43.

Ford, C.E. (1988) CAL for a newcomer. *The CTISS File*, **6**, 60-63.

Gardner, N. (1987a) The CTI: an interim assessment. *The CTISS File*, **6**, 6-7.

Gardner, N. (1987b) Integrating computers into the university curriculum: the experience of the UK Computers in Teaching Initiative. *ACM-SIGUCCS*, **15**, 425-431.

Greenhalgh, R. (1987) Facilitating the evolution of more effective CAL strategies. *Computer Education*, **55**, 9-10.

Hart, M. and Lesquereux, J. (1988) Promoting the use of IT across the curriculum. *Computer Education*, **55**, 4-5.

Hirscheim, R., Smithson, S. and Whitehouse, D. (1988) Microcomputer use in the humanities and social sciences: a UK university survey. *The CTISS File*, **5**, 3-6.

Jones, S. (1986) Conference report: IUSC Workshop Bangor. *The CTISS File*, **2**, 11-12.

Littler, S. and Williams, W. (1988) CTI project report: the Cardiff experience. *The CTISS File*, **5**, 7-16.

Maddison, J. (1983) *Education in the Microelectronics Era.* Open University Press, Milton Keynes.

Marland, M. (1981) (ed) Information skills in the secondary curriculum. *Schools Council Curriculum Bulletin 9*. Methuen.

McDonough, R. (1986) The Anaeas project: one year down, two to go. *The CTISS File*, **2**, 40-41.

Murphy, P. (1986) Information technology in Manchester schools. In Ennals, R., Gwyn, R. and Zdravchev, L. (eds) *Information Technology and Education*. Ellis Horwood.

Papert, S. (1980) *Mindstorms – Children, Computers and Powerful Ideas*. Harvester Press.

Ruthven, K. (1984) Computer literacy and the curriculum. *British Journal of Educational Studies*, **32**, 2, 134-147.

Telford, J. (1988a) *Cleveland Educational Computing Centre: Thematic Review 2: Computers in Primary Schools*. CECC.

Telford, J. (1988b) *Personal Communication*.

Trainor, R. (1986) Introducing microcomputers into history teaching and research: the DISH project. *The CTISS File*, **2**, 14-17.

Van Houwelling, D.E. (1987) The information network: its structure and role in higher education. *Library Hi Tech*, **5**, 2, 7-17.

Waddicor, M. (1986) Report of a workshop held on the topic of the CTI projects in the humanities. *The CTISS File*, **2**, 6-8.

6. Contract work in the development of curriculum materials: some issues and problems

P J Rodbard and N D C Harris, *Faculty of Education and Design, Brunel University, UK*

Summary: Historically, universities employed a number of full-time research staff on a permanent basis to work on externally funded projects. Contract work, often sponsored by industry, tends to require full-time staff but on a short-term contract. These extreme variations of research sponsorship create a variety of problems both for individuals and the host institutions.

CURRENT FINANCING OF UK UNIVERSITIES

An important indication of the research activity of a department has always been its publications. Many university and polytechnic annual reports list publications. The CVCP/UGC Working Group in its 1986 statement suggested that a performance indicator could be the percentage of staff in a cost centre who had not published in the previous three years. The sort of published works which are used as a measure of successful practice may include books, journal articles, conference papers and contributions to edited books. Some assessments may only include journal articles (Gillett, 1986).

Individuals undertaking projects funded by research grants experience little difficulty in publishing their findings. Unfortunately the private sponsors of many short-term contracts are reluctant to give permission for publication of any findings. The reluctance could be for a number of different reasons; perhaps the two most common would be that the information acquired either may not show the organization in a favourable light, or that it would be commercially unwise to let others see confidential information. Therefore a large number of short-term research contracts may not provide any publications which would enhance the reputation of the host institution by illustrating both the range and quality of the work undertaken. The reputation of the individuals concerned in these type of contracts would also suffer by their not being able to publish, which may make recruiting more difficult.

UK universities and other higher education establishments are currently being forced by reduced grants and ever-increasing costs to review and extend the methods whereby additional income is obtained. Until recently research was viewed not as a major source of income but as a means for the pursuit of pushing forward the boundaries of knowledge; the reputations of individuals and institutions were subsequently enhanced. However, recent financial pressures have forced all institutions to review their research practices and expectations as a possible solution to generating much needed funds and being identified as the top research institutions (Becher and Kogan, 1987).

Many universities have adapted well to this new challenge and have attracted sufficient research contracts to make a significant contribution to their income. Southampton and London Universities, for example, have both achieved a creditable 23 per cent of their recurrent income from research grants and contracts during the period 1985/86 (UGC Statistics, 1987). This report also shows that the income gained from research grants and contracts has risen a staggering 103 per cent over a five-year period and 18 per cent in the last year alone (see Table 1).

Source of income	1980–81 (£M)	1984–85 (£M)	1985–86 (£M)	Percentage change since 1980–81	1984–8
General recurrent income					
Exchequer grants	979	1258	1312	34	4
Fees and support grants	269	283	313	16	11
Other sources	69	127	133	92	5
All sources	1317	1668	1758	34	5
Specific recurrent income					
Research grants and contracts	202	349	410	103	18
Other sources	45	103	127	185	23
All sources	246	452	537	118	19

Table 1. *Income of universities: 1980–81 to 1985–86 (UGC, 1987)*

Much of the income from government-funded research bodies provides finance for research staff. In some cases, particularly in science and engineering, equipment can also be provided. However, the survival income relates to overheads. Funding for overheads from government research bodies is often limited to a small proportion or appears as a block grant one or two years later at about 40 per cent.

In comparison, contracts with industrial, commercial and public utilities currently attract overheads of around 50 per cent or more with these being paid sometimes in advance but more frequently quarterly, or at least much more quickly. The host institution receives a relatively immediate income allowing the possible temporary investment of any monies received. It is not surprising that the Committee of Vice Chancellors and Principals would like to see the overheads for research and development increased to between 100–150 per cent of direct staff payment costs.

If this increase is implemented it will probably be paid reluctantly by industrial concerns who may have previously obtained technological developments on the cheap. The losers would of course be those individuals or institutions that undertake research and development into education or the social sciences because this vastly increased rate would make it extremely difficult or impossible to attract any sponsors from industry, professional bodies, the charitable concerns or, particularly, local education authorities.

RESEARCH STAFF

Research workers are often attracted because they can register for higher degrees which may be linked with the sponsored research. Longer contracts provided either by grants or private sponsors provide an ideal time-span in which to undertake this kind of work, enhancing personal satisfaction and career development. Unfortunately, many private contracts are of one year duration making higher degrees dependent upon acquiring new contracts. This leaves the individual with the prospect of not being able to complete their degrees should the funding stop.

The recruitment of full-time research staff is very difficult because of the extremely precarious nature of the employment. Often two or three contracts are necessary to make up the research worker's salary. One solution to this problem is to recruit part-time staff, perhaps seconded from local authorities or other institutions. In reality, teachers engaged on part-time contract work receive little if any financial reward for their efforts. However the major problem appears to be getting the teachers released to undertake this type of part-time or even full-time research work. Local authorities may well be prepared to second teachers for educational research and development work, but often headteachers and governors are extremely reluctant to release suitable teachers, especially in shortage subjects.

For the individual teacher, there are few incentives to attract them to undertake the considerable workload associated with research and development work. Often no extra money is involved.

A solution to the problem of release and payment is to engage teachers to work in their own time on private contracts (with appropriate monitoring and support). In this way teachers can be paid but the possibilities for any publications are subsequently reduced unless materials for schools can be generated which acknowledge or identify the author(s). What is the market for such materials?

DEVELOPMENT OF CURRICULUM MATERIALS

The financial pressures affecting our educational system over the last few years have resulted in a continual decrease in real terms on book expenditure. The Book Publishers Association have found that the Book Price Index has decreased up to an alarming 60 per cent in the metropolitan districts for the secondary sector during the period 1978/86. The average figure for England and Wales during the same period is 44 per cent (see Table 2).

When this reduction on book expenditure is combined with a wealth of new examinations and initiatives, then the situation presents a special opportunity for commercial organizations. They can provide up-to-date learning materials at little or no cost for teachers which help to alleviate the awkward predicament in which they find themselves: that of providing modern professional quality learning materials that are cheap, stimulating and, most of all, appropriate to the syllabus being taught (Rodbard and Harris, 1988).

There is a considerable range of different learning materials currently on offer to teachers which are produced by commercial organizations at little, or no cost. They vary from printed materials in the form of posters, booklets, leaflets, books, information sheets and activity cards to more expensive productions of slides, films, videos, computer software and, soon, interactive videos.

	Secondary			
	Spending Per Capita	Spending Per Capita	% Change	% Change
	1978/79	1985/86	RPI	BPI
	£	£		
Average London	8.08	16.57	+9.7	−23.3
Average English Counties	6.66	11.11	−10.7	−37.6
Average Metropolitan Districts	7.32	7.92	−42.1	−59.5
Average Wales	6.05	8.53	−24.6	−47.3
Average England/Wales	7.31	10.92	−20.1	−44.1

KEY   RPI - Retail Price Index
        BPI - Book Price Index

Table 2. *School book expenditure*

PUBLICITY OR LEARNERS NEEDS?

Teachers engaged in developing curriculum materials under a commercial contract can find themselves torn between writing to suit the sponsor and writing to meet the needs of learners, teachers and schools. This can create a major dilemma for the individual, especially when pressure is brought to bear to increase the advertising aspects. This must be tactfully but forcefully resisted because it is vital that teachers and schools welcome the material to supplement existing resources rather than to reject any material out of hand because of apparent bias or blatant sales pitches.

A number of responsible commercial organizations have recently invested enormous sums for the production of suitable materials for schools. The Electricity Council has gone one step further by making considerable funds available for practising teachers in a variety of subjects to develop syllabus-related learning materials, monitored and supported by Brunel University. This is an innovative step on the part of this organization to tailor learning materials to the requirements of schools, teachers and examinations.

Such developments are possible by short-term contracts with the host institution which not only coordinates but provides the specialist support necessary to enable the eventual production of good quality materials. However, commercial organizations can undergo unforeseen circumstances or policy changes which result in changing the required work during the contract. To enable a flexible approach, a research and development contract may be tightly worded providing realistic objectives, but with a let-out clause which creates an unpredictable element for the research worker. A change in direction, perhaps half-way through a development contract, would not only have wasted a considerable amount of time and effort, but it would substantially reduce the amount and perhaps the quality of the eventual material produced.

The host institution in constant liaison with the funding organization can ensure that any materials developed are in harmony with the interests of the organization without over emphasis on marketing. Extreme tact and diplomacy may be necessary by both parties to overcome this difficult and potential conflict area. Ultimately the funding organization is paying the bills and it will want at least some of its perceived needs met or it will find another route.

Therefore rather than the host institution turning down a potentially lucrative contract, considerable effort has to be made to find common ground on which to build a working relationship where the eventual results would not impede the reputation of either party. Any material subsequently produced will at least have had constructive screening throughout its development stage, rather than the alternative which is the organization going it alone perhaps regardless of the needs of schools, teachers and pupils.

CONCLUSIONS

All the problems illustrated so far add up to an extremely insecure existence for research and development staff. Those who take up either full- or part-time contracts must view the work as being of a very temporary nature because the possibilities of continuous contracts are rather more remote.

The way to increase the vital revenue from research work is not for universities to price themselves out of the market by vastly increasing overheads but to provide a professional service which will both enhance their reputation and ensure many more contracts to come. One simple way to achieve this is by increasing the job security and the incentives necessary to attract and retain experienced staff who have the abilities to pursue, acquire and successfully complete essential contract work.

The conflicts for universities are short-term financial gain versus long-term reputation; short-term employment contracts versus investment in experience. The financial pressures tend to encourage the short-term approach while tradition rests with the long-term approach. How many more research staff can we train, use and lose? How much investment and loss of productive output goes into training? How much does the rest of the educational system gain from what we lose (eg in training of teachers in research and development, development of curriculum materials)?

REFERENCES

Becher, T. and Kogan, M. (1987) *Calling Britain's Universities to Account*. Education Reform Group, London.

Gillett, R. (1986) Serious anomalies in the UGC comparative evaluation of performance of psychology departments. Paper from Department of Psychology, University of Leicester.

Rodbard, P.J. and Harris, N.D.C. (1988) Commercially sponsored learning materials in the classroom. In Mathias, H., Rushby, N. and Budgett, R. (eds) *Aspects of Educational Technology XXI*. Kogan Page, London.

The Educational Publishers Council (1987) *School book Expenditure*. The Publishers Association, London.

University Grants Committee (1987) *University Statistics 1985-1986, Vol.3*. Universities' Statistical Record, Cheltenham.

Section 2:
Improving learning with the new technologies

7. Hypertext and compact discs: the challenge of multimedia learning

Jacquetta Megarry, 5 *Glencairn Gardens, Glasgow, UK*

Summary: The role of the computer should be organizing and representing knowledge to give the learner easy access and control, rather than trying to create a model of the user and seeking to prescribe his or her own route through it. Hypertext is high-level software through which the user explores and interacts with knowledge in a non-linear and interactive way. Not only can users pursue a variety of suggested routes through the material, they can also create new pathways for themselves and others to follow, forging new links, recording comments and suggesting extensions. Hypertext is inherently multi-user, blurring the distinction between author and reader. Hypermedia is the name sometimes given to the multimedia capability of hypertext, emphasizing presentations in which users can combine, edit and orchestrate sounds, graphics, text, moving pictures and computer software, at the click of a mouse.

Compact disc technology provides the perfect partner to hypertext, offering extremely dense, robust and flexible storage. Products such as CD-ROM (compact disc read-only memory) and CD-I (compact disc interactive) and technologies such as DVI (digital video interactive), offer immense scope for multimedia learning. Educational technologists face an urgent challenge to harness the unprecedented potential of this combination.

BEYOND WORDS

The era of mass education has been dominated by the spoken and written word. Schools, colleges, universities and, more recently, agencies of distance learning, have been brokers of learning that (outside mathematics) is overwhelmingly verbal. Yet large areas of our brains are dedicated to decoding and interpreting still and moving images and to processing raw sound as opposed to verbal descriptions of sounds. For many learning tasks, multimedia methods can be not only more appropriate than verbal ones, but also more efficient. Frequently they are more motivating.

Computer-assisted learning (CAL) has already shown great promise, but has also been largely confined to verbal learning. Too many computers are still used as page-turning devices, despite their immense capability for more flexible and interactive styles of use.

Systems for creating and editing computer graphics have tended to be primitive and labour intensive, with crude presentation of low-resolution images, sometimes in monochrome, seldom with any subtlety of shading or saturation. Realistic visual information has been confined to the hitherto analogue world of interactive video. Such systems are riddled by hardware incompatibilities, proving expensive both to create and to deliver; they make excessive demands on the user, requiring expertise to set them up and being greedy for desktop space. These features are unhelpful to both learners and teachers.

The convergence of computing and compact disc technologies is about to produce an all-digital, interactive, compact multimedia learning medium. It will also, by Western standards, be affordable, ultimately even cheap. To exploit such a system, we must break away from the habit of thinking about a computer screenful as a 'page' and from the notion of reading text in linear fashion. Hypertext is the key which can unlock the vast potential of compact disc knowledge bases and put them under the control of the learner. To understand how, we need a profound shift in our paradigm of computers in learning.

DATA, INFORMATION, KNOWLEDGE AND EXPERTISE

Much of the CAL hitherto developed suffers from the failure of its designers to recognize the continuum running from data, through knowledge and wisdom, to expertise. Many enthusiasts, lacking both a background in cognitive psychology and the commonsense of any nursery teacher, have operated on the 'empty-bucket' model of the learner, assuming that they have only to pour in facts to send the learner away better informed and wiser.

Knowledge is not merely a collection of facts. Although we may be able to memorize isolated undigested facts for a short while at least, meaningful learning demands that we internalize the information: we break it down, digest it and locate it in our pre-existing, highly complex web of interconnected knowledge and ideas, building fresh links and restructuring old ones. 'The difference between an expert on a subject and the rest of us is in part that the expert breaks down new information into more relevant chunks than we do and has more knowledge to connect it to' (Anderson, 1988).

Computers have long demonstrated their excellence at data processing and have also become useful as information systems. However, they are only just beginning to tackle human knowledge and expertise. The process has been handicapped by the lack of an agreed theory of human learning, let alone an agreed theory of instruction.

In recent years, a false trail has been laid by 'intelligent tutoring systems' that try to model the learner (based on no better evidence than an occasional key-press), and seek to optimize the 'treatment' according to the system's decision about what the student needs. To treat the learner as a dumb patient and the computer system as an omniscient doctor is both perverse and arrogant. Furthermore, a prescription based on the wrong diagnosis can be more damaging than no treatment at all. As Gaines (1987) demonstrates, control theory is inadequate for many industrial processes where insufficient data is available, let alone for the immense task of modelling human learning. It is more prudent to use the computer system to model the knowledge base and to give the learner freedom to choose how to interact with it.

Giving the learners more autonomy may also make them more effective. Experience in grasping or recreating the structure of a knowledge base is an important part of a learner's development. Educators have tended to assume that they must always structure and prepackage knowledge, selecting and assembling learning resources (for example, textbooks, study guides and audiovisual media). Too often we hand the learner an itinerary rather than a map of the terrain and a survival kit. This partly stems from the logistical problems posed by handling authentic source material and raw images. To solve them, we need not only powerful and friendly software tools, but also very large and robust multimedia storage. These needs are respectively met by hypertext and compact disc media.

HYPERTEXT AND HYPERMEDIA

Hypertext is high-level software through which the user explores knowledge in non-linear and interactive ways. It contains elements of word processing, outline processing and information linking, but deliberately sets out to blur the distinction between author and reader. It is essentially a multi-user system (like a computer conference to which anyone can contribute), and subsequent users may benefit from all previous contributions (Mason, 1988). Thus hypertext not only allows users to pursue a variety of suggested trails through the text, they can also create new pathways for themselves and others to follow, forging new links, recording comments and suggesting extensions.

If, on borrowing a library book, you found that most pages had marginal notes and cross-references from every previous reader, you might be dismayed. As someone who loves books and hates censorship, I should be outraged if certain pages had been torn out or amended. But computer systems allow users the option of viewing the 'clean' or annotated version, taking a guided tour or browsing at will. Although Old Testament scholars will naturally expect unrestricted access to the original text in full, they might also appreciate the option of guided tours with commentaries through the eyes of Jesus, St Paul, Martin Luther, the Pope and the Prophet Mahomet.

Hypertext systems control who is allowed to insert links and who (if anyone) is allowed to amend or even delete sections. Weyer (1988) identifies some options that hypertext systems might offer the learner:

Request	System's interpretation
Tell me	Give me the facts, no embellishments
Inform me	Give me facts plus background and other viewpoints
Amuse me	Find interesting connections or perspectives
Challenge me	Make me find or create connections or insights
Guide me	Suggest pathways but let me browse
Teach me	Provide step-by-step guidance

Hypertext thus supports a learning style radically different from linear reading or viewing, and different again from traditional interactive CAL. Suppose you wish to find your way around a large text database; hypertext lets you pursue cross-references, conduct keyword searches of encyclopaedic databases, consult dictionaries, check etymology or find synonyms or translations very simply. Mechanisms vary, but a popular one is to click the mouse on a 'button' (a live area on the screen which is somehow highlighted). Clicking on a button produces some action. For example, a window might open to display more information (eg an explanation or translation) or an illustration (eg an image or sound). Navigation is helped by creating 'bookmarks', making back-tracking easier, and providing concept maps. Such techniques are important since many large jumps can make it all too easy for the learner to 'get lost'.

Hypertext stems from seminal work published by Bush (1945), followed-up by Engelbart (1963) and Nelson in the early 1960s. The term 'hypertext' was coined by Ted Nelson in 1965, although it took over 20 years to enter the language. Nelson's 'Project Xanadu' was a system with the modest goal of linking, online and in real time, just about all the knowledge in the world, adding new knowledge as it became available, and allowing anyone to locate information through an indexing system that searched for ideas (however they were expressed) rather than for specific words or strings. While none of the hypertext products so far released approach this ideal, two recent ones are clearly steps in that direction: 'Guide' and 'HyperCard'.

OWL International's 'Guide', released for Apple (1986) and IBM compatibles (1987), was the first significant hypertext product for microcomputers. Guide can cope with very long documents (such as the Bible) as well as some fascinating mixtures of media. HyperCard takes its name from the metaphor of an index card, although each screen (of up to 32 kilobytes) is much more flexible than a card system suggests. Cards are grouped in 'stacks' with a common basic design and purpose, and a HyperCard stack may be a valuable knowledge base or educational product in its own right. For example, FingerSpell is a HyperCard stack in which each word can be shown in sign language, and/or prompted and/or spoken under user control (Markman, 1988). 'Stackware' (whether sold or freely shared) may be left unprotected to encourage local adaptation. 'Scripts' (programs) are written in HyperTalk, a language which is easier for users to modify than

File Edit Search Option

≡☐≡≡≡≡≡ Multimedia encyclopaedia ≡≡≡≡≡

Distribution The kingfisher is found in every European country, though it is not common. Both sexes have highly coloured plumage.

Nesting It nests in a hole in the bank, usually near water. 6–8 glossy white eggs are laid at a time, 22 by 18.5 mm approx.

Feeding It feeds on insects, shellfish, minnows and small fry, watching its prey from a high vantage point. After an almost vertical dive it catches the fish underwater in its spear-like bill.

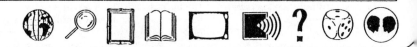

Figure 1a. *Screen from a hypertext encyclopaedia article on the kingfisher*

traditional programming languages.

Apple's late 1987 launch of HyperCard, and its crucial decision to 'bundle' (ie include at no extra cost) a copy with every new Macintosh, made hypertext an overnight buzzword at conferences and in the computer press. In Seattle in March 1988, Bill Atkinson (HyperCard's creator) told an international conference how astonished he had been by the public response: over 800 HyperCard stacks had been published in magazines and exchanged on bulletin boards within the first six months. Danny Goodman's 'Complete HyperCard Handbook' became an instant bestseller, with 150,000 copies in print within three months (Goodman, 1987). The hypertext bandwagon was rolling.

Hypertext gives users interactive control over not only text, but also sounds, photographs, graphics, moving pictures and computer software, weaving them into a seamless carpet of knowledge. Multimedia presentations can be combined, edited and orchestrated quickly and intuitively. Some authors distinguish multimedia applications by referring to 'hypermedia' rather than 'hypertext' (eg Meyrowitz, 1988), but I prefer to use 'hypertext' generally, since one neologism seems sufficient and 'hypermedia' lends inappropriately plural connotations to a singular concept.

Figure 1a, and its continuation Figure 1b, present screens from an imaginary hypertext encyclopaedia article on the kingfisher.

Bold print represents cross-references that are available at one hop. The globe icon evokes distribution maps, and the magnifying glass zooms-in for more detail. The picture-frame

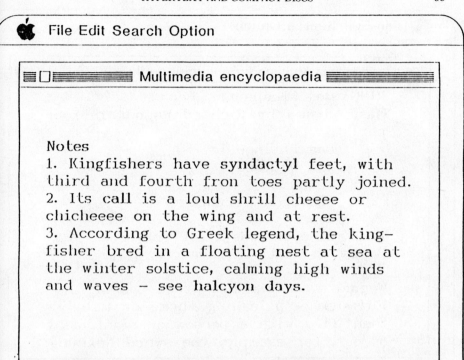

Figure 1b. *Screen from a hypertext encyclopaedia article on the kingfisher (continued)*

icon might conjure up a carousel of photographs or anatomical diagrams, while the television icon could elicit a short above-and under-water sequence of the kingfisher diving for fish. In between, lies the scrapbook icon which is used to 'cut and paste' text and images into a personal album which is saved to disc and can also be printed. The loudspeaker icon evokes a sample of kingfisher birdsong, while the question-mark icon produces a series of quizzes on the kingfisher's habitat, anatomy and food chains. Questions would, of course, be illustrated whenever appropriate and the quizzes would be available at various levels of difficulty and language level, giving the user feedback on answers and pointers to further points of exploration. The dice icon would lead the player into an interactive simulation game on the river ecosystem, and the talking heads are selected to switch between half-a-dozen languages for screen messages and commentary, and so on.

Figure 2 demonstrates that precisely the same set of icons and conventions lend themselves to quite different subject matter. Clicking on Wagner leads to a screen on the composer's life, including significant places and dates. A location map is available with more detail in key areas: for example, there are contemporary engravings of the Bayreuth Festival Theatre (cross-section and interior view). Clicking on 'leitmotiv' gives access to a library of all the leitmotive in Wagner's music, which can not only be heard in high-fidelity recording, but also shown in musical notation and juxtaposed with the relevant parts of the libretto. Pairs of languages (such as German and English) can be displayed in

File Edit Search Option

Multimedia encyclopaedia

RING, des Nibelungen, Der
Music drama by Richard Wagner in four
parts:
          Das Rheingold
          Die Walküre
          Siegfried
          Götterdämmerung

The full cycle was first performed at
Bayreuth Festival Theatre.

Wagner's music makes great use of the
leitmotiv – a leading theme or melody
identified with a person or significant
object, for example, the sword Nothung.

Figure 2. *Screen from a hypertext encyclopaedia article on the Wagner's music*

parallel texts. The quiz option includes leitmotiv recognition with graded levels and user control over contextual clues presented visually and by libretto. With a continuous performance time of around 18 hours for the Ring cycle, the advantages of random access are obvious.

COMPACT DISCS AS MULTIMEDIA STORAGE

Perhaps the above sounds fanciful? Although it does not describe any single existing product, I have already seen every feature described above at some stage of development, mostly somewhere between drawing-board and commercial reality; my forthcoming book (Megarry, 1989) gives chapter and verse. Grolier's pioneering multimedia version of the 'American Academic Encyclopaedia' already does much of this and more besides, and is among the very first compact disc interactive (CD-I) discs scheduled for release in autumn 1989 (Cook, 1988). By the early 1990s, products with such features will be consumer items aimed at mass markets in the US, Japan and Europe. They will be published in compact disc format: a shimmering disc 12 cm in diameter, smaller and more robust than a floppy disc, and with immensely greater storage capacity.

Compact discs (announced in 1982) have been the most successful consumer product ever brought to market. Over 65 million CDs were sold in the first two years that they were available, and over 10 million players in their first three years. Player prices fell from $1,000 or so in 1984 to around $150 by 1988. Outside specialist applications, the days of black vinyl records are clearly numbered.

In 1985, Philips/Sony launched CD-ROM (compact disc read only memory) in which high-fidelity sound is replaced by data, but manufacturing techniques and disc size are identical. A single CD-ROM holds around 600 megabytes (ie over 600,000 kilobytes) or enough to store all 100 million words in 1,500 full-length paperback novels. All 23.5 million addresses in the UK have already been pressed on to a single CD-ROM, and all the telephone directories in Europe would fit on just two such discs.

CD-ROM drives are computer peripherals, at first linked to IBM compatible PCs, and since 1988 also to Apple systems. Early products were in vertical niche markets, notably as a means of distributing large medical, bibliographic and financial databases and reference works. Published CD-ROMs multiplied rapidly: new titles in the first few years increased from 2 in 1985, 12 in 1986, 80 in 1987 to 200 or more in 1988. An important educational application is based at the UK Open University, where ECCTIS not only developed large databases of educational opportunities on CD-ROM, but also pioneered updating methods such as Softstrip and data broadcasting (Frogbrook, 1988).

The next stage according to Philips/Sony is CD-I (compact disc interactive) announced in 1986 and due for consumer launch late 1989. The joint standard specifies how the 650 megabytes available can hold still frames (up to 7,800), audio (from 1.2 hours of CD quality stereo to 19.2 hours of speech quality mono), text and graphics (up to 150,000 pages), partial-screen moving video, animated graphics, or can trade off any combination of these. The program that controls the presentation is also stored on the CD-I disc. A recent book documents not only the standard but also range of applications, from the Grolier multimedia encyclopaedia to simulated golf, from a French phrasebook to interactive detective mysteries (Philips International, 1988). CD-I players will feed into domestic television sets, and are expected to cost around $1,000. They will also play audio CDs; indeed owners of suitable CD players may be able to upgrade to CD-I with an accessory plugged into its digital inputs and outputs. CD-I is a self-contained consumer durable, not a computer peripheral like CD-ROM, although a keyboard is a likely optional extra.

Meanwhile, General Electric has been developing clever compression techniques to overcome what it regards as CD-I's Achilles' heel: its inability to cope with full-screen full-motion video. DVI (digital video interactive) is a technology in two parts. The first step is to compress video into a tiny fraction of its original space with little loss of quality. Step two is to provide boards (which will be plugged into users' computers) which provide sufficiently fast decompression to allow real-time playback of moving video. The result is that DVI can already squeeze 72 minutes of full-screen full-motion video with audio on to a single CD-ROM (or two hours of half screen, or comparable trade-offs).

DVI technology is advancing rapidly as demonstrated in Seattle in March 1988, compression was already being performed 60 times faster than at its first showing the year before. High-quality results require a remote compression service in which, even using specialized and expensive hardware, each frame takes just over three seconds to compress. However, the DVI team also demonstrated 'edit-level video' which allows instantaneous capture, manipulation and playback on the user's IBM AT or compatible. This provided adequate quality to capture the lightning dexterity of a live juggler on stage. Edit-level video gives PC users desktop control of studio-style video and audio effects, and the immense advantage of immediate feedback while developing a presentation.

Significant pilot applications of DVI include 'Design and Decorate' and 'Palenque'. In the former, users design a custom living room, selecting size and shape, wall covering, furniture and fabrics; the room can be viewed from various angles, edited and transformed at will. Accurate colouring and high-quality textures are important to the realism. Palenque is a high-budget project of General Electric jointly with Bank Street College of

Education, in which children control surrogate travel through an ancient Mayan site, with access to multimedia databases on the rain forest, the Maya, maps and glyph writing. The user controls the surrogate movement (body and eye movements) intuitively, using a joystick.

DVI is a technology, not a product. It can work not only with CD-ROM, but also with hard discs, with WORMs (write once read mostly discs) and other digital storage. Initially, at least, it is aimed at corporate IBM users. Nevertheless, General Electric's plans for consumer-oriented DVI applications may result in products that compete head-on with CD-I. At the Third International Microsoft Conference (Seattle, March 1988) not only was the rivalry between CD-I and DVI obvious, but other CD technologies were also vying for attention, including CD-V (compact disc video) and CVD (compact video disc). The latter two are completely different and totally incompatible. Until the market-place of the early 1990s makes a choice, we cannot be sure which of these formats will prevail. What is certain is that we need immense imagination and powerful creative tools to exploit such systems. By the time we have worked out which learners and which applications should command priority, and how to manage the learning resources, the necessary hardware will be in place. The task of deciding what to do with it is urgent.

Clearly, rich and extensive multimedia databases demand considerable space: 600 megabytes is quickly eaten up by moving video and high-fidelity sound. Even using DVI-style compression, one compact disc will not always be enough. No matter, thanks to the link with the mass-market world of audio CDs, jukeboxes are already available, ranging from a few hundred dollars for domestic units to $13,000 for the 240 disc CD-ROM jukebox announced by SOCS Research Inc for shipment in July 1988. Hardware prices can only come down. Whether we know how to exploit the learning potential of so much online data (around 150 gigabytes, or enough to store a sizeable library of around half a million books) is another question.

WHY IS COMPACT DISC DIFFERENT?

Readers with a sense of *déjà vu* may be asking themselves how all this differs from the hyperbolic claims made for a succession of new media from teaching machines to so-called advanced interactive video (as in the Acorn/BBC Domesday system). Only history can prove me right or wrong. However, four features of CD media contrast strikingly with laser videodiscs, perhaps the most recent of the 'false dawns' of technology in education:

- A CD bought anywhere in the world works on a player bought anywhere. This is a by-product of the Philips/Sony commitment to standards and contrasts sharply with the worlds of microcomputer and colour video hardware.
- Audio CD is an internationally successful product with proven consumer acceptability. The newer CD formats use almost identical technology and benefit from falling unit costs for disc pressing and making player/drive and jukebox mechanisms.
- CD drives are small enough to be built into cars and current PCs, can sit happily on televisions in homes, offices and hotels, yet are large enough to accommodate increasingly powerful on-board computers.
- CD is an all-digital technology, whereas laser videodiscs store both images and sounds in analogue format, and AIV videodiscs mix analogue storage with digital data in partial replacement of a sound track. There are strong reasons why all-digital media are likely to prevail over analogue or hybrid media. Digital coding makes for easy integration of data of different types, for powerful manipulation, efficient compression/decompression and a means of reconciling international colour television standards.

In common with laser videodiscs, CD formats are generally read-only; the user can neither alter nor erase their contents, whether by accident or on purpose, and to update them the supplier must either replace the CD or create an illusion of merger with new data in the computer's internal memory (Frogbrook, 1988). These restrictions may be more apparent than real, since the computer can present information from various sources seamlessly. Also, in late 1987 Philips/Sony announced draft specification for write-once compact discs (CD-WO), which write data for both CD audio and CD-ROM in two-kilobyte blocks.

SOME APPLICATIONS

With space to provide sensible groupings of languages, and the capacity to mix high-quality speech with sound effects and images, CD media offer unprecedented opportunities for multilingual editions of reference works, for language learning, for individuals with special needs and for multimedia self-study of both academic and practical skills. As Europe progresses towards a single market of over 300 million Common Market citizens, with free movement of people, goods and services targeted for 1992, the scope and need for such publications are immense.

Here are some examples of applications, many of which already exist in part, in various combinations of existing technology:

- Interactive atlas of Europe: zoom in on the country, region or town; click to switch between political, physical, economic or language-grouping colouring; links to national census data and pan-European databases; choice of six languages for menus, labelling and database information; windowing for juxtaposition of photographs of different regions; cross-sections with subterranean and submarine information.
- Traveller's friend: available in railway stations, hotel rooms, campsites and provides tourist information on the region and its major cities and tourist attractions, with information about local customs and history; choice of language track with language-learning option.
- Public domain software (shareware) library: supported by options for interactive tutorial, reference information or online help delivered by synthesized speech and/or screen messages; options to print-out teaching materials such as overhead projector transparency masters and worksheets.
- Learners with special needs (adults or children): versions customized to suit needs, for example, visually handicapped users can control the font size to suit near vision, with synthesized speech backup; deaf users call up enrichment material and visual aids such as time lines for past and future tenses.

CONCLUSION

Hypertext is a significant software development because it concentrates on improving the learner's control over a knowledge base, instead of trying to model and control the user. Compact disc technologies are important because they offer high-density, mass-produced, all-digital international distribution media. The synergy between hypertext and compact disc is without precedent. The challenge that educational technologists face in harnessing their capacity and flexibility is awesome.

After leaving full-time education, adults continue to learn but are largely self-taught. Hypertext can support us in our exploration of large multimedia knowledge databases, helping us to be autonomous and thus develop our knowledge structures. This mode of adult independent learning is too powerful to be confined to the technocratic few.

ACKNOWLEDGEMENTS

I would like to thank everyone who read and commented on earlier drafts of this paper, notably Chris Bell, Eric Deeson, Peter Frogbrook, John Twining, Norman Willis and David Walker.

REFERENCES

Ambron, S. and Hooper, K. (eds) (1988) *Interactive Multimedia*. Microsoft Press, Washington and Penguin Books, Middlesex.

Anderson, T. (1988) Beyond Einstein. In Ambron, S. and Hooper, K. (eds) *Interactive Multimedia*. Microsoft Press, Washington and Penguin Books, Middlesex.

Bush, V. (1945) As we may think. *Atlantic Monthly, 176*, pp10-108. Reprinted in Lamber, S. and Ropiequet, S. (eds) (1986) *CD-ROM: The New Papyrus*. Microsoft Publishing.

Cook, P. (1988) An encyclopedia publisher's perspective. In Ambron, S. and Hooper, K. (eds) *Interactive Multimedia*. Microsoft Press, Washington and Penguin Books, Middlesex.

Engelbart, D.C. (1963) A conceptual framework for the augmentation of man's intellect. In Howerton and Weeks (eds), *Vistas in Information Handling*. Spartan books, Washington.

Frogbrook, P. (1988) Compact disc read only memory for publishing educational data. *British Journal of Educational Technology*, **19**, 1, 66-67.

Gaines, B. (1987) From teaching machines to knowledge-based systems: changing paradigms for CAL. *Proceedings of the International Conference of Computer Assisted Learning in Post-secondary Education*. University of Calgary, May 1987.

Goodman, D. (1987) *The Complete HyperCard Handbook*. Bantam Computer Books, New York.

Markman, M. (1988) Epilogue: HyperCard. In Ambron, S. and Hooper, K. (eds) *Interactive Multimedia*. Microsoft Press, Washington and Penguin Books, Middlesex.

Mason, R. (1988) Computer conferencing: a contribution to self-directed learning. *British Journal of Educational Technology*, **19**, 1, 28-41.

Megarry, J. (1989) *Compact Discs and Computers: Converging Technologies*. Kogan Page, London.

Meyrowitz, N. (1988) Issues in designing a hypermedia document system. In Ambron, S. and Hooper, K. (eds) *Interactive Multimedia*. Microsoft Press, Washington and Penguin Books, Middlesex.

Philips International (1988) *Compact Disc Interactive*. McGraw-Hill, New York and Kluwer, Netherlands.

Weyer, S. (1988) As we may learn. In Ambron, S. and Hooper, K. (eds) *Interactive Multimedia*. Microsoft Press, Washington and Penguin Books, Middlesex.

Note

HyperCard, HyperTalk and Macintosh are trademarks of Apple Computer Inc.

8. Computer-assisted learning for those who know what to do but don't

W Bruce Clark, *Institute for Computer Assisted Learning,*
University of Calgary, Calgary, Canada

Summary: The area of industrial safety training has become one of growing concern in Canada on the part of both industry and government. In the spring of 1987 The Alberta Gas Ethylene Company received a grant to explore the use of interactive video as a training medium for plant safety in the petrochemical industry and enlisted the aid of the Institute for Computer Assisted Learning at The University of Calgary. What became apparent was that the task was not merely one of testing a particular medium but also of developing a product which would address the perceived problem that workers knew how to work safely but often didn't; a motivational and sensitization problem rather than a procedural one. The product that was developed consisted of a game/simulation which incorporated two interactive videodiscs and the supporting computer program, and was delivered using the IBM InfoWindow System. The video footage consisted of scenes and scenarios shot on site at the AGEC plant. Two types of tasks were posed for the users: hazard recognition tasks in which they were required to beat the clock in order to score, and decision-making tasks in which they were required to participate in the scenarios portrayed and try to prevent accidents from happening. A reward/feedback structure was devised that would reinforce behaviour rather than entice the user to engage in unsafe practices. The product has been installed in two sites at the plant, made an integral part of the safety training programme, and is currently being subjected to external evaluation.

BACKGROUND

In April 1987 the Institute for Computer Assisted Learning (ICAL) was approached by representatives of The Alberta Gas Ethylene Company (AGEC) for assistance in developing a computer-mediated instructional package targeted at improving plant safety. Plant safety is a significant industrial and government concern both in the province of Alberta and in Canada generally at this time; perhaps in no industry is it receiving more attention than in the petrochemical industry where workers are constantly in danger of exposure to materials that are toxic, carcinogenic and/or explosive. In spite of the attention paid to matters of safety, accidents still happen, largely a matter of carelessness. Special programmes by both the provincial and federal governments provide assistance in developing new approaches to safety training. AGEC had received a grant from one such programme to explore the use of interactive video as a technique for plant safety training.

   ICAL is one of a number of institutes at The University of Calgary, along with the Knowledge Science Institute, Arctic Institute, Sulphur Institute, and Institute for the Humanities. It was created in 1984 in response to the perceived need to provide an interdisciplinary vehicle for the support of computer-mediated instruction at the University. Part of its role was therefore to provide support to the campus, but a second part was to engage in research and development. The funding structure of ICAL is such that it is largely dependent on contracts from industry and government to support itself. It has tried to avoid competing with the private sector by not taking on work in which the private sector is already engaged. Rather it prefers to engage in novel problems. As it turned out, the safety issued presented by AGEC fell into the category of novel problem.

As it was first presented to ICAL, the instructional problem to be addressed at AGEC consisted of teaching standard operating procedures in the area of safety which would be comparable in form to teaching any standard operating procedures, be they cleaning a vessel or flying a plane. Furthermore, it was hoped that the training would be able to be generalized to out-of-plant behaviour (for example commuting to and from work, and behaviour at home). It was noted that workers who would not think of exposing themselves to toxic chemicals at work might, for example, not stop to think about the impact of varnishing a floor in the basement without proper ventilation.

It was perceived that what was needed was to devise some mental checklist for safety factors and then to teach that checklist. As discussions progressed, however, (and they progressed over three months before the nature of the problem was finally resolved) it became apparent that the issue was not a matter of lack of knowledge. The workers at AGEC were among the most safety knowledgeable and safety conscious in the world and additional exposure to checklists was not likely to address the problem that, in spite of all the knowledge and consciousness, accidents and near accidents still happened.

The problem rather could be traced to two factors:

- the fact that workers occasionally grew nonchalant just as handlers of poisonous snakes sometimes do; and
- sometimes the unexpected occurred suddenly and workers reacted before they thought. For example, if one's co-worker is suddenly overcome by toxic gas one's instinctive response is to rush in and rescue them rather than take the necessary precautions to protect oneself first.

In light of this the problem became one not of knowledge, but of motivation and sensitization.

The instructional development problem became one of how to develop a product which would address these two factors. It appeared that recognition and decision making were the two types of tasks that would have to be incorporated in any product that would improve motivation and sensitization. Sensitization would also require that users be shown the potential outcomes of poor decision making. A decision was made early in the development process to resist the temptation to 'reward' poor decisions; there were to be no scenes in which the plant blew up, for example.

THE FINAL FORMAT

Given the two tasks identified above, it was decided to design a product which included a game component to deal with recognition speed and a simulation that would deal with decision making. It is habitual to describe unexpected situations in gas plants as the work of 'gremlins' so the game component was constructed, pitting the player against the gremlins and against the clock.

In Level I of the game the gremlin deals six cards and the player selects one. This determines which of a series of stills containing multiple hazards is presented to the user. The user must identify the hazards within the set time period. Correct selections are rewarded, incorrect selections penalized through a point system. To accommodate such variables as psychomotor skills on the part of the players, baseline data from early rounds is used to adjust the time allowed in subsequent rounds. Level II of the game was constructed much the same as Level I except that the hazards are more subtle. In Level III the hazards are presented as motion sequences which must be interrupted, then the hazard identified.

While the challenge of constructing the game was to avoid making the hazards blatantly obvious, the challenge of constructing the scenarios was more complex. First, the total package must be usable by both operations and maintenance workers and what would be meaningful for the one would not be acceptable to the other. Second, scenarios must be constructed in such a fashion as to involve the player actively in a decision-making role.

It became apparent as the planning progressed that a single scenario would not be sufficient, that one would have to be developed for maintenance and a second for operations. The next challenge was to identify the context for each scenario. Finally it was decided to produce a scenario of repairing a leak in a natural gas pipe for maintenance, and entry into a vessel for the operations scenario. Multiple paths would be created through each scenario which would be non-recoverable (ie if the player failed to prevent a hazardous activity at the point of its appearance, the scenario would proceed along successive paths which would be logical outcomes of the presence of that hazard). The selection among alternate possible paths would be randomly determined, thus causing the scenarios to appear different to different users and different in successive uses by the same user.

While feedback from the game section was restricted to a point system, in the scenarios feedback consisted of:

- watching the scenario play out to its logical conclusion; and/or
- receiving comments back from the system.

These were weighted as to importance and affected the final score accordingly.

There is always the concern in programs of this type that inappropriate behaviour will be reinforced through spectacular devices like fires and explosions. An effort was made in this program to reward appropriate actions and to keep feedback for inappropriate actions as low-key as possible. For example after one particular poor choice the user received only the textual message: 'Because you used a steel hammer around gas, the spark caused a small fire which resulted in this section of the plant being shut down for two days. Don't expect a rise this year.' On the other hand, a rising gauge marked recognition of hazardous situations and appropriate decisions.

THE MEDIUM AND ITS CONSTRAINTS

The method of instruction had been predetermined by the terms of the contract, it must include interactive videodisc. While there are a host of instructional dangers associated with having solutions searching for problems, in this case there appeared to be a comfortable match between what was perceived to be the problem and the mandated solution. Safety issues lend themselves to video representation. The conceptualization of how the product would perform made the use of videodisc alone insufficient. The high degree of interactivity that was required implied Level IV videodisc: the integration of videodisc and computer with the capability of overlaying computer text and graphics on the videodisc image. It was decided to employ the IBM InfoWindow system which would permit this mix of video, text and graphics, and had as well a touch-sensitive screen. The touch-sensitive screen was important to permit rapid identification of hazards.

What became apparent in planning for the scenarios was that in spite of the volume of information that can be stored on a videodisc (54,000 frames on a single-sided disc) this does not permit a very extensive programme when multiple paths are required.

If one assumes but three options at each point, to go down four levels in a scenario requires 363 segments. If one assumes only 10 seconds per segment, this requires 20 minutes of running video. To go down five levels would require 60 minutes of running video. In many cases it requires more than 10 seconds of video per segment, and three paths from each point is conservative when you are working in the area of plant safety. This was further complicated by the need to produce scenarios in two areas.

Partial solutions came in producing two videodiscs rather than the one originally planned, in terminating some paths rather than carrying them all to their logical extension and in re-using video segments in different paths where possible. The latter did not affect the design of the product substantially but it did provide some surprises in the continuity for the film crew who had to shoot the video! Continuity had to be maintained from several shots to a given shot and from the given shot to several others.

The second constraint was the search time on the videodisc player. The IBM InfoWindow employs the Pioneer 2000 laserdisc player and start-up time to move the playback head is approximately 1.3 seconds. Once moving, the difference between skipping one track and passing across the entire disc is only about half a second. That second-and-a-half break when a new segment is being accessed can provide an annoying interruption in playing continuity unless steps are taken to distract attention. Information on the safety disc was laid out in such a fashion that jumps happened either after the user interrupted a sequence or at least when the perspective of the shot changed.

A final constraint appeared unexpectedly during post-production. The plans for the program called for the possibility of the video freezing on a frame once the player interrupted a motion sequence, and permitting the user to then touch the screen to identif' hazards. At the time this approach was devised, it was planned to shoot the video on film and then use the 3-2 pull-down technique to convert the film to videotape for mastering. This process would have permitted freeze-framing while maintaining a virtually still image. For budgetary reasons, at the time of filming it was decided to switch from film to Betacam. This resulted in a substantial cost-saving both in filming and post-production. Unfortunately with Betacam it is not possible to freeze on any frame selected from a motion sequence because of the jittering effect on the screen. To compensate for this, additional still frames had to be added during post-production. After a user touched the screen the program then had to jump to the associated still frame. This does not reduce the overall effectiveness of this program but does detract from its finesse.

USER INTERFACE AND MANAGEMENT

As noted above, the InfoWindow provides the facility of touch screen and this was employed as the normal means by which users interacted with the system. Because this wa' planned as an integral part of safety training at the plant, some monitoring facilities were built in to track its use. All workers at the plant were assigned passwords which made it possible to track usage of the system and also to store records between uses. One of the company's hopes was that employees would be able to use the system when they had time available during slow times in their shifts and that they would continue to use it. This necessitated making provision for them to continue at the point where they left off in the previous use.

First-time users were automatically introduced to how the system worked. On subsequent uses they had a choice of whether or not to review the introductory material. In subsequent uses they could also choose whether to play the game or engage in a scenario. First-time users however were directed to the game first.

EVALUATION

The conditions of the granting agency required that the product be evaluated by an external evaluator and that process is now underway. To facilitate the evaluation, auditing capabilities were added to the program which make it possible to track every user's paths through the program and identify which choices were made. In order to protect user anonymity the audit trail cannot be used to trace performance back to the user. Since the evaluation data have yet to be analysed, it is premature to speculate upon the effectiveness of the product. Informal reports indicate that the system is being used, that users find it easy to use, and that the hoped-for challenge is indeed there. They are also successfully identifying hazards (including some that were not noticed during filming). It is, however, too early to tell whether the use of this novel program will increase sensitivity to safety issues on the job.

'Safety: A Personal Choice', the videodisc described in this paper, is copyrighted by NOVACOR/The Alberta Gas Ethylene Company.

9. Learning with computers: CBT in practice

Professor J R Beaumont, *Business and Management,*
University of Stirling, UK

Summary: The scale of the training task facing all sectors of British industry across all levels of staff is large and increasing. Management is beginning to recognize that, in certain circumstances, computer-based training (CBT) materials can be a most cost-efficient and educationally effective means of providing the necessary training. Moreover, the attractions of good CBT material can be linked to the recent rapid developments in distance and open learning. In this paper CBT materials developed for information presentation and quality assurance training are described. Specific issues underlying their development, authoring and packaging are raised. For completeness, the discussion is broadened to consider more general issues related to learning with computers, particularly in business and management training.

BACKGROUND

Recent much-publicized reports (involving the National Economic Development Office, the Manpower Services Commission and the British Institute of Management) have highlighted that most managers in industry in other countries are educated and trained to a higher level than in the UK. It is also important to distinguish between business education and management training and development. Much of the emphasis to date in this country is on the former, the latter is often *ad hoc* involving different experiences from employment movement; career paths generally comprise early specialist work to which a management role is added.

The benefits of formal and systematic policies for continuing education and training, particularly in this IT age, are only now being recognized. To remain internationally competitive and increase productivity, managers at all levels must be aware of the potential power of new technology and acquire the pertinent skills.

While the focus of this discussion is 'learning with computers', for management training this focus should be complemented by a consideration of 'learning about computers' and their role in the organization. Many of the failures of IT relate to inadequate implementation, an issue which is often not addressed in the teaching environment.

At the outset it is important to appreciate that this additional 'intellectual resource' has to be learned by students rather than taught to them in a conventional way. As a form of discovery learning the use of computers in teaching is characterized by activity rather than passivity; as an ancient Chinese proverb says:

I hear and I forget
I see and I remember
I do and I understand

Let students actually participate and think for themselves! Do we give them sufficient opportunity for self-motivated, semi-independent and creative thinking?

In terms of learning about computers, a cogent argument can be made that computer literacy is important in management training. Even if management can avoid 'hands on' experience of computers, they will not be able to avoid the impact on their business and decision making. In one sense this is the fundamental perspective of teaching about computers in business and management.

Computer-based training is starting to be recognized by many organizations as a most cost-efficient and educationally effective means of providing certain types of training (although it is recognized that much of the early commercially available CBT material for 'drill and practice' was of a poor quality that unfortunately undermined progress in this area).

OVERVIEW OF COMPUTER-BASED TRAINING (CBT)

In any consideration of the usefulness and relevance of computers, it is necessary to examine both the nature of the medium and the objectives of our training. Management are aware of the benefits of computer-based simulations as tools in their decision making; they provide a risk-free environment in which to consider the potential impacts of alternative decisions. Moreover, it is now being recognized that the computer is a better medium for presenting particular types of material to be learned, especially when there are repetitive procedures and/or systems with emphasis on detail and accuracy.

Nature of CBT material

From the outset, it is essential to dismiss the perception that CBT material is a modified extension of wordprocessing (or desktop publishing). Professional authoring by educationalists is a prerequisite to ensure that CBT material exploits the full potential of this medium for the users' benefit.

Both examples of CBT material, which are discussed in the next section, were developed on the backcloth of a 'hypertext' rather than a text environment. Hypertext offers a new representational structure for information (numerical, textual and graphical) which is founded on associations/relations rather than the simple linear progression of paragraphs in a textbook or notes in a lecture. This structure provides a flexible, bespoke learning environment for users and, by employing the computer, the constraints of the paper medium can be overcome. People think by associations and therefore it is important that this learning environment can be captured for users. This learning environment is active and flexible.

It would be incorrect to view hypertext as the only suitable backcloth. Interactive microcomputer videodisk technology will obviously have an important role to play in the development of CBT material. Further in the future with artificial intelligence, 'expert systems' could offer responsive mechanisms for individual tuition.

Distance and open learning

In practice, one of the real attractions of this educationally sound direction for certain types of training is its cost-effectiveness. Moreover, in some specialist areas there remains a shortage of suitably qualified trainers with appropriate experience. The recent impetus behind the attractions of good CBT material can be linked directly to the rapid developments in distance and open learning.

For the company providing the training, the advantages of CBT material include:

- the capability to satisfy the envisaged increase in demand which is often geographically dispersed;

- the opportunity directly to incorporate the skills training within the working environment; and
- the measurement of student progress against stated objectives (audit trails capturing a student's learning path can be incorporated within the software to facilitate monitoring).

In practice, careful monitoring of user-support is very important.

For the student, attractions of this novel medium are strengthened by the fact that directed progress can be self-paced (with repetition as required). It should be emphasized that, in comparison to other more traditional teaching methods, the students rather than the teachers have much greater control of the learning environment as they are able to select and arrange the material as they desire. Good CBT material permits practice and application of newly acquired skills and knowledge (often with feedback about difficulties and potential advantages).

DEMONSTRATOR CBT APPLICATIONS

As a basis for broadcasting the awareness of the potential benefits of good CBT material, two 'demonstrator' projects are described briefly:

- quality assurance; and
- information presentation.

The discussion highlights some of the different contexts in which CBT material can be employed.

From the experiences of producing both demonstrators, it is pertinent to make some general comments regarding development, authoring and packaging. Both products benefited from direct and positive involvement of the end-user client in their development. If the *modus operandi* of software firms rigidly to follow a detailed written specification from project commencement had been adopted, the final product would not have been as useful for the prospective trainees. Moreover, the involvement of end-user trainers meant that they felt part of the generation process and, as a consequence, were more likely to respond favourably to the CBT material as part of their overall training armoury. The upfront costs of producing specific CBT material (which are, hopefully, paid back through its use by a large number of users in the future) are compounded by the need for experienced authors who are not only familiar with the software (such as hypertext for the examples in this paper) but also, more importantly, possess training backgrounds and can therefore relate directly to potential problems facing users. Some practical background in education is a prerequisite; software familiarity can develop over time through practice. In terms of packaging, both products were based on stand-alone personal computers using a mouse. Touch-screen options were considered for the Glasgow Garden Festival demonstrator because of its use in an exhibition.

Quality assurance

1988 has been termed 'quality year' and quality assurance is essential for any manufacturing company. Management, however, recognize the practical constraints imposed by paper-based documentation for both updating procedures and staff training.

The first CBT demonstrator is for training staff about printed circuit board (PCB) manufacture. This work was undertaken for Wang (UK) Limited and it is important to stress that their senior staff's collaborative involvement in the specification and design of the CBT material was essential for success.

The demonstrator shows how the hypertext documentation can handle cross-referencing of material directly and automatically, and how diagrams and pictures can be accessed as required. Quality-assurance checklists are linked with work instructions and users are guided through complex procedures in their own way. Audits of quality assurance action can also be undertaken to assist real-time monitoring and planning processes. In this way the CBT material is acting as a decision-support tool.

Information presentation

The second CBT demonstrator was developed as part of the promotion of th Glasgow Garden Festival. In this instance the CBT material acts as a structured information provider informing visitors about the city's history, culture, geography and industry. As the tradeable information sector develops, for many information providers it is essential to avoid an 'information overload' situation. In the demonstrator the structured hypertext environment enables increasingly detailed information to be accessible from lower levels and careful screen design ensures the most suitable presentation (including maps) of the information of interest.

From the garden festival demonstrator it is clear that CBT material would be very relevant for marketing; replacing the conventional glossy brochure (by showing solutions to prospective clients' problems). A related application could be to enhance customer service, for instance in the financial services sector, by guiding a customer through the maze of products and services. Some form of intelligent knowledge-based management system would probably need to be incorporated to help in this advisory role.

For completeness, in terms of application, it is necessary to note the obvious application area: CBT material to replace applications software manuals which are generally unhelpful, if not misleading!

SOME CONCLUDING COMMENTS

Training is such a vital ingredient for the future wealth of our nation that we must explore and exploit advances in information technology to determine which medium is the most suitable for particular messages. CBT should not be thought of as a panacea, it should be seen as an integral component of an integrated multi-media training system. The use of computers in training disappointingly remains confined to small groups of interest (often, unfortunately, the quantitative methods team). For the desirable integration of computers with traditional approaches there is a need for more universal acceptance through demonstration that computers are useful and relevant in integrated teaching activities.

For long-term progress, it is important to consider our training strategy and, particularly, the extent to which it is modified by a computer-based learning experience. In this context the increasing importance of distance and open learning merits careful scrutiny. It is believed that computers can be consistent with the behavioural approaches to 'programmed learning', primarily for an individual's instruction and self-development. While recognizing the difficulties involved in undertaking the research (and indeed actual implementation of computers in training remains a problem given scarce resources), there is nevertheless a surprising paucity of research into the educational impacts of computers. Objective assessments are likely to be difficult but it is important for us to know whether technology is driving our messages. Whatever benefits to the students, the computer must by complemented by human support.

Irrespective of the assistance computers can offer, the burden of responsibility must remain with the teachers (who should, therefore, be aware of the strengths and weaknesses of these potentially powerful tools in particular situations). Given the growing access to personal computers which have increased processing speed and high-quality graphics capabilities, the applications of CBT can be expected to expand rapidly over the next couple of years. The limitations are no longer imposed by technology but by the imagination of training course designers!

10. An approach to intelligent access to laser discs

M R Kibby and J T Mayes, *Scottish HCI Centre, University of Strathclyde, Glasgow, UK*

Summary: The ideas reported derive from work carried out on the StrathTutor project funded by the University Grants Committee (UGC) under the Computers in Teaching Initiative (Mayes et al, 1988). The starting-point for the project was a general dissatisfaction with the way in which computer-based learning was developing (or failing to develop) in higher education and learning, coupled with some views about the issues that would need to be addressed if the challenge posed by developments both in hardware and in software was to be met. We describe here how these issues are now perceived and how we attempt to resolve them.

THE ISSUES

Intelligent learning systems

Traditional computer-assisted learning (CAL) programming in which all links between frames must be made explicit in the authoring process, represents a necessarily limited and cost-ineffective approach to educational computing. There is now a general expectation that future progress will lean heavily on artificial intelligence (AI) techniques. However, the aim of building a system that performs as an intelligent tutor, adapting its instructional form and content to the individual student, represents a highly complex and currently intractable problem. It is not surprising, therefore, that most intelligent learning systems developed to date have tried to limit the problem. The predominant approach is to take a formal domain encompassing highly procedural and well-analysed tasks, such as the Anderson et al geometry and LISP tutors (Anderson et al, 1985), modelling the problem-solving process with a production rule set. This expert system approach to learning essentially views the student's knowledge as a subset of the expert's and insofar as the student's behaviour deviates from the idealized model embodied in the rule-set, then the student is in error and must be corrected (Clancey, 1984). Even in a limited domain, there remain substantial problems in describing efficient teaching strategies by a set of rules.

Browsing in large databases

There is a recognition that developments in technology are to some extent forcing the pace, in particular the development of interactive laser-discs and CD-ROMs, with fast random access to very large numbers of high quality images. There is also a recognition that the various electronic media are converging into one system of vast potential which demands instructional techniques that are capable of exploiting its educational potential to the full (see O'Shea, 1988).

An important way forward is to regard learning as one of the kinds of interaction that 'users' will have with increasingly sophisticated and complex data structures. Canter, Rivers and Storrs (1985) discuss how it is no longer sensible to consider data sets as knowledge that is simply searched. The general activity of navigation through databases encompasses such varieties of interaction as browsing, scanning, wandering and exploring. Hammond and Allinson (1988) propose the use of metaphor as a navigation aid and discuss the example of a travel metaphor as a design principle. Hypertext systems such as Guide or HyperCard which are tools for organizing screen-based information, present similar navigation problems. The act of navigation in hypertext may be regarded as constructive exploration or nugatory 'globetrotting' (Duncan, 1988).

Knowledge representation

Having the capability to store large and complex knowledge structures, and being able to design navigation aids to help learners in their exploration of the content, does not diminish the problem of how to organize that knowledge in the first place. This is a fundamental problem since the organization of the knowledge to be acquired can scarcely be achieved without adopting at least an implicit theory of instruction. The design of the links between frames in programmed instruction demands prerequisite assumptions about the nature of learning, at least for the particular material involved. These assumptions must then be reflected in decisions about when the student is to be directed to a particular frame.

Conventional authoring languages require the author to specify the next frame to be presented in the context of every possible interaction, which has been termed address-orientated by Osin (1976). More recent approaches to this problem, each adopting particular views of the underlying learning process, involve organizing the knowledge into such forms as semantic networks (Carbonnel, 1970), production rules (Clancey, 1983) or error libraries (Johnston and Soloway, 1983). These are knowledge-orientated approaches in which some interaction between the coding of the content and the nature of the learner's responses determines the instructional sequence.

Development costs

Estimates of development ratios of around 100-150 hours of preparation for each hour of instruction are common for address- orientated authoring, which is currently tolerated but which contributes extensively to the high development costs of training materials. As with other software, the development costs do not fall as fast as the price of the hardware.

The problem is one of linkage; as more frames are included, so the number of links between them which need to be introduced, debugged and adjusted increases at an even greater rate. If there are N frames, then there are $N(N-1)$ possible links between them, of which a fraction k are meaningful. The problem can be seen to be one of order $Npage^2$. With a videodisc, there may be tens of thousands of frames available. Even if a subset of these, say 1,000, is incorporated into a training package, then in comparison with conventional material containing only one tenth of that number, the linkage problem will be 100 times worse. If the problem is mitigated by restricting the organization of frames into simple networks or hierarchies, then the richness of the available material is lost. The BBC Domesday discs, for example, demonstrate the variety of data which may be incorporated. Here, however, the wide range of analyses which may be performed on selected numerical data contrasts with the relatively limited access to graphic data by means of a network of links. An interesting (in a learning context) but semantically difficult enquiry such as: 'Where is there a thatched cottage like the one in the picture?' presents problems.

STRATH TUTOR

StrathTutor codes knowledge by requiring the author to index each frame, like earlier attempts such as SMITH (Osin, 1976). However, it departs radically from previous systems by requiring no coding at the level of the organization of the knowledge. It codes no links between frames, either directly or in the form of sequencing rules. Neither is any modelling of the student's developing understanding attempted, and in that sense StrathTutor is not a tutoring system at all. Instead, StrathTutor attempts to provide a maximally supportive environment for 'learning-by-browsing'. That is not to say that it lacks a pedagogic strategy, however. On the contrary we regard it as an example of a reactive learning environment (Brown, 1983). Unlike other such environments, such as simulations or computer languages aimed at the discovery of logical or mathematical concepts, StrathTutor can be conceived as an exploratory system for interacting directly at a conceptual level with almost any kind of knowledge-base.

Salient features of StrathTutor

Authoring requires no programming and no coding at the level of the organization of the learning material (no links between frames are explicitly represented, no instructional sequencing necessary). Knowledge is represented as attributes; associations to related frames are generated by the use of pattern-matching heuristics. Up to 60 attributes can be used throughout a tutorial to code each frame of text and graphics. Links are computed at run-time by pattern matching heuristics, according to the type of interaction which the learner initiates. By representing knowledge separately from frame contents and by deferring linkage until the link is required, StrathTutor exhibits some of the features associated with intelligent systems. Some of the heuristics are derived from a simulation model of human memory (Hintzman, 1984).

The learner can explore the knowledge base in a number of different ways:

- by selecting from the progress menu. As each frame is displayed an algorithm determines and displays the titles of the three most related frames from those still unseen. Next is a default option which chooses the 'closest' frame;
- select by title or select by attribute are options in which the learner can interrogate the knowledge base rather in the manner of querying a database;
- a guided tour will allow the learner to see all frames that are coded with the combination of attributes that the learner has selected; and
- areas of interest within a frame must be designated as hotspots by the author and allocated attributes. They may subsequently be selected by learners as requiring further investigation as part of their exploration. Another algorithm determines and displays the closest frame to the attribute configuration coded on that hotspot. Hotspots may be linked to a window displaying specific ancillary detail as a hypertext facility.

Complete learner control. Progress through the material is entirely a matter of choice by the learner. Browsing in StrathTutor is largely conceptual: the learner is required continually to search for links between frames at the level of the underlying concepts (attributes). For example, at any time the learner may choose a menu item which will list attribute names common to the present and the previous frames.

Self-testing. The learner may also elect at any time to undertake a test of his or her developing understanding of the material. The quiz menu allows the learner to attempt to identify the hotspots on two frames that have maximum overlap in terms of attributes. Feedback is given in the form of a game score and, if requested, a 'best answer'.

StrathTutor has been implemented on the Apple Macintosh. A number of tutorials are used experimentally in teaching undergraduate students in bioscience.

EVALUATION

Some early and tentative investigations into the effectiveness of Strath Tutor in facilitating learning are describe in Mayes et al (1988). Further attempts to evaluate our approach to the construction and presentation of learning material have centred on two different evaluation techniques.

The first is the analysis of trace-files generated automatically each time the learning system is used. Such trace-files analyse the learner's choice of progress from one frame to the next, the time spent on each frame, the setting of a number of user-controllable characteristics, and the use and success the learner has with the quiz options. Pre- and post-tests were administered to the 17 subjects who were undergraduate and postgraduate students with little knowledge of the test domain, glaciation. The data was aggregated together to provide 21 variables describing each subject and their interaction with the material which was analysed by pair-wise correlations (or 2×2 contingency tables) and by rule induction. There was significant learning by the subjects: post-test/pre-test differences were inversely correlated with pre-test scores and with the total score in the quiz. Other interactions of significance included the number of frames seen with percentage of time the learner back-tracked, and quizpoints with percentage of time hotspots were visible (outlined). However, these may not be casual relationships and it is difficult to draw further conclusions apart from recognizing that visibility of hotspots assists in understanding the material or scoring points in the quiz. Nevertheless, this kind of analysis has uncovered several aspects of the interface where redesign should lead to a more comprehensive use of the tools.

The second approach to evaluation has been some preliminary trials with the technique of constructive interaction (O'Malley et al, 1985) in which pairs of subjects are videotaped while using the learning system. This has proved to be particularly effective because one subject is required to justify further progress through the material by convincing the other of the appropriate mouse-driven action to take, thereby exteriorizing at least some part of the learning processes. Since subjects unfamiliar with the Macintosh computer were used in all the experiments described here, learning includes how to use StrathTutor as well as learning about the subject being studied. One interesting but preliminary conclusion is that subjects become so engrossed in the task of learning that they forget how to navigate within the system. This can lead to concentration of one or few modes of use, rather than employing the full range of tools at their disposal.

DISCUSSION

The intelligent approach to linking laser disc frames into learning packages described here has considerable potential for the development of learning and training materials. First, there is potential for time- and cost-cutting in utilizing conventional frame-based materials produced by laser disc technology in comparison with computer graphics, although the latter clearly has a role in specialized contexts. The greater saving is likely to come about through the formation of intelligent links between frames in contrast to the present universal requirement for manual linking. Our experience with StrathTutor has been that it is possible to construct learning materials with a development ratio of 30-40.

As a consequence of our approach, there comes a change in learning style. Instead of fixed or limited paths in the learning material, control is given to the learners in a learning-by-browsing environment who can go in whatever direction they wish. However, they are not left to flounder. They are given tools, which are exclusively mouse-driven, allowing access to the underlying knowledge base to aid in the formation of the concepts necessary to understand the learning material. Objections from those who envisage only one route to learning in a particular domain, are met by pointing out that individual learners differ in their requirements and that no area of knowledge is structured in a linear manner, or even as a tree. Our evaluations indicate that subjects certainly learn from the system and that the learning is durable and conceptual. The system provokes much learner-centred discussion when used by pairs of subjects. This confirms subjective observations made during class use.

We contend that interactive learning systems such as StrathTutor are more appropriate to the new electronic milieu in which education and training will be taking place. They have the potential to utilize the contents of laser discs and other sources of information in a more flexible manner than traditional systems, from both the authoring and learning aspects. There is a number of technical and programming problems to be overcome before a laser disc learning and training package based on our approach can be built. A 'frame' in the training sense may be represented by a video sequence running for some seconds. For example, how is a StrathTutor hotspot to be defined in an animation, in dynamic coordinates? Does this have to be done manually or can the frames themselves be analysed to track particular objects intelligently? With many thousands of frames, how can the real time computations be carried out? Are there short cuts, or alternative knowledge representations? Is the task of assigning attributes to each still or animated frame still too great, even in comparison with formal links?

REFERENCES

Anderson, J.R., Boyle, D.F. and Reiser, B.J. (1985) Intelligent tutoring systems. *Science*, **228**, 456-62.
Brown, J.S. (1983) Learning by doing revisited for electronic learning environments. In White, M.A. (ed) *The Future of Electronic Learning*. Lawrence Erlbaum, NJ.
Canter, D., Rivers, R. and Storrs, G. (1985) Characterizing user navigation through complex data structures. *Behavioural Information Technology*, **4**, 93-102.
Carbonnel, J.R. (1970) AI in CAI: an artificial intelligence approach to computer-assisted instruction. *IEEE Transactions Man-Machine Systems*. **11**, 190-202.
Clancey, W.J. (1983) GUIDON. *Journal of Computer Based Instruction*. **10**, 8-15.
Clancey, W.J. (1984) Methodology for building an intelligent tutoring system. In Kintsch, W. (ed) *Methods and Tactics in Cognitive Science*. Lawrence Erlbaum, NJ.
Duncan, E. (1988) Proceedings of the first UK meeting on Hypertext, Aberdeen, 17-18 March.
Hammond, N. and Allinson, L. (1988) Development and evaluation of a CAL system for non-formal domains: the hitch-hiker's guide to cognition. *Computer Education*. **12**, 215-20.
Hintzman, D.L. (1984) MINERVA 2: a simulation model of human memory. *Behaviour Research, Methodology, Instrumentation and Computing*, **16**, 96-101.
Johnston, W.L. and Soloway, E. (1983) PROUST: knowledge-based program understanding. Report: Yale/CSD/RD285, Yale University, Department of Computer Science.
Mayes, J.T., Kibby, M.R. and Watson, H. (1988) StrathTutor: the development and evaluation of a learning-by-browsing system on the Macintosh. *Computer Education*. **12**, 221-9.
O'Malley, C.E., Draper, S.W. and Riley, M.S. (1985) Constructive interaction: a method for studying human-computer interaction. In Shackel, B. (ed) *Human-computer Interaction*. North-Holland, Amsterdam.
O'Shea, T. (1988) Proceedings of the Fifth International Conference on Technology and Education, Edinburgh, March 1988.
Osin, L. (1976) SMITH: how to produce CAI courses without programming. *International Journal of Man-Machine Studies*. **8**, 207-41.

11. An interactive troubleshooting unit for logic circuits using an expert system

Keith Barker, *Computer Science and Engineering Department, University of Connecticut, USA*

Summary: An interactive troubleshooting unit has been built to help the user understand the steps necessary to the efficient debugging of logic circuits. An expert system is activated when the simulator and verification unit results do not agree. Results indicate a high rate of user success in finding the errors but a simple hierarchy of reasoning should replace the detailed analytical descriptions provided at present.

INTRODUCTION

In the educational environment students are expected to understand, learn and develop as a result of performing set tasks that are designed to achieve specific objectives. The staff to student ratios in the science and engineering colleges mitigate against the contact time and attention necessary to ensure that the learning does in fact take place. The only measurable parameter is the outcome of the directed piece of work.

There is insufficient time for the expert to spend with the learner and so the student is hardly ever exposed the exploratory and diagnostic thoughts and reasonings of those who, through time, have grown to understand the techniques and philosophies of problem solving. Not only is the student deprived of a valuable source of learning but also the means of monitoring, evaluating, assessing and providing feedback are missing.

The use of expert systems is now seen, in many contexts, to aid the diagnosis of problems where the solution is the only objective. Automatic test equipment enables faults to be found rapidly and efficiently by skilled or non-skilled users but such a facility is not designed specifically to promote understanding on the part of the user.

CONTEXT

Computer science departments have grown out of two academic areas: those of mathematics and electrical engineering. In the former case they tend to be based in the arts faculties with an emphasis on software and basic science, whereas in the latter case they are found within engineering and have an emphasis on hardware understanding and applications. Students in engineering-based computer science and electrical engineering departments are expected to learn about digital logic in theory and its use in practice.

Laboratories are an essential part of a course in engineering and provide reinforcement of the theory as well as providing a vehicle for skill development. Design is also a fundamental component which cannot be ignored and is found in both the lecture and laboratory situations.

Because of the high student to staff ratio and the less-than-enthusiastic commitment to laboratory work on the part of many academics in American universities, the practical supervision of undergraduates is mainly in the hands of teaching assistants (TAs). These are graduates who are studying for higher degrees and who need the financial assistance of a TA position. Thus the effective learning of the undergraduate students may be coincidental while trying to achieve the short-term objectives of a particular assignment.

Good students will work on their own, will experiment to push forward the boundaries of their knowledge and will grow as a result. Those with less drive and foresight will aim to achieve only the short-term objectives and will neither develop the basic understanding of the current topic nor the skills and techniques to translate what they have learned to other situations.

OBJECTIVES

The objective of this project is to try to build an expert system that will replace the instructor in the 'advisor mode' by being present at all times to offer advice and answer questions. The topic for this investigation is digital logic circuit design at the level of small-scale integration (SSI) components in a protoboarded design.

After the specification of the assignment, students follow the usual procedures of design, building and testing. All three of these steps can usually be achieved without a great deal of difficulty. Design techniques can be learned and hand or computer tools are available. Building has a large skill component which includes layout and signal routeing. Testing involves generating sensible test signals and accurately recording the results. The interpretation of these results and comparison with the expected values lead to a quantitative measure of success in the total project.

Unfortunately, the major problem in this procedure arises when the results of the testing do not agree with the expected results or are apparently not correct. Here is where troubleshooting or debugging must begin and this aspect of practical work is the one that causes the most problems. Students do not often know how to set about resolving the differences between the expected and achieved results. They do not know how to decompose the problem into workable sections, they cannot identify the suspected area of the fault and cannot reason their way to identifing the circuit component in error or locating the wiring fault.

The interactive prototype system that has been implemented is intended to work at the troubleshooting stage to help a student to identify the errors in the circuit and to provide an environment in which the student can develop his or her own expertise in troubleshooting faulty circuits.

THEORY

Troubleshooting activity in circuits can be described under two categories: that associated with problems in the field and that in the developmental stage of a design. For example, field troubleshooting could be the exercise of finding the fault in a piece of hardware that has been working correctly but now is malfunctioning. Developmental troubleshooting would take place on a piece of hardware in the laboratory during fault diagnosis in the protyping stage. The former of these two types has resulted in a great deal of work in customized test pattern generation to identify faults in engineered products. However, the laboratory prototype fault-finding procedures need to be based on a good set of rules even though expertise tends to generate a general set of heuristics as well.

Existing technologies

The D-algorithm (Roth et al, 1967) uses the topographical gate-level description of a circuit, the concept of path sensitization and the notion of signal propagation. The basic idea is that, when a certain fault is suspected, the algorithm tries to derive a test pattern which can propagate the error to the primary outputs when applied to the primary inputs.

The fault modelling and fault dictionary technique (Hayes, 1985) is concerned with the systematic and precise representation of physical faults in a form suitable for simulation and test generation. In the dictionary, each fault has a signature which consists of the characteristic function of the erroneous response produced by the fault. The disadvantages of this method include the limitation of fault coverage since some faults cannot be modelled, and the impracticality of modelling all possible faults in complex circuitry.

Reasoning from first principles

This stems from a basic understanding of the devices and the type of circuit to be tested so that layers of categories for failure are able to be determined. For each suspected candidate of failure the circuit model, in simulation, is checked to see if a failure in that element could contribute to the measured errors at the outputs. This is done using a two-way tracking algorithm which postulates a single error at a time. The information needed clearly to identify the error or errors may not all be available at the circuit's terminals and further interactive probing may be necessary.

LEARNING PHILOSOPHY

The general philosophy in this learning environment is that the user interacts in a conversational mode (though not using natural language) with the expert system as they both provide input to the solution of the problem. Assuming that the circuit does not test as expected, then the expert system will postulate one error at a time and make a suggestion as to how to find it. This may require probing of a signal level at a point other than the outputs, and the user has to respond correctly to this. The expert system will then use this extra information to focus on the suspected error.

If the user does not know how to find the information that the system requires, a 'HOW' display prompt is available. If the user does not know why the system is suggesting this action then a 'WHY' display is also available. In the same way that one would expect a student to listen to the offerings of a live instructor one assumes that someone wanting to learn would absorb the arguments presented in the displays. All the 'HOW' and 'WHY' responses are logged in files for future reference by the user.

IMPLEMENTATION

The system is hosted on a PC-AT compatible with 1MB of RAM and a 30MB hard disc. The connection between the computer and the circuit under test (CUT) is via a Hewlett Packard PC Instrument system using the Digital Multimeter (DMM) unit for probing and the Digital I/O unit for input and output. The CUT is built on a protoboard which is connected to the I/O unit with ribbon cables.

The computer software has four basic program components beyond the operating system:

- Simulator: built to have a spreadsheet input.

- HP PC Instrument software: a commercial package that controls the input and output of signals to the PC.
- Verifier: to check the simulator output against the CUT.
- Expert system: having 60 major rules.

Simulator

This program allows the user to describe the connectivity of the circuit design by entering the links between the circuit elements in a spreadsheet-like fashion. Checks are made in the input process and any likely errors are flagged immediately. The simulator produces the outputs in the form of waveforms from a series of test vectors generated by producing all the input-variable combinations in sequence.

HP PC Instrument software

This software provides the capability of connecting eight different units to an external circuit. The units themselves are simple boxes with no controls and the software creates a CRT display that mimics the front panel of a conventional instrument (eg a DMM display and controls or oscilloscope screen). All input and output functions are displayed on the PC screen and all controls are driven from the screen menus. This control can be achieved by a touch screen or cursor movements from a mouse or the arrow keys.

Verifier

This part of the program checks the outputs of the simulator against the outputs of the CUT as obtained from the I/O unit. Since the verifier, using the HP PC Instrument system, is very fast compared to the simulator, the number of tests possible is limited by the simulator software. This is because the test vectors are applied to both simulator and hardware verifier at the same time. If the number of inputs is less than or equal to ten then exhaustive testing of the simulated circuit and the CUT is used. Random testing is used for circuits with input variables greater than ten (that is, more than 1024 tests in the exhaustive mode).

Expert system

When the simulator and verifier results do not agree, the expert system can be activated to postulate likely faults. The faults are categorized from high to low priority as follows:

Fault	Example
Absent-minded fault	Power supply is off
Assembly fault	Wrong pin number used
Defective component	Burnt chip
Design fault	Exceeded maximum fan-out

The system does not assume only one fault but suggests the likely candidates for failure in order of priority as indicated. On correction of one fault the expert system will proceed to the next until all faults have been located and corrected or the system runs out of hypotheses!

In some cases there is not enough information available to make a clear judgement and extra probing is required. The value, measured through the digital multimeter, is used by the expert system to decide the next step. The advantage of the DMM is that any voltage level can be measured, whereas with the digital I/O only high and low levels are indicated.

RESULTS

Many tests were performed on a wide range of circuits, having an average complexity (levels of logic) of 5.2 and an average number of inputs of 4.3. In each case the error was found by the system and the 'WHY' file produced contained the correct reasoning to find the error.

Subjective tests on users to determine the effectiveness of the screen interface have lead to modifications to clarify the messages and have pointed to inadequacies of the user's understanding of the constructed circuit topology.

CONCLUSIONS

Within the limits of SSI combinational logic circuits, the total system will simulate the circuit, verify its operation against the simulator and lead a user through the reasoning to find an error or errors. It produces a file of the reasoning process from the inferences in the expert system, which can be useful in retrospectively examining the debugging process. However, the results indicate that the detailed reasoning is not efficient for good learning and a hierarchy of explanations is being prepared.

In general this indicates that, although the debugging process and the learning process have to be executed simultaneously, the presentation of responses on the screen have to concentrate on one or the other.

REFERENCES

Hayes, J.P. (1985) Fault modelling. *IEEE Design and Test Computing*, **2**, 2, 88-95.
Roth, J.P., Bouricius, W.G. and Schneider, P.R. (1967) Programmed algorithms to compute tests to detect and distinguish between failures in logic circuits. *IEEE Transactions in Electronic Components*, EC16, **10**, 567-580.

ACKNOWLEDGEMENTS

The author acknowledges the contributions to this work by Shuk Wan Chan and Rao Cherukuri who have implemented the system and provided much of the testing procedure.

12. The opportunities presented by the use of the Modula-2 language in the education of electronic engineers

Mike Collier and Graham Sims, *Department of Electrical and Electronic Engineering, Plymouth Polytechnic, UK*

Summary: Universal panaceas do not arise that often so it is a pleasure to be able to report on one! This paper argues that the new computer-programming language Modula-2 is far more than an extension of existing languages and could revolutionize whole areas of engineering design and practice. In particular, the authors draw upon their experience of teaching electronic engineering undergraduates to prognosticate a new methodology for degree-level teaching.

The paper presents a view of current teaching practice and outlines the skills required of future electronic engineers for which the authors believe Modula-2 provides impressive facilities. The language is shown to address this educational challenge on three fronts: through the destratification of design expertise, the promotion of transferable personal skills and the provision of an engineering development environment.

In arguing this case the paper presents a brief history of the Modula-2 language and an overview of the salient features.

WHAT ARE ELECTRONIC ENGINEERS?

The nature of electronic engineering has changed so radically over the last 20 years that the current discipline is far removed from its origins in the valve and transistor age.

The emphasis today is on the creation of systems and sub-systems capable of being incorporated into marketable products. Although electronic engineers still have specialisms and preferences they need a wide range of analytical and design skills to meet the multi-disciplinary requirements of system design.

THE CHALLENGE OF THE NINETIES

The next decade will require widely experienced systems designers capable of lateral thinking. The cult of the boffin, the narrow technical expert who cannot relate or communicate outside his field, will be demythologized.

A prime requirement will be technologists with a mobility of expertise across the whole hierarchy of electronic systems design. Although 'electronics' suggests electrons, the processors of the future may use optical and molecular devices. The important skills will be those that can create information systems across a broad range of hardware.

THE INTEGRATION OF ELECTRONIC DESIGN

As the discipline of electronics evolved, there emerged a number of distinct activities associated with the design of total systems. Because of this diversity of techniques it was

Figure 1. *Nineties Jobcentre*

common for designers to specialize in one particular field somewhere between chip design and expert systems. The situation was fragmented with an assembly-language expert often acting as a mediator between the hardware designer and the high-level language programmer. The spectrum of activities can be represented on the electronic engineers' 'tree of knowledge' shown in Figure 2.

In the past this range of specializations has often proved a hindrance to design projects. The current industrial emphasis on systems design means that an electronic engineer is no longer restricted to the electronic components of a digital system, he or she must also be capable of interfacing with a program or operating system. The struggle for identity between electrical engineers and computer scientists is coming to an end:

> 'The former are prone to see the microprocessor as just another component and the latter view a lower-level language than Ada as belonging to the dead world of hieroglyphics. The truth is that the worlds of software and hardware have converged and there is remarkably little difference between them.' (Clements, 1984)

In education, software has traditionally been regarded as a separate topic from hardware. However, in embedded computer-system design the two are now inseparable and it is necessary to teach a common design technique which is appropriate to both. This should involve top-down design, modularity, structure and testability. In seeking to unify the field a common medium of communication and specification is required and it is here that Modula-2 can make a contribution.

HOW ARE ELECTRONIC ENGINEERS TRAINED?

Engineering degree courses are typically structured in a bottom-up manner. The approach in electronics is usually to start with the smallest unit, the electron, and impart an understanding of semiconductor physics followed by devices, circuits, logic and building up to microprocessors. From here courses climb the ladder of complexity through assembly-language programming to high-level languages. Finally, systems and functional specification are explored and the whole area bound together with some concepts of management and marketing.

Expert Systems

Logical and

Mathematical

Operations

Data Structures

and Algorithms

System Configuration

Assembly Language

Chip Level

Operations

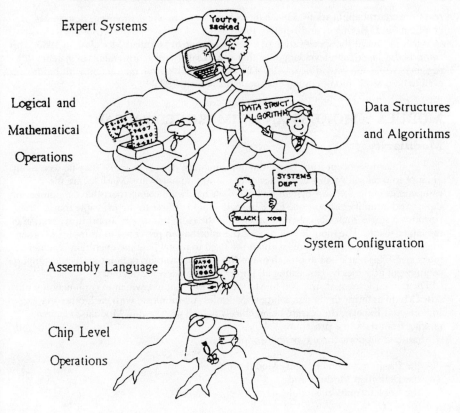

Figure 2. *Electronic engineers 'tree of knowledge'*

As early as 1979, in the great self-analysis of engineering (Finniston, 1979; Lawrence, 1979), voices were calling for a reversal of the process so that engineers developed their skills in a top-down manner. Lewin argued, by analogy with Karl Popper's theories, that since engineering was committed to open systems, non-unique solutions and the production of artifacts, the aim should be to produce systems engineers rather than applied scientists (Lewin, 1979).

The problem with implementing a top-down strategy of teaching in electronics lay with the non-integrated nature of the discipline. Among the many disparate factors was the fact that communication between designers and computer systems used a variety of linguistic modes. The emergence of the Modula-2 language has changed the picture.

A MINI-HISTORY OF MODULA-2

In the 1970s a team under Niklaus Wirth at the Eidgenossische Technische Hochschule in Zurich produced the specification for the computer language Pascal. This was a block-structured, high-level language particularly suited to top-down problem solving by stepwise refinement (Jensen and Wirth, 1978). However, Pascal did exhibit some deficiencies as a language for the full spectrum of electronic engineering applications. Being a high-level language it did not permit easy access to the host machine's hardware or operating system. Thus it was unsuitable for the writing of operating systems and many real-time control applications. Hence the C language was often employed, despite its cryptic nature (Kernigan and Ritchie, 1978).

Wirth produced the specification of a new language to be called Modula-2 in 1980. This comprised a single high-level language that would satisfy the requirements of system designers while also providing low-level facilities to enable close interaction with hardware, even to chip level, and operating environments (Wirth, 1985).

MODULA-2: MORE THAN AN IMPROVED PASCAL

Modularity

The modularity concept from which the new language derives its name may be seen as an attempt to treat software design in a similar manner to hardware. Modules are the components of the software system and like their hardware counterparts have a number of inputs and a number of outputs. Each module should adhere to the principle that it performs a single, logically coherent task and is therefore not simply an arbitrary section of the larger whole. The module will process the information presented to its inputs in order to generate the required outputs without the need to reveal how the operation is achieved internally. This black box approach to modules both maintains data integrity and supports commercial activities by concealing all implementation-specific details.

The highest level of abstraction in Modula-2 is the Module, which in conjunction with other Modules forms the design solution. Modules communicate with each other via Imports and Exports, the 'cargo' being objects (which may be any Modula-2 element ranging from data to a procedure).

Modula-2 supports three types of Module:

- the Program (main or client) Module;
- the Definition Module; and
- the Implementation Module.

A Program Module is distinguished by the absence of Exports, it may only Import (hence 'client'). Exports are defined in the separately compiled Definition and Implementation Module pair, which are known collectively as a Library Module. Library Modules are independent, portable resources available to all Modules.

The Definition Module specifies the names and properties of the objects available for Import from the Library Module, and therefore provides the defined interface. The Implementation Module contains the actual code required to provide the operations specified in the Definition Module. This information is not relevant to the client and can be disregarded or hidden. Hence the Implementation Module is the black box with the Definition Module acting as the interface between it and the client Modules.

Low-level facilities

To support portability a standard library is defined for Modula-2. To ensure system-dependent features do not jeopardize this, a 'System Module' (which defines the low-level facilities provided by the language) is contained within this library. The objects contained in the System Module allow the programmer to manipulate the host computer at the level of assembly language (address generation, register operations etc) without having recourse to an assembler.

Concurrency

In order to exploit parallel architectures and to provide multi-tasking on conventional computer architectures, the System Module also contains objects to support concurrent

Figure 3. *The three types of Module in Modula-2*

processes. This will help guarantee that Modula-2 can meet future computational needs.
(For a more detailed discussion of the syntactical differences between Modula-2 and Pascal see Dettmer, 1986.)

DESTRATIFICATION OF DESIGN SKILLS

Project teams using Modula-2 no longer need individuals specializing in particular aspects of the design process. This language allows them to plan, project and program across the board. Within educational institutions it is possible to set assignments and projects which utilize skills and knowledge throughout the electronics area. These can be specified and communicated in terms of Modula-2 Definition Modules, and the detailed solution worked out in suitable Implementation Modules.

PROMOTION OF TRANSFERABLE PERSONAL SKILLS

Awareness is increasing that graduates in all disciplines need an armoury of personal skills to function effectively in team and management situations (Arnold and Donaldson, 1988). The production of these skills among electronic engineering undergraduates has often been an uphill task and therefore the adoption of a language such as Modula-2, which implicitly demands and develops these characteristics, could widen the educational experience of the students. Three skills in particular are highlighted: teamwork, communication and the building-up of a tool box.

Teamwork

Whereas so many of the activities and assignments in a traditional degree course are individualized and it has been a struggle to produce meaningful group work, Modula-2 is a realistic training ground for developing teamwork skills. The language is ideally suited to the team-programming situation because the Import and Export features of the modular structure allow separately created objects with defined interfaces. Thus projects of lifelike complexity, hitherto difficult to simulate, can be undertaken in groups with facilities being available for monitoring the contribution of each member.

Figure 4. *Capabilities of Modula-2*

Communication skills

Written communication is a skill needed in all development and manufacturing communities. Often the presentation of design proposals and ideas lacks any common format. By approaching the design of a system through the writing of a series of Modula-2 Definition Modules, a conciseness and clarity of communication is achieved which, while not in the form of literary English, does promote lucid communication in the verbal medium. It may even be argued that Definition Modules may be expanded by the use of comment sections to embrace both the specification and algorithm of the design solution. This will lead to a corresponding increase in efficiency and maintainability.

Software tool-box

Modula-2 permits, even encourages, the user to create a set of personalized Library Modules which can be accessed with ease by any software application they design in the future. Thus an electronic engineer can develop a 'tool-box' of useful software tools and carry these with them throughout their career.

TOWARDS AN ENGINEERING DEVELOPMENT ENVIRONMENT

Since Modula-2 comprises both a language and a set of software-development utilities, it provides its own environment for software generation.

With a truly modular structure it is possible to design software for testability. Test points can be interfaced between modules so that by breaking the links between modules open-loop testing can be performed. This is already done widely at hardware level and Modula-2 merely extends the testing techniques in a consistent fashion through the software components of the design. Very often a module may be the interface to a hardware circuit, in which case the hybrid system achieves a degree of homogeneity which should delight true system engineers.

The efficiency of project management benefits from an integrated development environment in which top-down design is fostered. The design problem can be decomposed by stepwise refinement into a series of Definition Modules, and these can be further refined to Implementation Modules containing the finer details.

ACCOLADES OR BRICKBATS

Novelty is often greeted with suspicion and Wirth's new language is no exception. There is still considerable scepticism and inertia within British industry and academia and competition from Ada (ANSI, 1983) (which is now virtually mandatory for defence contracts) is mounting.

On the other hand, arguments about the relative speed of assembled and compiled programs are slowly fading with the optimization of compiler design. Benchmark tests at Plymouth Polytechnic indicate that Modula-2 can hold its own for speed with the best of structured languages (Sims, 1987).

INVERTING THE CURRICULUM

The bottom line of the above discussion is that Modula-2 is a computer language which will integrate many of the disparate skills of the electronic engineer. In engineering departments this language makes possible curricula which use a top-down approach in the educational process. The specializations which withheld popularity from Lewin's proposals (Lewin, 1979) have been unified into a continuous weave of design skills.

It should now be possible to consider degree courses in which the first year comprises a solid grounding in design principles, problem specification and algorithm design. The later years of the course would lead on to mathematical methods, system architectures, memory arrangements, logic and chip architectures. Through all of this would run the thread of engineering design. Without doubt, this represents an inversion of the traditional inductive engineering curriculum.

REFERENCES

ANSI (1983) *The Programming Language Ada Reference Manual*. American National Standards Institute, Washington, ANSI/MIL-STD-1815A.

Arnold, J. and Donaldson, M. (1988) Development of transferable personal skills in degree courses. *Polyteach*, **2**, 1-2. Plymouth Polytechnic.

Clements, A. (1984) Education and computer technology. *Software and Microsystems*, **3**, 4.

Collins, S. (1987) Modula-2: a babel fish for chips? *IERE Colloquium on Modula-2*, London, 1987.

Dettmer, R. (1986) Pascal and Modula-2. *Electronics and Power*, June 1986, 435-439.

Finniston, M. (1979) *Engineering Our Future*, HM Stationery Office.

Jensen, K. and Wirth, N. (1978) *Pascal User Manual and Report (2nd edn)*. Springer-Verlag.

Kernigan, B.W. and Ritchie, D.M. (1978) *The C Programming Language*. Prentice Hall, New Jersey.

Lawrence, P.A. (1979) Engineering and the national context *Electronics and Power*, May 1979, 359-361.

Lewin, D. (1979) The relevance of science to engineering: a reappraisal. *The Radio and Electronic Engineer*, **49**, 3, 119-124.

Muller, C. (9187) Modula--Prolog: a programming environment for building Knowledge-A systems. In Kriz, J. *Knowledge-based Expert Systems in Industry*.

Pierce, R. (1986) Ada goes into service. *Electronics and Power* June 1986, 433-434.

Sims, G. (1987) *Modula-2 Benchmarks*. Internal Report, Department of Electrical and Electronic Engineering, Plymouth Polytechnic.

Wirth, N. (1985) *Programming in Modula-2* (3rd edn). Springer-Verlag, Berlin.

13. The collaborative development of compuer-based training in a process industry

P Chapman, *Imperial Chemical Industries, UK*
Q Whitlock, *Dean Associates, UK*

Summary: This paper describes a project to produce computer-based training units for supervisors and operators in the chemical processing industry. The project was administered by the Chemical Industries Association (CIA) with primary funding by the Manpower Services Commission (MSC) and a substantial 'in-kind' contribution from the individual companies taking part in the scheme.

This was a large-scale operation. In all some 20 people were actively involved with the project at one stage or another and well over three hours of computer-based training (CBT) sequences were the outcome. Those involved represented the CIA itself, six major companies in the chemical processing industry and two firms of consultants.

Several aspects of the project are worthy of review. We have chosen to focus on a particular feature of the resourcing of the project, namely the effect of using teams composed of authors based in many different locations working together and with consultants to produce the courseware.

INDIVIDUALIZED LEARNING IN THE CHEMICAL INDUSTRY

Individualized approaches to learning have been employed in the chemical industry for the past 30 years, albeit rather intermittently. Programmed instruction was used extensively in many of the bigger chemical companies between the mid 1960s and 1970s. These companies bought in, commissioned or developed programmes for process operators on a wide range of topics and procedures. The Chemical and Allied Products Industry Training Board stimulated these initiatives by funding research and development. Other bodies such as the Programmed Instruction Centre for Industry provided information and research expertise on alternatives to classroom instruction.

In the decade 1972-82 the use of individualized materials dwindled, partly due to disillusionment with commercially available programmes and partly due to the shortage of good instructional designers. The CAPITB was abolished in 1980.

THE ARRIVAL OF PERSONAL COMPUTERS

In the early 1980s interest in self-instruction re-awakened as personal computers came on the scene. The awareness grew of the possibilities of using these devices as the means of delivering more realistic interactive training programmes. It now becomes possible to develop far more effective sequences not only for the initial learning of procedures but, more significantly, simulations of invisible processes. For example, the production of refrigerant could be demonstrated with unlimited repetition, under the learner's control.

In chemical plants of the late 1970s and early 1980s initial experiments with computer-based learning programmes were confined to isolated enthusiasts working on personal computers like the Commodore Pet or the Apple. In this respect the industry differed from the world of finance. Banks and credit companies typically took the mainframe route, exploiting the availability of branch terminals which staff used regularly in the performance of routine tasks.

This rather random pattern gave way to to a more systematic approach under the stimulus of the MSC's Open Tech Programme. In the ICI group, for example, a substantial Open Tech project led to open learning as a general approach and CBT as a specific medium obtaining widespread exposure in the industry. Within about two years, ICI set up open learning development teams in no fewer than nine locations all with a CBT capability. Similar developments were taking place in BP, Shell, Exxon and other leading members of the CIA.

SCOPE OF THE CIA PROJECT

In the spring of 1987 the CIA formulated the plan which led to the project we are describing. The general scope of the project was to produce examples of CBT which would benefit the Association's firms and generate an understanding of the problems associated with its development and use. The project aimed to assess three specific aspects of course development in CBT:

- the resources required for the design of courseware;
- the feasibility of designing and developing courseware in teams drawn from different locations; and
- the relative suitability of different subject matter at each location.

This plan was based on a feasibility study which the Association had carried out in the early months of the year. This study had drawn up a specification including the following features:

- potentially suitable subject areas for the industry;
- an estimate of the cost;
- some indication of existing competence within the collaborating companies;
- a set of guidelines for courseware development;
- a possible structure for the project; and
- key issues for the project to address (eg size of modules).

Overall management of the project was invested in a steering group. This group comprised representatives of the six companies collaborating in the project as well as the Manpower Services Commission and the CIA itself.

In order that the participating companies could monitor the CBT development process as closely as possible, the steering group decided that the design of courseware would be assigned to trainers and other specialists already working in the industry. However the coding of the CBT sequences in the selected authoring language was undertaken by a specialist contractor. The language in question is not easily mastered by trainers lacking computer programming skills and in the time available it would have been unreasonable and undesirable for the authors to learn both lesson design procedures as well as coding.

THE CHOSEN SUBJECT MATTER

As regards the subject matter, the project focused on the development of three courses on subjects most relevant to the needs of the industry. These were the safe use of scaffolding, the safe handling of chemicals and problem solving for process workers. Each course was intended to serve as initial training for newly appointed operators and as revision material for supervisors and other experienced staff.

The programmes on scaffolding and chemicals handling were conceived as discrete packages which could be used in stand-alone mode for initial learning or revision. By contrast, the problem-solving programme is stage four of a six-stage course. A problem-solving model has been introduced in the earlier stages. The CBT unit is designed to enable operators to practise the application of the model with two simple cases and then to apply it under supervision to a problem in the plant.

COURSEWARE DEVELOPMENT TEAMS

The courseware for each of the three topics would be developed by a different team drawn from two or more of the collaborating companies. Typically a team comprised four or five members representing two or three companies and three or four different sites. In one case team members were drawn from Teeside, Edinburgh and Aberdeen.

All the authors were knowledgeable in the subject area of their choice and most of them had considerable experience as practical trainers. However only one person in each team had previously designed any individualized learning material in computer-based or other form. Hence, although the authors were to receive a short formal course on CBT design, Dean Associates (the consultants who delivered the training) were retained to advise the development teams as well as to provide liaison between authors and programmers.

DEVELOPMENT PLAN

The timetable for the project is shown in Figure 1. The four-day authors' course was the formal opening of the project. The course covered three areas:

- training design;
- CBT planning documentation; and
- an overview of the capabilities of the authoring system to be used on the project.

Four days is by no means excessive for an event of this kind even for experienced trainers. While most instructors are, or claim to be, proficient in the practice of basic design skills such as task analysis, objectives setting and questioning, it is our experience that these fundamental abilities need to be enhanced substantially if a good trainer is to perform effectively as an author. To take a simple but important example, most instructors, however experienced, have great difficulty in framing questions for cognitive material which do anything more than test recall.

DESIGN DOCUMENTATION

It also became clear that more time could have been spent practising the pre-coding design documentation or, to use the term coined at Control Data, programmable ready material (PRM). The development teams started with an outline specification and objectives for their topic. They then had to define the course content, structure that content into manageable units or modules, devise tests and write the learning sequences. The outcome of these tasks was a set of documentation which a competent coder should be able to convert into CBT sequences. It comprises a course map showing the overall modular structure of the course including pre- and post-tests; a flow-chart showing all the possible routes through the programme; and a set of screen design sheets each of which depicts the text and graphics the author wishes to display on a particular screen.

This documentation was passed first to the training consultants. After checking, it was sent for coding. Since the coders had no direct contact with the authors it was crucial that

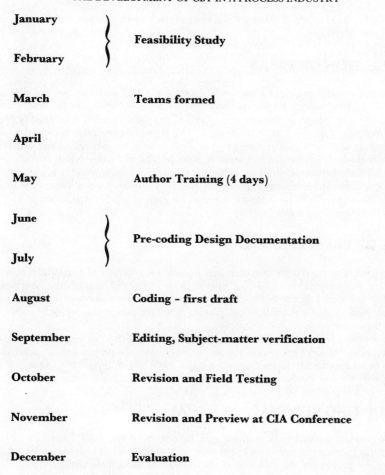

January		
February	}	Feasibility Study
March		Teams formed
April		
May		Author Training (4 days)
June		
July	}	Pre-coding Design Documentation
August		Coding – first draft
September		Editing, Subject-matter verification
October		Revision and Field Testing
November		Revision and Preview at CIA Conference
December		Evaluation

Figure 1. *Chemical Industries Association CBT Project: Timetable 1987*

the documentation prescribed precisely both the visible features of a screen (text and graphics) and the invisible features (eg routeing and scoring).

EARLY PROBLEMS WITH DESIGN

The first instalments of the PRM revealed two major problems. First, most authors relied too much on the coders' ability to interpret their full intentions. Many screen design sheets lacked guidance on how exactly graphics were to be presented and how textual screens were to be built up. This was not intentional corner cutting so much as a misunderstanding of the role of the coder.

The second, and less unexpected deficiency, lay in the limited element of interaction. Most educational technologists would place interaction at the top of a short list of essential criteria for CBT.

These firsts drafts lacked that feeling of productive interchange which inexperienced authors find so hard to acquire. Later reworkings of the materials demonstrated a distinct improvement in technique.

ALLOCATION OF TASKS

Since the individual members of a team were based at different locations they could only arrange to meet for periodic reviews at about four-weekly intervals during the four months of the development phase. In the intervening period members assumed responsibility for the development of specific aspects of the topic. This proved a reasonable *modus operandi* for the scaffolding and chemical-handling projects. Both these topics subdivided into discrete areas, each of which was treated as a separate module. The problem-solving programme contains no such natural subdivisions. However, the accompanying workbook is an important adjunct and one team member assumed responsibility for this. One of the two practice cases to which the problem-solving model is applied was likewise allocated to different members of the team.

ROLE OF TEAM LEADERS

As the project progressed it became clear that in each team the role of team leader had been interpreted very differently. In one case the team leader did most of the course design even before the team had effectively formed. In another the originally designated team leader adopted more of a watching brief, playing very little part in the detailed development work.

These attitudes reflected the differing management styles of the two team leaders and would not normally be of great significance. However, since the project was intended as a learning experience for all the participants it might have been appropriate to agree a team leader specification at the outset of the project.

SUPPORTING TEXTUAL MATERIAL

All three projects included accompanying text. Indeed few, if any, CBT courses for occupational training can operate without such adjunct materials. However, an interesting feature of this project was the evolution of the strategy for using these texts.

As in many other training schemes, the content of the initial learning programmes included a combination of procedures and concepts (or knowledge).

As development work proceeded it became clear that the conceptual material comprised a combination of what T F Gilbert has called 'Domain Theory' (that is, facts and principals essential to the understanding of a specific operation) and more general concepts of topics such 'What is a Chemical?'. In this latter case the team concerned originally planned to deal with the topic in a computer based sequence. Second thought led to this material being included in the workbook and eventually it was dropped altogether as it became clear that it was inappropriate.

The final version of the text contains reference material relating directly to the points covered in the CBT units and is considerably slimmer than the first draft thereby enhancing the probability that it will be used. A similar process occurred with the scaffolding text, the final version of which combines a glossary and the illustrations referred to in the tests. In addition to the text, the chemical-handling package included performance aids in the form of colour printed cards of the common hazard warning symbols. Likewise the problem-solving course included an algorithm which an operator can use as an *aide-mémoire*.

CMI ASPECTS OF THE COURSE

One area of the development work which was handled largely by the consultants was the drawing up of a specification for the computer management function within the courseware.

Each course was designed so that it can be used by only one student at a time if student records are required. These records comprise a post-test score and a time record. It is possible for someone other than the 'signed on' student to browse through a course if no records are desired. Instructors have a special method of signing on to look at student details, and reset the student record when a student has completed the course. When a student finishes, the data are printed out.

THE EVALUATION PHASE

Both the constraints and advantages of the collaborative approach were again in evidence during the final phase of evaluation. The first opportunity to inspect the materials was at a meeting in mid-August of the steering group, including the team leaders. Here the first drafts of one module for two of the projects were available.

Over the next few weeks each team had to assemble locally to review the programmes before transmitting their initial reactions to the programme managers. At this stage, the comments related mainly to general features such as appearance, colour and use of functional areas of the screen rather than details about the content. This process was repeated as the first completed courseware became available in mid-September. By this time comments were also being received from accredited experts in the various subject areas.

A month later the material was ready for field testing. Each team arranged for its own programme to be trialled at each of the team member's locations. They also arranged to trial the programmes of the other teams.

All the programmes were tested with both operators and supervisors. Generally both student performance and reactions were positive although instructors and supervisors tended to be less enthusiastic than operatives. Here it is worth noting that the programmes included pre- and post-tests for both the individual modules and the overall programme. Thus a knowledgeable supervisor can bypass the core teaching material altogether.

CONCLUSIONS

To conclude, we would like first to summarize the problems and advantages of CBT development by collaborating teams and then make some recommendations for future operations of this type. The problems fall into two major categories: didactic and logistic. In the didactic category we would cite the lack of design skills for distance learning. This was revealed in both the earlier difficulty authors experienced in writing interactive sequences and the uncertainty in handling topics as opposed to procedures.

Logistically the lines of communication between individual team members and the coders were sometimes stretched to the limit. Many of the authors, if not all of them, simply added the new commitment to their existing workload. Not surprisingly there were occasional clashes of priority.

Finally, the lack of prototyping capability clearly handicapped some of the less experienced authors who found it very difficult to visualize how their 'on paper' designs would appear on screen. The collaborative strategy does nevertheless hold a number of attractions. First, team working generates an esprit de corps and commitment on the part of the developers which reflects the 'amateur' spirit in its original sense. Between them, team members spent hundreds of hours and travelled thousands of miles to achieve their objectives.

Secondly, the very fact that the development teams represent many of the leading companies in the industry will lend a credibility to their efforts among their peers.

Finally, from a technical point of view, while the multi-site operation clearly handicaps communication it does provide an exceptional opportunity to try out draft courseware with a large and varied sample of the target population. This is a distinct advantage over most occupational training projects which tend to suffer from under testing of draft material.

On the basis of our experience with this project our recommendations to those planning a similar large-scale collaborative venture are as follows:

- when setting up development teams ensure that individuals receive intensive practice in interactive design and preparation of PRM;
- arrange for authors to meet coders at a preliminary stage;
- make some provision for fast prototyping of initial courseware;
- programme development time for authors before the project begins; and
- clarify the role of team leaders.

14. A study of microcomputer usage in an occupational therapy unit for adults with severe learning difficulties

Jane Galushka, *Department of Psychology, University of Keele, UK*

Summary: The microcomputer has great potential in special education and promises to be an effective and powerful educative tool. Different managerial practices in using the microcomputer can influence its potential effectiveness. This study examines microcomputer use in an Occupational Therapy Unit in Stoke-on-Trent. By a process of participant observation, interview and analysis of records a detailed profile of the Unit was constructed on how microcomputers were used. The results are discussed in relation to five factors which appear to be of importance in influencing the use of the microcomputer: context of innovation; locus of innovation; support for innovation; implementation of innovation and determinants of innovations.

INTRODUCTION

The goal of this study is to identify the factors which are central to the effective use of microcomputers in special education. The microcomputer has a great potential for providing flexible environments which are conducive to learning (Kidd and Holmes, 1982). Getting the most out of a microcomputer and tapping its full potential is not an easy business. What we consider to be appropriate use of the microcomputer can be purely subjective, nevertheless there is some agreement as to the identity of a few malpractices. Kelly (1984) provides a good description of these. He believes that it is more imaginative and less restrictive to view the microcomputer as a powerful learning resource as opposed to a 'sophisticated teaching machine'. Many agree with this view (eg Papert, 1980; Chakera, 1984). As yet no comprehensive study has been made into what factors might be important for the introduction and subsequent use of the microcomputer in special education.

From the literature five factors appear to be of importance for Innovation in general:

- Context of innovation. The attributes, style and culture of organizations can affect the rate and kinds of innovations that occur within them (Merton, 1965).
- Locus of innovation. Where in an organizational hierarchy, initiatives for innovation projects originate can have consequences for the future course of innovatory ideas (Lindbald, 1984).
- Support for innovation. Creative innovators can gain support for their ideas by forming coalitions with organization members who share similar individual goals to themselves (Litterer, 1967).
- Implementation of innovation. The ability of innovators to implement ideas will often depend on their ability to specify goals and to define approaches which accommodate goals. Bower (1965) stresses the ability to separate planning from execution.

– Determinants of innovation. Resources such as staff, equipment and funding can influence policies and restrict goal considerations. Technology or 'technical know-how' is also important in putting an innovative idea into action.

The above five factors provide a framework within which we can view the introduction and subsequent use of microcomputers in special education. Little previous research has been done in this area, particularly for adults in special education. Sheingold and her colleagues (1983) looked at how different school systems in normal education used microcomputers. Six trends emerged which appear to have implications for microcomputer use including the emergence of new roles. Goldman (1987) conducted a survey of special administrators in America. A wide variability was found in levels and methods of microcomputer adoption in the education of those with mild learning difficulties. One major factor which emerged from this study was the high level of cooperation between special and normal education in such areas as hardware and software allocation and staff training.

There seems to be a need to study in detail what factors influence the use of microcomputers in special education centres in Britain. This paper reports a study which examines microcomputer use in an Occupational Therapy Unit in Stoke-on-Trent. By process of participant observation, interviews and analysis of records a detailed profile of the Unit was constructed.

METHOD

The Occupational Therapy Unit

The Occupational Therapy Unit is attached to an old hospital which has taken on the role of a residential home for physically and mentally handicapped adults. The ages of the residents range from 30 to 80 years old but the majority are in their 40s. The Unit provides day-care facilities for 87 residents whatever their handicap. According to a report from the Unit, each resident is offered at least one session a week depending on their needs. The main aim of the Unit is to provide an environment and facilities that will improve each individual's quality of life and enable them to lead as independent a life as possible. A microcomputer was obtained in October 1986 and has became a regular feature of activities at the Unit.

Participant observations

Over a period of ten weeks in the winter of 1987 the Unit was visited once a week. By working alongside the staff, observations were made of how staff work with residents on the microcomputer, the goals and priorities of the manager and methods of achieving goals.

Interview

A structured interview with the manager of the Unit took place during two 30-minute sessions. Questions were raised in the key areas of:

– management and resources;
– computer equipment and resources;
– decisions to purchase a microcomputer;
– microcomputer usage in the Unit; and
– evaluation of the microcomputer.

Analysis of records

Staff at the Unit keep records of who they use the microcomputer with, for how long they use it and with what software, together with general comments on performance. Records from October 1986 to October 1987 were analysed. For each of the 13 months, the average time spent on the microcomputer, the average number of sessions and number of programs used were calculated. The same calculations were carried out for each individual who used the microcomputer.

SUMMARY OF RESULTS

Participant observations

The main aims for the microcomputer in the Unit are stated for all to see on a wallchart in the Unit. These are:

- to provide mental stimulation; and
- to develop and improve hand-eye coordinations, motor movements and perceptual skills.

The microcomputer is set up in the same room where all other activities in the Unit occur. It is partly separated from other activities by a cupboard and a curtain partition. Sessions are scheduled on the microcomputer in the morning and afternoon of every day.

Microcomputer use

The staff at the Unit work with ten to fifteen residents a week, each resident may be given between one and two sessions using the computer in a week.

It was observed that when staff are using the microcomputer with individual residents they do not in general follow an explicitly defined set of objectives. Consequently they have no method of assessing how well a person has done on a programme. This is something the manager is aware of and is working towards changing; a planned set of objectives is being implemented, for example, in teaching the concept of time.

Once the staff have set up the microcomputer and decided what software to use, they will either stay with the individual and give prompting and encouragement or they will leave the residents alone to get on with the work. It is not clear what factors determine these modes of behaviour.

Staff interest

Of the staff at the Unit, the manager shows the greatest interest in the microcomputer. The assistants seem to show an indifference, apart from one who has had some prior experience.

Access to and use of experts

One major decision made by the manager at the Unit was to arrange for the software engineer of the Computer Applications to Special Education (CASE) team at Keele University to visit once a week. His role is to provide on-site advice, training and help, and to work with individual residents. It was observed that very few of the projects the software engineer was asked to work on were allowed to continue to completion.

Relationships within the organizational hierarchy

The manager of the Occupational Therapy Unit has to work with other professionals in the hospital such as psychologists, speech therapists and nurses. She is often required to carry out tasks with the residents on the specific recommendations of these people. It was observed that there was very little cooperation or cohesion between these professionals, they often work in isolation from one another on identical goals. Furthermore none of these other professionals are involved with the microcomputer work.

Interviews

Management and Resources
The manager has five assistants on her staff. Both the manager and the assistants work on a part-time basis. The staff have varying experience within the Unit ranging from years to weeks. Attendance at training sessions is optional but highly encouraged.

The budget for computer equipment is not fixed, however the manager has been able to accumulate a substantial resource of hardware, peripherals and software.

Decisions to purchase a microcomputer
The decision to purchase a microcomputer at the Unit resulted from the personal interest of the manager. From an initial interest and excitement she sought to find out more about the potential role the microcomputer could play in the Unit. She was able to consult several different people from varying disciplines, including an Occupational Therapy Interest Group on microcomputers. Through her contacts the manager was able to obtain a BBC microcomputer on loan. Then with the permission of the Hospital Manager the mobility money of about ten residents was used to purchase a microcomputer and equipment.

Analysis of records

From Figures 1 and 2 which show the average number of sessions and length of sessions over the 13 months, two points emerged. First, no general pattern of use over the months is apparent. Secondly there are wide differences between the months. In contrast, the average

RESIDENT	% TOTAL SESSIONS	RESIDENT	% TOTAL TIME
MC	18.30	MC	28.87
LS	17.24	LS	17.17
NT	5.04	HS	5.03
AS	4.77	JB	4.10
HS	3.97	NT	3.82
SN	3.97	AS	3.32
CM	3.71	JD	2.88
JD	2.91	DC	2.41
JH	2.38	CM	2.37
NS	2.38	SW	2.30

Table 1. *Percentage of total sessions and time spent on the microcomputer for ten residents given the most access to the microcomputer*

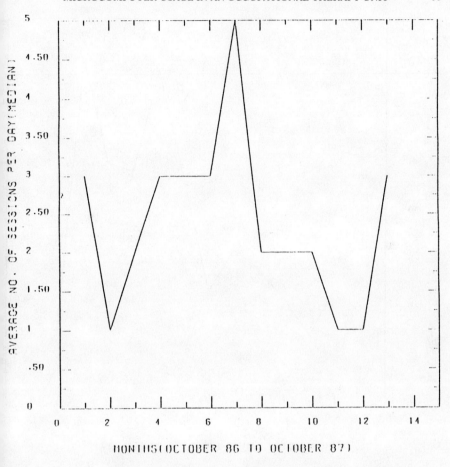

Figure 1. *Average number sessions per day over time*

number of programs used in a session remained constant over the 13 months.

Analysis of the records also showed that over 13 months, 42 individuals were given access to the microcomputer. Some were given just a couple of sessions while others were given over 20. Such wide variability in access also occurred among those who were given the most access, the majority of whom were on mobility allowance (Table 1).

DISCUSSION

In this study three main methods of investigation were implemented: participant observation, interview and analysis of records. No method alone elicited sufficient information to describe exactly how microcomputers are used. Each method proffered information unique to a particular area. There is, however, scope for this technique to be improved which will be considered in relation to five areas of discussion.

Context of innovation

The Occupational Therapy manager works in relative isolation from the other

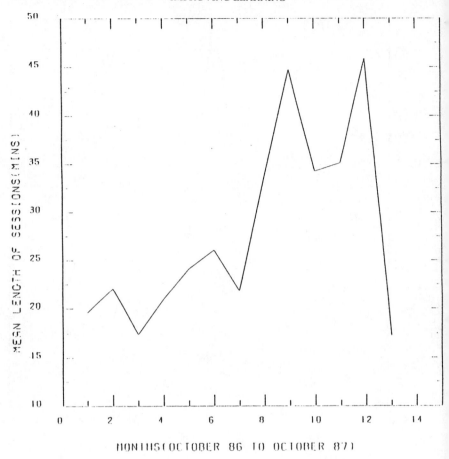

Figure 2. *Mean length of sessions over time*

professionals in the hospital. She did not therefore involve them in her plans for the microcomputer. The Hospital Manager was the only person in the hospital hierarchy who had an influence on the plans. The isolationism of the Unit has implications for microcomputer use which will be considered in the other areas of discussion.

Locus of innovation

Staff in education are usually seen to be on the receiving end of decisions about change. This is not so at the Occupational Therapy Unit where the innovation described came from 'within' in the shape of the manager. There may be a danger that when one person is very active in the decision-making process, people, particularly top managers, come to rely too heavily on that person. If that person leaves then the project can be neglected or abolished. This 'single activist' phenomenon appears to be a symptom of the isolationism of the Occupational Therapy Unit and is something which needs to be investigated further.

The traditional view of educators as formalized by House (1979) is that they have few incentives for innovation because they do not like the uncertainty of not knowing how it will affect their learners. This was observed not to be the case for the Occupational

Therapy manager who found great incentive in knowing that the microcomputer would affect the residents in a very positive way. This incentive was fuelled by her interest and motivation. Ager (1985) believes that a major determinant of the use of microcomputers will be levels of staff interest and commitment. It was noted that the manager's staff did not appear to be very interested in the microcomputer. Levels of interest, therefore, appear to require further investigation.

Support for innovation

The Occupational Therapy manager was able to marshal support from the hospital manager for the microcomputer. It was observed that occasionally she had to resort to political lobbying in an attempt to secure the future of the microcomputer. The exact nature of the 'coalition' between the two managers would need to be studied further in order to ascertain the nature of the conflicts and compromises and how high a priority the microcomputer is for the hospital manager.

Implementation of innovation

The implementation of the ideas of the Occupational Therapy manager did not follow any specific goals or defined approaches. There was no clear policy, for example, on when staff should remain with individuals during their sessions. There seems to be a need to study planning and execution of plans in more detail.

Determinants of innovation

The resources that the manager has available to her appear to be important. The five assistants work on a part-time basis so the manager never has the full staff available to her at any one time. This can be restrictive in terms of time available to engage in certain activities. That the manager is the only qualified occupational therapist suggests a limitation in expertise.

The diversion of money from another project to fund the microcomputer might have been a low-priority project since no separate fund was created specifically for it. The implications of this for the implementation of the microcomputer need further study.

While the Unit has quite a substantial amount of equipment it is not always working and it often takes quite a while for repairs to be completed which can restrict microcomputer use.

The manager has created a network of technical support for herself which involves many disciplines and professions. This network, however, operates from outside the Unit, there is no internal technical support system. This is likely to be another symptom of the isolationism of the Unit which warrants further investigation.

CONCLUSIONS

This study has initiated a method which has begun to provide a picture of what factors influence the use of microcomputers. The method does, however, need improvements to highlight further details. These are:

- consequences of isolationism;
- single-activist phenomenon;
- levels of interest;
- nature of 'coalitions';
- planning and execution of goals; and
- resources and technology.

What emerges from this study is that we cannot look at individual managerial practices in microcomputer use in isolation from the organizations in which managers work, the people within that organization, and the resources and expertise that are made available.

REFERENCES

Ager, A. (1985) Recent developments in the use of microcomputers in the field of mental handicap: implications for psychological practice. *Bulletin of British Psychological Society*, **38**, 142-145.

Bower, M. (1965) Nurturing innovation in an organization. In Steiner, G.A. (ed.) *The Creative Organization*. University of Chicago Press, Chicago and London.

Chakera, E. (1984) Contrasting approaches to the learning processes in special schools. In Kelly, A.V. (ed) *Microcomputers and the Curriculum*. Harper and Row.

Goldman, S.R. (1987) Special Education administrators policies and practices on microcomputer acquisition, allocation and access for mildly handicapped children. *Exceptional Children*, **53**, 4, 330-339.

House, E.R. (1979) Technology versus craft: a ten year perspective on innovation. *Journal of Curriculum Studies*, **2**, 1, 1-15.

Kelly, A.V. (1984) Microcomputers and the curriculum: Uses and Abuses. In Kelly, A.V.(ed) *Microcomputers and the Curriculum*. Harper and Row.

Kidd, M.E. and Holmes, G. (1982) Strategies for change: the computer and language remediation. *Programmed Learning and Educational Technology*, **19**, 3, 234-239.

Lindbald, S. (1984) The practice of school centred innovation: a Swedish case. *Journal of Curriculum Studies*, **16**, 2, 165-173.

Litterer, J.A. (1967) *The Analysis of Organizations*. Wiley, New York.

Merton, R.K. (1965) The environment of the innovating organization: some conjectures and proposals. In Steiner, G.A. (ed) *The Creative Organization*. University of Chicago Press, Chicago.

Papert, S. (1980) *Mindstorms, Children, Computers and Powerful Ideas*. Harvester Press, Brighton.

Sheingold, K., Kane, J. and Endreiweit, M.E. (1983) Microcomputer use in schools: Developing a research agenda. *Harvard Educational Review*, **53**, 412-432.

15. Computer interfacing in the physics laboratory

N R Foster, M A S Sweet and H I Ellington, *Robert Gordon's Institute of Technology, Aberdeen, UK*

Summary: Three packages interfaced to a BBC microcomputer for use in secondary school physics have been developed. These are:

- an inexpensive optical spectrometer used with a diffraction grating to measure wavelength of light;
- an opto-detector combined with a slotted disc which allows an investigation of the concepts of velocity and acceleration, enabling both graphs and printouts of the instantaneous distance travelled, and velocity reached to be given; and
- a linear displacement transducer developed at RGIT which has a resolution of less than one-hundredth of a millimetre. This has been linked with a software package that makes it possible to explore the concepts of stress and strain involved in Hook's Law and enables calculation of the Young's modulus of a wire to be undertaken.

The project is also concerned with measuring the success of the packages in meeting their predetermined objectives. One of the packages, Young's modulus, has already been subjected to preliminary testing using young people from local schools in the Grampian Region and first-year degree students. The emphasis of this paper is upon this one package with only brief references to the others. Testing methods used have been criterion-referenced pre- and post-tests, questionnaires completed by the students and illuminative evaluation. So far illuminative evaluation has been used as a development aid rather than for assessment.

INTRODUCTION

This project, which is jointly sponsored by Robert Gordon's Institute of Technology (RGIT) and the Scottish Council for Educational Technology (SCET), was begun in the Autumn of 1986 after initial work by the project supervisory team had shown that there were certain physics experiments which could benefit from the use of microcomputers as experimental tools. Our aim is to produce a number of different packages using various transducers for interfacing to the BBC range of microcomputers, which will instill physics principles by practical exercises in the laboratory as an adjunct to formal teaching methods.

THE PROJECT

Following discussion with SCET, it was decided to target the packages at the Scottish Certificate of Sixth Year Studies (CSYS) physics level with perhaps some overlap to Scottish schools' Higher grade and first-year physics at tertiary educational level.

The next question which arose was 'how much of the work involved in measurement and calculation should the computer do?' One early experiment had used a microcomputer to measure the velocity of sound. Because all calculations were performed internally and the result printed out, this failed to involve and educate the student. This was obviously undesirable, it was resolved that a set of learning objectives be drawn up for each package and that steps be taken within the package to instill the corresponding principles through a practical learning experiment. Also, each package would undergo testing and assessment using local school pupils and RGIT students to ascertain how well these learning objectives had been met.

When considering possible experiments to develop into packages, we have found it particularly fruitful if there are compelling and valid reasons for an approach employing a microcomputer. There are a number of possible valid reasons (for example, where measurements to be taken are complicated or monotonous to conduct). This could lead to the learning objectives of the experiment being obscured. Another case might be an experiment where the measurements need to be taken so rapidly that manual operation is ineffective.

In an effort not to produce too closed a package, it was decided to stimulate the students' ingenuity by suggesting further applications for the transducer used in each package and emphasizing this aspect for further project work since this is a large part of CSYS physics. The team is also aware of a secondary set of objectives associated with each package for at least some of the students, namely learning how to utilize electronics in order to solve practical problems. For this reason, full details of each transducer, including its underlying principles and its operation and calibration, are included with each package. This will have the added benefit of assisting in expanding the range of applications for each transducer.

THE PACKAGES

An upper limit on cost to the user of 0 per package was kept in mind throughout the project. SCET standards of software programming and compatibility across the complete range of BBC microcomputers have been adhered to.

An inexpensive optical spectrometer

This package investigates the properties of prisms, diffraction gratings and double and multiple slits. A turntable is driven by a stepper motor which is controlled by a BBC microcomputer. A photodiode mounted on the edge of the turntable detects the varying light intensity. Reading these values from the photodiode, the microcomputer draws a graph of intensity against angle.

An investigation into the concepts of displacement, velocity and acceleration

The object of this package is to demonstrate the concepts of displacement, velocity and acceleration in operation in order to reinforce the theoretical aspects. A pulley on an axle has a cord joining a vehicle on a linear airtrack to a hanging weight. On the same axle is a slotted disc. As the weight falls, causing the vehicle to accelerate, the microcomputer counts the number of slots which pass an optical detector and displays the results graphically.

Measurement of Young's Modulus for a wire and related concepts

Outline

Design specifications for this transducer included the need for accuracy and reproducibility. In order to be attractive to schools, it had to be simple and inexpensive to produce. The transducer is known as a linear displacement transducer (LDT) and, using

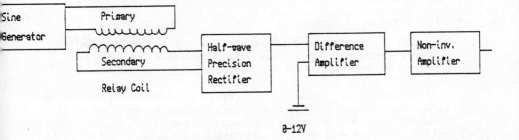

Figure 1. *Schematic diagram at transducer*

the BBC microcomputer's built-in analogue to digital converter (ADC), is capable of resolving displacements to one- hundredth of a millimetre.

Referring to Figure 1, the sine wave generator outputs a constant amplitude alternating voltage which generates a magnetic field. Variations in coupling efficiency between the primary and secondary coil, caused by the moving core, lead to changes in amplitude of the output voltage which then undergoes further signal processing before being fed to the analogue-to-digital (ADC) input on the BBC microcomputer.

The base-board of the apparatus is attached to a wall. A vertical wire is fixed at the top of the apparatus, fed through the LDT and at the bottom a set of weights is hung. The LDT registers any change in length of the wire due to the amount of weight suspended from it and displays the results as a graph on screen.

The student is asked to measure the length and diameter of the wire. These results are then entered via the keyboard which enables a value for the Young's Modulus to be calculated. The microcomputer will not display its result until a reasonable value for Young's Modulus has been entered by the user.

Learning objectives
The following are the major learning objectives which this package has been designed to achieve. The student should be able to:

- define the terms 'stress' and 'strain' for a wire, explain the physical significance of each term and evaluate each quantity;
- state the relationships between stress and strain for a wire in terms of Young's Modulus and explain the significance of the elastic limit;
- plot a suitable graph of either stress versus strain or displacement versus force and use this to calculate from the value of Young's Modulus for the material of the wire; and
- state the order of magnitude value of Young's Modulus for the material of the wire.

Present stage of development
The package has already undergone testing and validation. Two methods were developed to ascertain how well the package met the above educational objectives. First, the package assessment paper to find out how much the student had learnt from the package. Secondly, a questionnaire to elicit the student's own reaction to the package. (Details of both appear in later sections.)

Package distribution to schools in the Grampian Region has been made possible with the help of the local Educational Resources Service who have agreed to produce the transducer in kit-form with the software being given to schools free on request.

THE YOUNG'S MODULUS ASSESSMENT PAPER

Introduction

An important part of the project is to ascertain how packages have performed in
fulfilling their learning objectives. Since 'Young's Modulus of a wire' is the first
package to undergo testing, a standardized approach had not initially been decided
upon.

The assessment paper consists of questions designed to determine how effective the
package has been in achieving its predetermined objectives. It is attempted by all
students as an 'open book' type of assessment. As well as this paper the students and
teachers were asked for comments on the package's ease of operation and clarity of
instruction and theory, together with any faults which the students might have
discovered while using the program.

The first schools all completed the assessment paper after they had used the
program and arrived at a value for the Young's Modulus of a wire and thus had
become familiar with the necessary theory. All the resultant marks from these groups
were very high. In an attempt to establish a control group, further school groups were
split into two. The first group attempted the paper before conducting the experiment
and the second group completed the paper afterwards. Initially no time limit was set
on the assessment paper and results from both sections were quite similar. However,
the time taken by the two groups to complete the paper varied noticeably. Those
students who sat the assessment paper before they had seen the package took up to
one- and-a-half hours to complete it, while those who had used the package before the
assessment paper completed it in as little as 20 minutes.

Results and statistical analysis

To date, seven schools have tested the package at RGIT. The results of the package
assessment papers are shown in Table 1. The results are not clear-cut. There are two
main reasons for this. First, the sample size is small. Secondly, a consistent approach
to the way in which the assessment paper was conducted had not been finalized.

The mean mark of students who sat the assessment paper before conducting the
package is 21.5 with a standard deviation of 2.7. The mean mark of students who
completed the paper after conducting the package is 23.2 with a standard deviation of
3.4.

Using the Student's t-test for small samples, the test statistic for the two samples was
calculated to be 1.4. From tables, for a sample with 35 degrees of freedom, t(5 per
cent) = 2.0. Hence the difference between the two means is not statistically significant
at the 5 per cent level. This implies a need for more data and a standardized
approach towards the assessment paper. More data will become available when the
package is distributed to schools throughout the Grampian Region.

No significant conclusions can be drawn from the results of RGIT students who
completed the assessment papers. However, referring to Table 2 later in this paper, it
is clear that the students benefited from the experience and found it to be enjoyable.

Alternative methods for the interpretation of the assessment paper

- Set a time limit on the paper. This is possibly the most obvious course of action.
  However, setting such a rigid limit could prove to be counter-productive. Since the
  students have come to use the package voluntarily, any strict enforcement of time
  limits could lead to resentment or a lack of care being taken over the paper which
  would tend to invalidate any results gained.
- Change the paper into a 'closed book' type of assessment. This implies the need for

Mark out of 30	Number of students: Before	After
15	1	0
16	0	0
17	0	1
18	0	2
19	1	1
20	2	3
21	0	3
22	2	0
23	2	2
24	2	5
25	1	2
26	0	1
27	0	2
28	0	3
29	0	1
Total no. of students	11	26

Table 1. *Results of the package assessment papers from schools*

some form of traditional 'chalk and talk' by the teachers before the students attempt the assessment paper. Whilst this is likely to be the most direct method of discovering how successfully the package has achieved objectives, it could be seen by some teachers as an implied criticism of their methods. Since the need to establish a good working relationship with the teachers is essential to the project this idea will not be used.
- A scheme of time penalties or weighting. By asking each pupil to take a note of the time taken by them to attempt the assessment paper, a mean time for attempting the paper could be calculated. For every five minutes over this mean a mark could be deducted from the final total. Similarly, a mark could be added to the final total for every five minutes under the mean time.

For the data extracted from assessment papers to be meaningful, a consistent approach to their interpretation needs to be arrived at. Using time limits in schools and time penalties for groups at RGIT as outlined above, the team feels this has now been done.

THE YOUNG'S MODULUS QUESTIONNAIRE

Introduction

The questionnaire was designed to elicit how the student had felt about the package, how well it had got over the concepts described earlier and whether they would like to see other experiments conducted in this way. The results are mainly from students at RGIT.

How helpful did you find the section on experimental procedure and operation of the apparatus?

Very Helpful	Quite Helpful	Not very Helpful	Not at all Helpful
59.09	22.73	13.64	4.55

How clearly were the concepts of stress, strain, elastic limit and Young's modulus explained in the section theory?

	Very Clear	Fairly Clear	Not very Clear	Not at all Clear
Stress	36.36	63.64	0.00	0.00
Strain	31.82	68.18	0.00	0.00
Elast.Lim.	22.73	54.55	22.73	0.00
Young's Mod.	18.18	68.18	9.09	34.55

Once the measurements had begun, how logical and easy to follow were the instructions?

Very Clear	Fairly Clear	Not very Clear	Not at all Clear
77.27	22.73	0.00	0.00

Overall how easy did you find the computer program to be?

Very Easy	Quite Easy	Quite Difficult	Very Difficult
59.09	40.91	0.00	0.00

How much experience have you had with computers?

A Lot	Quite a Lot	Very Little	None
9.09	36.36	36.36	18.18

Would you like to see other experiments computerized in this way?

Definitely	Probably	Probably Not	Definitely Not
54.55	36.36	9.09	0.00

Table 2. *Results of Young's Modulus questionnaire*

Results as a Percentage

Results are shown in Table 2.

The results of the questionnaire (Table 2) are encouraging and may well be a better way of arriving at the true worth of a package than the assessment paper, due to the difficulties in obtaining a valid control group. This will require further consideration when more data has been gathered.

CONCLUSION

The response to the project of both physics teachers and pupils has been extremely positive, with every school that has been involved being very keen to be included in further testing during the project. Further data for the project should become available upon dissemination of the packages to schools throughout the Grampian region and, ultimately, the whole of Scotland. With other packages still in the 'pipeline' it is considered that this project will have assisted the use of computers in schools as a practical tool and adjunct to teaching.

16. The microcomputer as a catalyst for change in educational technology: a Kenyan experience

Brian F Wray, *Project Director, Computers in Education Project, Aga Khan Education Service, Kenya*

Summary: In 1982 the Aga Khan Education Service, concerned with the appropriate introduction of new information technologies into schools, attempted a promising single school pilot project which has now been expanded to eight Kenyan schools.

In order to improve the quality of education as well as providing access to the technology, a school-wide introduction has been attempted challenging the teachers to find their own solutions to the problems faced by suggesting several alternatives.

The projects attempt to show the need for greater use of available technology for more effective and enjoyable education. The teacher is tempted away from the central classroom role to become more aware of a child-centred curriculum. This major change in philosophy has many difficulties, some of which still have to be tackled.

The results to date suggest considerations for future educational technology introductions, in particular the need to rethink the education of managers and providers of education.

INTRODUCTION

In 1982 the Aga Khan Education Service (AKES)[1], ever-concerned with improving quality in its units, investigated the applications of microcomputers in the secondary school within developing countries. After consideration of the then normal approaches, together with an extrapolation of future advances, an action plan was drawn up for a pilot project in a single Nairobi private school. This plan called for an appropriately broad introduction of the uses of microcomputers to the staff of the school, challenging them to devise solutions to the new possibilities presented by this technology. A major concern was to wean the teachers away from their didactic approach, towards a child-centred problem-solving approach which was one of the national goals of the newly introduced Kenya 8-4-4 curriculum.

The Project was set up with the following five objectives:

- to improve the quality of teaching by in-service teacher education using the microcomputer as a catalyst;
- to use microcomputers as a teaching resource in appropriate school subject topics;
- to provide the pupils with a basic knowledge of new information technologies, both to aid them in their studies and to make them aware of their technological environment;
- to improve the quality of the school administration through the use of appropriate information technology; and
- to appoint such members of staff as required so that the school can maintain its level of educational/information technology without the need of continued support by the project.

As a result of investigations into the effect of this pilot project on the teaching-learning environment, it was decided to attempt a phase II expansion of the same philosophy to eight schools around the Republic. Originally five extra schools were included; one private, four Government. Later two other Government schools, aided by AKES, were also added.

The Aga Khan Foundation (AKF)[2] made a major grant to cover equipment, software, media and training activities for a three-year period and, in line with its policy, has ensured that the effects of the innovations are being detailed by a full-time researcher. Having decided the equipment specification, an approach was made to the manufacturer, Apple Computers Inc, who generously donated all the required computers and peripherals together with their proprietary software. The project received interest in other circles and AKF was able to obtain co-funding from IDRC and Rockerfeller Foundation for the research component.

The Ministry of Education has continued to give the project its support by ensuring duty-free status for equipment, designating the various workshops as official and maintaining a concerned interest in the progress. The Head of State and the Minister of Education, as well as Ministry officials, receive reports at regular intervals from various sources.

THE IMPLEMENTATION

The schools chosen for the Project are distributed in three centres, Nairobi, Mombasa and Nakuru, which determines the nature of workshops and visits. Nairobi is centrally located with Mombasa being 500km away on the coast and Nakuru about 180km from Nairobi towards Uganda.

The introductory workshops were held on a town basis in August 1986, involving all the school staffs for 70 hours. These were designed to attempt to remove the 'fear-factor' of the technology as well as to give some insight into the possibilities it offered. Much of the time was spent with hands-on exercises working in small groups, providing experience not only of the tool but of possible classroom methodologies. The teachers expected to be told exactly what to do and how a particular piece of software would be used in their syllabus, and were uncomfortable at finding themselves in an open-ended situation which demanded that they bring professional experience to bear.

Each school received five Apple IIe computers together with disc drives, monitors, printers, applications software and a small quantity of CAL software, together with books for teachers and pupils. They further received a selection of magazines and could borrow software and books from a central library. This allows the schools to find useful software so that it may eventually be purchased for them. This scheme is very necessary since much of the 'recommended software' is of poor quality, unsuitable for Kenya or difficult to use. Software is purchased both from UK and US sources, based on reports in various educational magazines. Much of the 'best' is little used yet due to the philosophical changes required by the teachers. Teachers tend to change their ideas on the usefulness of software as they become more accustomed to the new methods.

The 18 months since the phase II introduction has been spent in encouraging experimentation with microcomputers, first as a tool for the teacher and more recently as a tool for the child. Monthly visits have been made to each school to assist and to resolve any difficulties which the staff have encountered in mastering aspects of the technology, most of which have been due to complete non-familiarity since only a handful of the 300 teachers involved had ever seen a computer before the introductory workshop.

Centralized seminars/workshops aimed at revising the educational methods have been held at which up to three teachers from each school have attended for either a weekend or a vacation week. These workshops, covering groups of subjects, attempt to show both the usefulness of different types of CAL programs and the methods of using applications programs for preparation, for management of the education process and within the classroom itself. Major concerns at each of these sessions were attempts to reinforce the idea of a child-centred approach and to make the material interestingly relevant by linking it to everyday experiences, including those within other subjects. The baseline research had underlined the fact that, while many teachers subscribed to a more liberal view of the education process, almost all only ever used a didactic approach in the classroom.

Other workshops have been aimed at improving the administration of the schools through the Bursars developing spreadsheets to satisfy their accounting needs, and through the Heads and senior staff developing the use of databases, wordprocessing and spreadsheets to keep better records which they can analyse in new ways, providing better information to staff, parents and children.

A major need of all development projects should be to ensure that the affected community is able to continue to function as a unit after the donors have withdrawn. Three workshops have been held for selected staff who have become the 'coordinators' between the project and their own schools. These sessions have dealt with technical aspects of the machines as well as the project philosophy. The coordinators now organize their own in-school workshops for new teachers, and have been given the opportunity of planning and operating the next holiday workshop for all staff.

LESSONS LEARNT BY THE IMPLEMENTERS

Some teachers have not moved from their original positions, in fact some have rejected the computer as irrelevant to their teaching. Given the experience in other countries, of slow take-up and rejection in schools, even where both the wider use of computers and of other educational technologies are more common, the actual 19 per cent reported average staff usage within the project appears to be a reasonable achievement.

Original baseline research data noted that the vast majority of teachers conduct classes by lecturing, dictating notes and demonstrating ideas on the blackboard. A prevalent idea seems to be that all facts must be written down, even if they are copied from the textbook on to the blackboard and hence to the pupil's notebook. This may have relevance when textbooks are in short supply, but it also happens when all the children have a copy. Unfortunately, the majority of locally produced textbooks make no concession to modern textbook design or the educational philosophy underlining it. Teachers appear to believe that children are incapable of understanding anything unless they have been told it by the teacher. The use of educational technology in many classrooms resembles a state of affairs which pre-dates Guttenburg and Caxton.

The first software which both teachers and children request is either testing or drill since these relate directly to the normal teaching-learning styles and they feel comfortable with them. Teachers are surprised that children can work through material which the syllabus puts later. In fact, we have found form 1 pupils working with chemistry programs designed for university level with apparent understanding, pleasure and no thought of the 'difficulty'.

The better-designed courseware (ie software and the accompanying material that a child, or group, should work through in order to gain mastery of a concept or topic) can be used by the pupils easily, with pleasure and with minimum guidance from a teacher. Group-working provides a better environment than children working alone but many teachers are unhappy with this situation since they are no longer in control. They report problems of time, noise and other factors but mostly appear uncomfortable at not being the focus of the class' attention. Some attempt to remedy the situation by sitting at the keyboard themselves!

The combination of didactic methods, poor reading, factually orientated examinations and a strictly hierarchical school system, tends to reinforce the notion of the school as a factory, albeit an inefficient one, turning out certificated products who only then start to learn about the real world. Teachers are teachers of subjects, not of children, being concerned that the definitions, processes and facts of their material can be regurgitated in the examination, even if they are never used afterwards. A new Secondary Examination will be held for the first time in 1989, and, if it follows the lead of the Primary one and the National Education Goals, should help redress the balance towards thinking.

A POSSIBLE DIRECTION FOR SECONDARY EDUCATION

It would appear that once again the human is being left behind by the technology. TV and video are not well used in schools, yet appear as a major source of informal learning. Books have been with us for several hundred years, yet millions in the West are illiterate, and it is suggested that the majority who can read still cannot use a book properly for learning or to find information quickly. The present surge of microprocessor-based educational technology equipment (computers, interactive video, CD-ROM, satellite communications etc) leaves most traditionally trained teachers reeling, preferring to closet themselves in the familiarity of subject-based fact dissemination. (Notice the trend, if money is available, of forward-facing computer laboratories, projection video and OHP of computer screens which once again put the teacher in front of the class.)

It would appear that we have the tools which will enable any motivated learner to learn facts and certain skills which at present are highly prized. Three major questions remain:

- Where is all the wonderful courseware we have been promised?
- How do we ensure that the learner is motivated?
- What is the role of the manager in learning?

Our institutions of higher learning have a major task in front of them. Their discipline constrained professors have to try to produce a whole new cadre of secondary-level educationalists who have a different perspective from those whom the same institutions have been producing for so many years.

I would suggest that two major and separate types of educational workers are required:

- those who can produce material which the learner can use with facility so that the learning process becomes enjoyable, efficient and effective; and
- those who can help the learners map their way through the various concepts and knowledge that is needed for them to develop in their world.

The Open University and others have made a worthwhile start on the former, although aimed at the post-secondary group. There are many teachers already able to produce good material, but their energies need to be consolidated into national efforts so that the fruits of their endeavours are available to a much wider audience. As this expertise is developed, together with the advances now being made in learning theory, it should be possible to build a vast library of good course material using the most appropriate technologies. If this is done as a national exercise, the cost, amortized over several generations, would be within the reach of even the poorest nations.

A more difficult task will be to provide the learner management. It would appear that none of our present models of educational institutions are appropriate, requiring new models to be tried in the near future. Most young children are naturally curious and become responsible at an early age; in Kenya one still sees pre-teenagers in sole charge of their family's cattle far from their homes. These cattle often represent the entire wealth of the clan. How many Western ten-year-olds have a family charge card?

The present school system seems to stifle curiosity and deny responsibility for learning (although not for failure!). The new manager will have to be aware of the learner's needs and desires, and of the opportunities afforded by courses and the possibilities for further development; and able to counsel and analyse difficulties, suggest solutions without a detailed knowledge of the subject matter itself, and know where and how to find help. For too long we have been training teachers of subjects, we now need to educate people who will help others to educate themselves properly.

Parents need to be actively involved in the total education of their children until adulthood. In a pastoral society this went unquestioned, all the clan had some responsibility for the child's upbringing and often took responsibility for several stages of progression through adult life as well. In the industrial society, children are pushed into child-minding factories where the parental responsibility seems to stop at the door once the fees have been paid. Possibly one of the first series of self-learning courses needed for this high-tech age is 'How to care for your child now they have achieved this stage in development'.

Notes

1. AKES is incorporated in Geneva with autonomous service companies in various countries including India, Pakistan, Syria, Tanzania, UK, USA, Canada and Kenya.
2. AKF is a major Third World foundation concerned with health education and community work. It provides seed money for projects which can act as models for future development by governments or larger NGOs concerned with development.

17. Covering the waterfront: findings from a programme of research on computers in education and training

David Hawkridge, *Institute of Educational Technology, The Open University, Milton Keynes, UK*

Summary: This paper discusses a long-term programme, begun in 1981, of four studies on computers in education and training. The studies were planned to follow close behind four successive waves of innovation:

- when microcomputers arrived in UK and US schools in the early 1980s;
- when microcomputers became valuable in teaching disabled children and adults;
- when microcomputers entered company training; and
- when microcomputers reached Third World classrooms in significant numbers.

All four studies follow a similar pattern starting with identification of learning needs. In each, the researchers have been journalists, reporting what others have told them and what they have observed, but also academics analysing critically the context within which learning is occurring. The issues discussed are more permanent than the hardware or software. Lastly, the studies lead to some predictions about each wave. In covering the waterfront in this way there is a risk of superficiality and sheer error. Since the methods are more qualitative than quantitative, the findings are for debate, rather than being 'facts' based on experimental or survey research.

INTRODUCTION

This is a personal story. In 1980, less than eight years ago, I began to get interested in microcomputers. Like many other educational technologists, my acquaintance with computers up to that time had been limited to mainframes. The first time I met one was in 1961 at the University College in what is now Zimbabwe, where we had a Hollerith card sorter and tabulator which helped me to analyse my PhD data. In 1965 I visited the United States and saw the beginnings of PLATO at the University of Illinois. PLATO later became a very large computer-assisted instruction project. Then in 1967 I moved to California and joined the staff of Project PLAN, a computer-managed instruction experiment in a dozen primary and secondary schools in several States. By the time I began my present job, in 1970, I needed no convincing that computers could be used in education, but mainframes were simply not cost-effective.

In 1980, however, other electronic media, particularly those that were most useful in distance education, were at the top of my research agenda (see, for example, Hawkridge and Robinson, 1982). If David Croom, of the publishers Croom Helm, had not visited me to discuss possible books, I probably would not have considered 'covering the waterfront'. After he had gone I began thinking about a long-term programme of research and writing about this innovation, the microcomputer, which was bound to change education and training because it was small, relatively cheap and, above all, under the direct control of teachers and students.

The four topics I shall discuss came to mind fairly easily, but I had no idea how long the programme would take, except that it would need at least eight years, at two years per study, and I was not certain at first about the order in which to tackle the topics. The four successive waves of innovation were not yet clear to me, though it was obvious that one was already hitting British and American schools.

NEW INFORMATION TECHNOLOGY IN EDUCATION

In 1981 I began searching the electronic databases and added to my collection of documents about computers in education. I visited old colleagues, schools, universities and factories in the United States and found much excitement about the new developments with microcomputers and telecommunications. There seemed to be a need for a basic book about new information technology in education to complement those that were beginning to appear about information technology in other spheres. After a year of research, I wrote that book (Hawkridge, 1983).

What were my main findings, bearing in mind that my research was neither of the survey kind nor experimental? First, that there were tremendous international political and economic forces behind information technology and that education was unlikely to escape their influence. Second, that the range of existing and potential educational uses was very wide, and increasing. Third, that the quality of the hardware far exceeded that of the available software. Fourth, that serious educational, social, political, economic and technical problems surrounded this innovation. And fifth, that the optimism among educationalists was only slightly greater than the pessimism. Nevertheless, microcomputers and their related technology were being used in schools in greater numbers each year, and more and more teachers were being trained.

NEW IT IN THE EDUCATION OF DISABLED CHILDREN AND ADULTS

During the first study, I came across the second wave of innovation, running a little behind the first: outstandingly successful examples of information technology being used to aid the education of disabled children and adults. Two Open University colleagues in the Institute of Educational Technology joined me. Tom Vincent specializes in using computers to alleviate learning problems of blind students, and Gerald Hales is a specialist on learning problems of deaf students. We obtained, from the Nuffield Foundation, a grant to study how new IT was being used to help disabled students in the United States and this country. It is a field in which optimism is tested pragmatically all the time, but where pessimism has little place.

We covered, between us, students who are speech-impaired, blind, deaf and physcially disabled. We did not cover the rest of the special education field, as some suggested we might, because we saw few examples of successful applications there. We started from the learning problems of people with these kinds of disability, and focused on how these difficulties could be alleviated by using information technology, particularly that based on microcomputers. With assistance from two American co-workers, we obtained data from all of the principal research and development centres in the United States, and visited several of them ourselves. Thus the second book in the series (Hawkridge, Vincent and Hales, 1985) draws together information from three sources:

- experience as reported in journals and elsewhere and as described by contacts we made during our survey;
- technical details provided by researchers and manufacturers; and
- advice and opinions from workers in this field.

Again, what were our findings? They are difficult to summarize, particularly because solutions for the problems of disabled children and adults must be fitted to the individual.

For physically disabled students the latest microelectronic devices and systems are smaller, easier to use and carry, faster and more powerful. They offer a wider range of options for learning to physically disabled students, whose input and output problems can now be more easily reduced or overcome. In many cases, the result is greatly improved communication between teachers and their students, and between students themselves. In fact, better education.

For blind and partially sighted students, many devices now exist which give access to printed material and help to overcome the enormous task of producing braille in sufficient quantity to meet the demand for reading material. Problems of communication with sighted people are being eased through braille-to-text conversion and by adding speech output to devices that produce text in a printed form. Fortunately, the inherent problem of using computers that are designed to produce visual output is being overcome by alternative tactile or audio outputs. Redesign of supporting software holds the key to sighted people. Workstations now integrate hardware and software into a convenient and accessible environment, usually adapted for each student.

For deaf students, especially those deaf from birth, being able to develop competent use of language is vital in the educational environment. Information technology makes this more feasible, particularly through visual interactive systems.

For speech-impaired students, speech handicaps can be overcome to a remarkable degree with synthetic speech devices. Most such students feel they are brought a step closer to interacting with other people and their environment, like everyone else. People who lose their speech through an accident or illness regain some of their old way of living. For those who have never spoken, the technology brings them into a new community based on speech.

Although optimism and technical progress abound in this field, we discovered a range of educational, social, political, economic and technical issues that required critical analysis. Based on these analyses, we advanced a number of fairly positive predictions, some of which have already come true and others which may if the research and development teams are successful. We concluded that the human element, rather than the technological, would always be paramount, with the technology at best a complement or merely a supplement.

COMPUTERS IN COMPANY TRAINING

Meantime, the third wave of innovation was building up. As soon as the manuscript for the second book was in Croom Helm's hands, I prepared a proposal to the Leverhulme Trust for a British study of computers in company training, and was awarded a grant. I tried, without success, to obtain funds from the United States to cover a study in that country, but American foundations look askance at British researchers! Instead, after some delay, the Open University provided just enough money for me to obtain the assistance of a Californian co-worker, Carole Hall, who became a co-author along with Wendy Newton, who was the co-worker under the Leverhulme grant. The three of us wrote the book last year and it appeared in January (Hawkridge, Newton and Hall, 1988).

During the fieldwork in 1986-87, we soon found that very little had been written about company experiences in using computers for training. There were primers on computer-based training (CBT), and one or two non-academic journals, but most of the writing was done by vendors, and naturally focused on their own products and services. They only mentioned companies in passing. We felt the field was wide open to us. On the other hand, it was not always easy to obtain the facts. Almost everywhere, however, we were greeted very warmly, perhaps because we were bringing news of what was happening in other similar settings. By the end of the study, we had visited about 50 companies, mostly large ones.

Once more, what were our findings? How is this third wave of innovation surging through companies and affecting their training? In hardware terms, training on mainframe computers is declining in the face of a very rapid increase in micro-based training, with or without interactive video. In software terms, many authoring languages are on the market, chasing a relatively small number of customers who want to develop their own training programs. Few of the languages are sophisticated enough to take trainers beyond computer-based programmed learning, but that is a beginning.

Artificial intelligence has yet to make its mark on the preparation of training programs. Generic programs for microcomputers, and generic videodiscs, both intended to carry out the same training in a large number of different companies at low cost per copy, are on the increase, but so are custom-made programs and discs used in only one company or group of companies. Overall, there is a very wide range of experience now available to learn from, as the Manpower Services Commission has been trying to tell companies in this country for the last two or three years. We have written-up much of it.

COMPUTERS IN THIRD WORLD COUNTRIES

I come now to the last wave of innovation, running behind the other three, but no less important and interesting. When I began this programme of research, there were virtually no microcomputers in Third World countries, and it was not clear how soon there would be, or even whether they would arrive at all. I only became sure in 1987 that there should be a fourth study in 1988-89. What finally convinced me was visiting a secondary school in Beijing, where I saw more computers, about 50, than I had seen in any British or American school. My conversations with the teachers there led me to prepare a proposal to the new Harold Macmillan Trust, which is specially interested in assisting education in the Third World. What I had in mind was a qualitative study in which a few teachers in each of a number of Third World countries would be co-workers, paid by the Trust, which has now made a grant for this purpose.

I asked two colleagues in the Open University Production Centre of the BBC to join me: one is John Radcliffe, Head of the Centre, who ran the BBC Computer Literacy Project that led to the BBC microcomputer. The other is John Jaworksi, Senior Executive Producer of OU mathematics and computing programmes. We agreed with the Trust that we would confine the study to Africa, Asia and an Arabic-speaking country, leaving the Americas to the Americans.

Invitations to participate went to China, Kenya (the Aga Khan Schools), Jordan, Mauritius, Singapore and Zimbabwe, and we hope that India and Sri Lanka may receive invitations shortly. Acceptance is only the first stage, of course, as we have to identify teachers who can take 10-20 days to do the fieldwork during 1988. This fieldwork will consist of visiting other schools using computers to discuss with the teachers a set of questions we have drawn up. We hope too that there will be meetings of these teachers towards the end of the year, to pool their experience and consider the future. One of us will visit each country, probably once at the start and again at the end of the fieldwork, and will meet Ministry officials to discuss policy.

Coordinating such a far-flung project is not easy, and we have already encountered problems of protocol. Teachers are not accustomed to being approached to be co-workers, but we want the study to include their viewpoint in particular. Already it is clear that there is an abundance of experience to draw on for the study, some of it successful, some of it not. And there are many policy issues under debate.

CONCLUSIONS

In covering the waterfront in this way I recognize, at a personal level, that there is a risk of superficiality and sheer error. I do not pretend to be an expert on computer-based training, for example, although I know quite a lot about what has been happening to CBT in British and US companies recently. Nor can I pretend to be a specialist on the problems of disabled students, despite learning a great deal about them during the second study. The reviewers, in being well-disposed towards the first two books, have indeed picked out a few errors, but I feel that undertaking this research programme has been exciting and worth while. Of course, by covering the waterfront in this way, I am now unable to keep up with developments on all four beaches. Fortunately, I have several colleagues who do so and write about the changes.

Finally, I must point out that since the methods are more qualitative than quantitative, the findings are for debate, rather than being 'facts' based on experimental or survey research. The issues are not likely to change, but as others accumulate experience and draw it together, and as the technology advances, these four studies will become obsolete in certain respects. No matter. Such is the nature of information and even of knowledge.

REFERENCES

Hawkridge, D. (1983) *New Information Technology in Education*. Croom Helm and Johns Hopkins University Press, London and Baltimore.
Hawkridge, D., Newton, W. and Hall, C. (1988) *Computers in Company Training*. Croom Helm and Methuen, Beckenham and New York.
Hawkridge, D. and Robinson, J. (1982) *Organizing Educational Broadcasting*. Croom Helm and Unesco, London and Paris.
Hawkridge, D., Vincent, T. and Hales, G. (1985) *New Information Technology in the Education of Disabled Children and Adults*. Croom Helm and College-Hill Press, Beckenham and San Diego.

Section 3:
Opening learning opportunities

18. Modularization: educational opportunity or administrative convenience?

Jose Rowe, *Essex Institute of Higher Education, UK*

Summary: Traditionally, higher education has been course-based with the criteria for the philosophy, design and evaluation being centred upon the course. The needs of the student and the employer are now being recognized as of greater significance and educational administrators are seeking to find new ways of satisfying market forces and making best use of increasingly scarce resources. This has led to a fresh look at the benefits to be derived from the modularization of courses.

This paper seeks to identify some of the issues involved and proposes that, suitably implemented and supported, the administrative convenience is also of potential educational benefit. Modularization provides both educational opportunities and challenges.

INTRODUCTION

This paper is offered as a personal view of the opportunities and challenges presented by the recent revival of interest in the concept of modularized courses. Having designed and taught an inservice course in computer education leading to a CNAA DPSE award, I had to come to the opinion that at the time of its review we should restructure it into a modular format. This seemed to be the best available solution to the reality of rapidly developing material, an increasingly broad spread of pre-course experience in our clientele and the desire to make the course as adaptive as possible to the circumstances and perceived needs of both teachers and their LEAs.

It transpired that my own decision coincided with the start of a move within the Institute to modularize all its courses. Also I found that on many of the validation and review visits I was making with CNAA panels there was an increasing tendency for course teams to move towards more adaptive and student-centred provision. Last summer I took part in the meetings held to determine a common policy and set of regulations for modular courses within our Institute and I arranged a national symposium for course leaders of computer education DPSEs to meet and discuss possible developments and formats for the future. Currently I am seeking to design modules in expert systems in a manner which enables them to be incorporated into a range of courses.

BACKGROUND

Modern tradition has been for higher education to be subject- specific in content and course-based in organization. Working in a university for 16 years the impression I gathered was that the framework in which teaching took place was based upon the model of a 'corpus of knowledge' to be imparted together with the acquisition of certain skills relating to the particular discipline.

In public sector higher education, the emphasis on initiation into academic life is quite often replaced by the concept of equipping students for particular professions; the course becomes a sequence of material as required by professional bodies (or at least the perception of what it is *thought* is wanted).

In most cases the emphasis is upon 'the course', its philosophy and its outputs, rather than on the nature of the student input. Even if it had ever been true that because students entered courses at 18 having passed the same A level they could be assumed to have a uniform background, the current requirement for institutions to provide for mature students with a variety of backgrounds and expertise makes this assumption totally invalid (see Figures 1 and 2).

Organisation   Content

(named) course based   subject(s) specific

hierarchical   corpus of knowledge

coherence of experiences   imparting of
(in relation to discipline)   relevant skills

possibility of options
(as permitted by timetable)

Presupposes:-

uniform intake ('A' level subjects and grades)

uniform age

similar experience

Figure 1. *Traditional programme of study*

NEED FOR CHANGE

Although modularization is not a new proposal, it has in the past been an administration-led mechanism introduced in order to maximize the efficient use of available resources. It has not necessarily led to the freedom of choice for students that is now being required. What started in the 1970s as a far-sighted restructuring is now becoming essential for survival.

In the past, academic or educational establishments have been accused of 'playing god' by claiming that as they had the subject expertise, they were in the best position to know what a student needed to learn. The present indications are that we are now in danger of

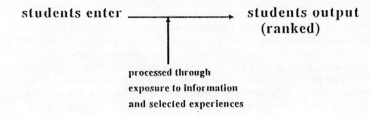

students enter ⟶ students output
(ranked)

processed through
exposure to information
and selected experiences

Course-centred model, with students
of similar age and background being
introduced to the academic or
professional programme designed to
equip them for an academic or
professional career in their chosen
field.

Figure 2. *Traditional model of study*

external pressures causing a shift towards employers (present or future) being cast as 'god'
(ie knowing what it is they need a student or employee to know). There is a certain irony
in this since it comes at a time when many employers are recognizing that there is a need
for employees with basic skills and the enthusiasm and capacity to learn and to be
adaptable to the retraining which will be an inevitable part of modern working life. The
students themselves often feel that they know their own needs best and judge a course on
their perception of its interest and relevance to their situation, this judgement often
changing considerably during and after a programme of study.

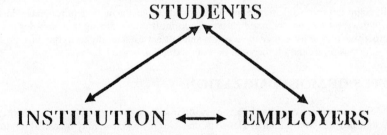

STUDENTS

INSTITUTION ⟷ EMPLOYERS

The Institution's role is to be both proactive and
reactive, with regard to the needs of society.

Figure 3. *Education and training provision tripartite collaboration*

It would therefore seem that a sensible compromise (in best British tradition!) is more likely to provide a better balance. I suggest that a tripartite collaboration between students, employers and educational providers is more likely to succeed than any of the parties operating without regard for the needs of the others (see Figure 3).

It is necessary for the healthy development of new ideas that institutes of education and research should play a proactive role in the provision of education and training programmes while at the same time endeavouring to operate in a manner that is responsive and sensitive to the needs of industry, commerce and the students themselves.

ADMINISTRATIVE REASONS FOR MODULARIZATION

Changes imposed from outside are putting pressures on institutions in a number of ways: market forces are resulting in new funding arrangements; the need to demonstrate the relevance of course provision and its credibility; and the ability to respond rapidly to the changing requirements of society. In addition, the change in the funding structure imposes a greater need to implement cost-effective delivery of courses and, where possible, sharing of resources (see Figure 4).

market forces

> **new funding arrangements;**
> **relevance of provision;**
> **credibility;**
> **speed of response.**

resource sharing

cost effective delivery

Figure 4. *Administrative reasons for modularization*

Recognition that students are individuals and employers have requirements which also vary between them has led to educational administrators realizing that in order to be competitive they must satisfy these needs and not act unilaterally as in the past. So one of the solutions promoted has become that of modular courses.

TYPES OF MODULARIZATION

Modular courses are evolving in a variety of guises, usually such as best to accommodate previous practice and thinking. Hence at one extreme a course may be called modular if it comprises equal sized units, some of which are compulsory and some of which may be optionally selected from a fixed pool of units. At this end of the range the compulsory and optional units may be available only to students registered on that particular course. This model shows no appreciable benefit to students or administrators.

At the other extreme is the model of a pool of modules from which the student may select in various orders with credit being accumulated over time. Modules are studied alongside a range of other students but usually with some rules determining the name (if any) of the final award gained (see Figure 5).

Possible Designations for Modules

compulsory;

designated;

acceptable;

pre-requisite;

co-requisite;

restricted;

integrative;

project.

Figure 5. *List of possible designations for modules*

Educational Benefits of Modularisation

for Students

focus on needs of student;

flexible provision;

adaptive;

recognition of experience.

Figure 6. *How students benefit from modularization*

POTENTIAL BENEFITS OF MODULARIZATION FOR STUDENTS

Modularized programmes can provide benefits to students in allowing recognition of previous experience and flexible provision in terms of both time and content. One of the strengths of a modular scheme lies in its capability to allow for credit accumulation and transfer over a period of time and across different providing agents. It should be able to be adaptive to the students' needs and changing circumstances in ways that are not possible for fixed content courses.

A major attraction for a potential student is for the programme to provide an individually appropriate course of study building upon existing strengths, remedying weaknesses and exploiting experience and present interests. It should avoid the problems of many holistic courses which offer inappropriate starting points, proceed at the wrong pace for the student, include irrelevant content (as perceived by the student) and introduce destructive competition (see Figures 6 and 7).

However, the benefits of peer group interaction should still be available with the potential environment for refining each others' ideas, sharing experiences, cooperation and team activities and the whole social climate that promotes learning (see Figure 8).

POTENTIAL BENEFITS OF MODULARIZATION FOR STAFF

An institute-wide modular programme has potential benefits to offer the teaching staff besides the pragmatic one of survival. It offers an opportunity to look at the material taught with a critical eye and no longer feel obliged to conclude something because it always has been there. The fact that the programme is now going to be institute-based may mean that topics which were not viable within the confines of any single course may

seeks to:-

build on strengths;

remedy weaknesses;

exploit interests and experience;

satisfy requirements;

avoids:-

destructive competition;

inappropriate starting point;

inappropriate pace;

irrelevant content.

Figure 7. *Aims of an individual learning programme*

peer group interaction provides:-

refinement of ideas;

social environment that promotes learning;

learning from exposure to different but related
experiences of other group members;

sharing and not duplicating experiences while
learning;

co-operation and team activity, using range of
abilities present in group.

Figure 8. *Benefits of group learning*

Potential Benefits of Modularisation

for Staff

opportunity for a fresh look at the 'what,why
and how' of the material presented;

wider contact between disciplines;

demonstration of greater relevance;

time for integration and support (rather than
re-design);

student experience as a resource;

easier up-dating.

Figure 9. *How staff may benefit from modularization*

be appropriate to offer to a larger clientele and contact with staff in other disciplines may become easier and more productive. Time which has been previously spent in revising whole courses can be focused on individual modules and their integration into different frameworks. The experience of students may become a more widely used resource, to the benefit of all participants (see Figure 9).

PROBLEMS OF MODULARIZATION

As with all change and innovation, modularization is best effected where there is visible commitment to the decision from the top. It then requires a sensitive introduction to those most closely implicated in the change. Too often there is inadequate recognition given to the need to invest additional resources in the first instance in order to make longer term savings. Practical support is especially needed as some staff may not be immediately convinced of either the necessity or the desirability of any change and this one in particular (see Figure 10). One disadvantage, from the student's point of view, of studying a collection of modules is the loss of the group ethos and dynamic that is present in longer courses of study. Positive measures may be required to replace this appropriately, as has been done with the Open University summer schools.

SOME REASONS FOR RELUCTANCE TO MODULARIZE

The reasons given against modularizing courses are quite varied; some staff are quite happy to support it as a principle but not for their course. In some cases I believe that the whole concept of proposed change is seen by staff as criticism of their past efforts and not as a new opportunity and challenge to meet changing circumstances.

For others the idea of modules runs contrary to their concept of a neatly packaged and labelled set of knowledge and experiences called a 'course'. This may be in part due to the traditional focus on knowledge as defining a discipline rather than a set of skills and processes some of which enable the student, and later the practitioner, to acquire and assess knowledge as required.

But probably the main problem is the success with which the concept of the holistic course has been adopted. The total course ethos which includes the concepts of coherence, progression and the evaluation of achievement via the assessment of objectives attained does, at first sight, appear threatened to the point of extinction by the adoption of modules which can be accumulated as and when required by the student. But is it? We must all be aware that what may be a most beautifully 'coherent' course programme to its deviser can seem a disjointed rag-bag of experiences to the student whose background does not match that originally envisaged. The coherence which seems to me important is the coherence as seen by the receiver, and this is a very individual matter. Similarly, progression is related to the personal starting point of the student and not an absolute entity.

I think that the challenge for the modular programme is to transmit to the student a sense of personal progression and coherence in their course of study, however timed. To do this successfully will require transferring some of the human effort previously put into formal teaching and using it for the assessment of relevant prior learning and counselling of individual students.

CONCLUSION

The revived interest in modularizing courses, while it undoubtedly has gained momentum due to the administrators' perception of market forces and the need to provide a more flexible response to student needs, does hold out the opportunity for a change in the focus

Need for sensitive introduction, as with any

innovation or change.

Requires visible commitment and support from

the top.

Has an initial requirement for additional resources

to accomplish the change.

Reluctance to modularise may be due to:-

**change being perceived as criticism of
past efforts;**

a liking for the convenience of 'labelling';

**the traditional focus on knowledge content
rather than processes of learning;**

**acceptance of the holistic view of a 'course'
as seen by the provider, rather than the receiver.**

Figure 10. *Problems of modularization*

of learning provision. Administrative convenience may well provide an educational opportunity of general benefit.

In order to maximize these benefits it seems important that the implications of modularization are thoroughly thought through and supported. A whole support structure for staff, students and employers needs to be implemented. A unified policy with regard to admissions, registration, assessment, module length and period of delivery needs to be agreed if students are to derive the advantages of credit accumulation and transfer which they seek.

I will conclude with questions which we tend not to ask, or assume to have affirmative answers, but which have recently been put to me. First, do employers (particularly of inservice students) care about or want qualifications for their employees? And the associated question, do the students want qualifications? In either case my own question is, should we not be extending the idea of profiling much more from schools to higher education, if not to replace course awards, at least to facilitate the interpretation of the credits gained under a modular programme?

19. The evaluation of open learning

Tony Prideaux, *Plymouth Polytechnic, UK*

Summary: The emphasis of the 'Open Tech' programme (funded by the Manpower Services Commission and the Seafish Industry Authority) seemed very biased towards the production of materials; it is felt that most projects placed insufficient emphasis on the support of the materials and that evaluation was, in many cases, of low priority. Experience gained with an evaluation of the Seafish Open Learning project gave me a desire to continue in this field and a conviction that the future of open learning will be decided by properly designed, operated and evaluated support systems.

Before beginning the main theme of this paper it is necessary to discuss the terms 'open learning' and 'evaluation' as they appear to have a range of accepted meanings.

OPEN LEARNING

MacKenzie, Postgate and Scupham (1975) note the difficulties in defining the term 'open learning':

> 'Open learning is an imprecise phrase to which a range of meanings can be, and is attached. It eludes definition. But as an inscription to be carried in procession on a banner, gathering adherents and enthusiasms, it has great potential. For its very imprecision enables it to accommodate many different ideas and aims.'

CET (1986) give their definition of the constituent parts of an open-learning system, Lewis and Spencer (1986) use a similar definition as does Race (1986). Most open-learning projects have their own definitions, all of which indicate various degrees of openness and closure caused by constraints. In Figure 1 a matrix has been used in which the degree of openness of a typical open-learning project could be measured: a total score of seven would be completely open, a score of 35, completely closed. Most learning, even in a closed environment, contains some elements of openness so the score will lie somewhere between open and closed.

It would appear that no so-called open-learning systems are completely open, all have constraints that create some degree of closure; most are as open as can be devised for their particular circumstances. The main feature common to all open-learning systems would seem to be that they are learner-centred as opposed to teacher or institution-centred.

EVALUATION

There appears to be a considerable difference of opinion as to the meaning of the word 'evaluation'. Rowntree (1981) notes the problems caused by the two different meanings used for the word evaluation on the two sides of the Atlantic Ocean. To most North American teachers the word evaluation means the same as student assessment. In the UK it usually refers to the appraisal of the course material and the methods by which it is delivered.

Biggs and Collins (1982) use the American meaning as does Curzon (1980). The

	open				closed
	1	2	3	4	5
Delivery method					
Previous Knowledge					
Media Used					
Place of study					
Time of study					
Pacing					
Assessment					

Figure 1. *Degrees of openness*

definition used as a guide in setting up the evaluation work carried out on the Seafish Open Learning Project work again came from Rowntree (1982).

'Evaluation is the means whereby we systematically collect and analyse information about the results of students' encounters with a learning experience.'

Although a short statement, this provided the best definition of evaluation in general that could be identified. The aim of evaluation in this project is to improve the materials, their tutoring and delivery. Harris, Bell and Carter (1981) describe this as typically formative evaluation as opposed to summative evaluation:

'Formative evaluation:
Evaluation which is intended to supply constructive and rapid information about what is happening in a particular situation, with a view to improving that situation.
Summative evaluation:
Evaluation which aims to enable potential users of educational material to assess its overall merits or shortcomings. As such, it is usually applied after development of the material has been completed.'

Having agreed the meanings of 'open-learning' and 'evaluation', the next question that must be asked is: 'Why does open-learning need evaluating?'

WHY EVALUATE OPEN LEARNING?

Ian Marshall (1986), in part 3 of *Training course in delivering open-learning schemes* states:

> 'To be successful, an open-learning delivery system must efficiently deliver high quality learning materials to satisfied students at an economic cost. You have to evaluate each of these areas objectively and look for ways of improving your performance based on the evaluation.'

One of the disturbing facets of the 'Open Tech' programme is the lack of information available on project evaluation. Only four case studies are available from MSC and information from individual projects is sparse. It is hoped that some form of evaluation has been carried out by other projects, but one is left with the feeling that some have produced materials without concerning themselves about delivery to the learner.

The Seafish Open Learning Project, although MSC Open Tech funded, had not commenced delivery by the end of the funding period. Seafish Industry Authority provided the funding required to launch the pilot phases of the project from their training budget, they also provided funding for a full evaluation of the project, the preliminary findings of which are now available. This is the only full evaluation of Open Tech funded materials that I have so far identified.

WHAT NEEDS TO BE EVALUATED?

Bosworth (1988) considers that it is just as important to evaluate the way materials are put into practice as to evaluate how good they are in the hands of a committed user. Stoane (1986) suggests that it is just as important to evaluate the tutoring system and the administrative system as to evaluate the teaching materials themselves. Jordan (1987) insists that the success of open-learning is in itself a potential danger, the ignorant or exploitative approach of some may bring the whole area into disrepute.

In a recent survey Hodgson (1986) stated that:

> 'Most distance learning literature and research appears to have been divided into two components:
>
> – the learning materials
> – support systems.
>
> Some authors feel that there has in the past been an undue emphasis placed on the former, ie learning materials, and not enough on the educational process of which they are but one, if important, component.'

It is therefore suggested that an appropriate way of evaluating open-learning is a three-pronged attack, as suggested by Stoane (1986), looking in depth at:

– the teaching materials;
– the tutoring system; and
– the administrative system.

Taking each of these in turn, the evaluation needs to be formative and to look in detail at the following aspects.

The teaching materials

- Do the materials fulfill the requirements?
- Are the materials 'user friendly'?
- Are there any errors in the materials?
- Do any parts of the material need changing?
- Do learners complete the material in the time allocated?

The tutoring system

- Are tutors' comments helpful?
- How long was the turnaround on marking?
- How many contacts were made with the tutor?
- How were the contacts made?
- Did the contacts solve the learners' problems?

The administrative system

- How efficient is the system?
- How good is the record keeping?
- How many complaints were there?
- How quickly were complaints dealt with?
- How easy is it for learners to obtain advice and counselling?

The suggested technique for obtaining and evaluating this information is discussed later in this paper.

PREVIOUS WORK IN THE EVALUATION OF OPEN-LEARNING PROJECTS

Apart from the work of the Open University and SCOTTSU, little published material on the evaluation of open-learning appears to have been produced in the United Kingdom. One paper from the University of Lancaster by Hodgson (1986), one school-based evaluation by Waterhouse (1982) and a project by the late Sam Rouse (1986) of the National Extension College have been identified. Lewis et al (1986) have produced a series of open-learning guides for CET, none of which deals specifically with the problem of evaluation. Stoane (1986) has produced a package for SCOTTSU on the evaluation of open-learning projects which will provide the basic information for future evaluators. A new publication from MSC, edited by Rowntree (1988), gives a strong pointer on the way forward for open-learning projects which may stimulate more evaluation. The most fruitful source identified to date has been the work undertaken at Athabasca University in Canada under Project REDEAL. Some useful work has also been undertaken at the University of Lund and at the Norsk Korrespondanseskole.

SUGGESTED METHOD OF EVALUATION

Stoane (1986) produced an open-learning package on evaluating open-learning, I have relied heavily on this work in my own evaluation procedures and would recommend it to any inexperienced evaluators.

My own experience in setting up and running an evaluation of the Seafish Open Learning Project, coupled with the feedback I have received while undertaking this work, make me feel that evaluation is an essential part of open-learning. I am not alone in this, at a recent conference at Lancaster University it was clear from several of the presentations that the need for evaluation existed and that it should be applied to the whole of the system, not just the materials.

As both the learners and tutors involved in most open-learning projects are scattered throughout the United Kingdom, it is difficult to undertake evaluation by some of the methods commonly used for this purpose; the only two that would seem to be practicable in this instance are:

- questionnaires; and
- telephone and/or face-to-face interviews.

In the present project, storage and retrieval of the information gathered was aided by use of a BBC Master computer with ViewStore database software. The BBC computer was chosen as, although not as powerful as many other systems available, it would be common to most of the educational establishments participating in open-learning projects. These centres also have the ViewStore ROM and data can therefore be exchanged by posting discs or by the use of modems and British Telecom lines, thus enabling all participants to monitor the progress of the evaluation. This strategy of involving the delivery centres throughout the process helped to motivate them in chasing-up students and tutors slow in completing questionnaires. The centres also felt less threatened as they were an integral part of the overall evaluation system.

Before starting to develop the questionnaires and interview techniques, reference to Rowntree (1986), Harris and Bell (1986) and Stoane (1986) produced the information needed to set up suitable questionnaires which were then evaluated by colleagues before piloting. After piloting, the revised questionnaires were sent to the delivery centres for distribution to students with the modules.

The strategy used had three separate questionnaires for the student, written in a format compatible with ViewStore. The three questionnaires dealt with:

- the student (personal details, qualifications etc);
- the materials (difficulties, tutor support needed etc); and
- audio-visual aids (access to equipment etc).

Additional questionnaire/report forms were devised to allow the tutor to feed back comments at the same time as reporting on the student to the delivery centre. The three questionnaires were again designed to work with databases and covered the following areas:

- the materials;
- the tutor/student relationship; and
- the tutor/delivering college relationship.

One further questionnaire/report was aimed at the delivery centres to enable them to give their comments on the relationships between the various organizations and individuals involved in the piloting exercise.

Checklists were written for the interviews, that for the student included the following questions:

- Did you enjoy the materials?
- Were the materials easier or more difficult than you expected?
- Did the package take longer than you expected?
- Did you get all the help you needed?
- Who helped you most often with the materials?
- Have you any comments?

The checklist for tutors was similar, both checklists contained a number of questions designed to allow the questionner to lead into the topic as the conversation progressed. If possible, the conversation should be recorded to help when writing-up the results.

Questionnaires were distributed with the materials; a sample of those returned who had completed the materials were telephoned for an informal interview, all those identified as drop-outs were also selected for interview. In addition, those students who had given constructive responses to the 'open' questions were contacted for additional information.

RESULTS

The results obtained from the pilot phase of the project are as follows:

- The evaluation strategy outlined above has seemed to work well in the pilot project with fairly small student numbers.
- A number of minor problem areas within the pilot phase have been identified and will be rectified.
- As a result of the information obtained, the Seafish Open Learning project is likely to continue.
- The evaluation will continue in a simplified form during the full implementation of the project.

CONCLUSION

In conclusion I would like to make the following points:

- Evaluation is an essential ingredient of successful open learning.
- Evaluation of materials alone is not enough to ensure success.
- Evaluation of support systems is probably more important than evaluation of materials.
- Second-grade materials may still enable students to achieve learning objectives.
- Second-grade support of open-learning may produce high drop-out rates and dissatisfied customers.

REFERENCES

Biggs, J.B. and Collins, K.F. (1982) *Evaluating the Quality of Learning, the SOLO Taxonomy.* Academic Press, London.
Bosworth, D. (1988) Embedded OL, *OLS News* **23**, 1.
CET (1986) *Open Learning.* CET Information Sheet 5, Council for Educational Technology, London.
Curzon, L.B. (1980) *Teaching in Further Education.* Cassell, London.
Harris, N.D.C., Bell, C.D. and Carter, J.E.F. (1981) *Signposts for Evaluating: A Resource Pack.* Council for Educational Technology, London.
Harris, D. and Bell, C. (1986) *Evaluating and Assessing for Learning.* Kogan Page, London.
Hodgson, V.E. (1986) The interrelationship between support and the learning materials, *Programmed Learning and Educational Technology,* **23**, 1, 56-61.
Jordan, N. (1987) Ensuring quality in open-learning, *OLS News,* 22 December 1987.
Lewis, R., Mead, J. and Paine, N. (1986) *Open Learning Guides 1-9.* Council for Educational Technology, London.
Lewis, R. and Spencer, D. (1986) *What is Open-Learning?* Council for Educational Technology, London.
Mackenzie, N., Postgate, R. and Scupham, J. (1975) *Open Learning Systems and Problems in Post-secondary Education.* UNESCO Press.
Marshall, I. (1986) *Training Course in Delivering Open-learning Schemes.* SCOTTSU, Dundee.

Race, P. (1986) *How to Win as an Open Learner.* Council for Educational Technology, London.

Rouse, S. (1986) *The Invisible Tutor.* National Extension College, Cambridge.

Rowntree, D. (1981) *Developing Courses for Students.* McGraw-Hill, London.

Rowntree, D. (1982) *Educational Technology in Curriculum Development.* Harper and Row, London.

Rowntree, D. (1986) *Teaching Through Self-instruction.* Kogan Page, London.

Rowntree, D. (ed) (1988) *Ensuring Quality in Open-learning.* Manpower Services Commission, Sheffield.

Stoane, J. (1986) *Training Course in Evaluating Open-learning Schemes.* SCOTTSU, Dundee.

Waterhouse, P. (1982) The supported self-study project 1981-1983, *Programmed Learning and Educational Technology,* **19**, 3, 261-266.

20. Open learning in schools: the TVEI Open Learning Network

Colin Crawford, *Scottish Council for Educational Technology, Glasgow, UK*

Summary: This paper examines the TVEI Open Learning Network in Scotland. This Network was established as a consortium of Scottish TVEI projects with an initial aim of producing and delivering materials, piloting, evaluating and modifying these materials in the light of evaluation of both students and tutor comment. The general background to the TVEI Open Learning Network is discussed with an examination of the National Certificate in general and educational issues which have to be taken into account in Scotland as a whole.

The materials themselves and their method of production are described. The question of providing adequate training through consultancy sessions with involved staff is examined and the issues arising identified.

INTRODUCTION

The TVEI Open Learning Network was established in 1986 under funding provided by the MSC to operate for three years. The Network is basically a consortium of Scottish TVEI projects with central facilities for the production of open learning materials and with local delivery of packages being carried out within each TVEI project. There are several specific objectives associated with the major aim of investigating methods by which access to SCOTVEC 'Action Plan' modules can be increased through open learning:

- the development of a number of learning packages;
- the dissemination of these materials throughout the TVEI network;
- the monitoring of these packages during delivery; and
- the revision of these packages as appropriate.

THE NATIONAL CERTIFICATE

The Action Plan was launched by the Government in 1983 to overhaul education and training for young people aged 16 to 18 in Scotland. The National Certificate has proved to be the way ahead in Scotland for all non-advanced further education. A modular programme of study is taken to gain the National Certificate; the majority of modules are of 40 hours duration, although there is provision for half, double and treble modules. Each module contains a module descriptor which states explicitly what a student should be able to do by the end of the programme of study. There has been a shift from norm-referenced exams to criterion-referenced assessment which is internal and continuous though externally moderated. Each module descriptor includes the performance criteria for each learning outcome. Since August 1984, there has been a dramatic uptake of the National Certificate and around 200,000 students from further education colleges, schools and community education centres have received certificates. There has been a 30 per cent increase in the uptake of non-advanced further education with in excess of one million student accesses to date.

THE SITUATION IN SCOTTISH SCHOOLS

Scotland in particular has undergone many changes in the educational field during recent years. Coupled with the introduction of many new certificated courses in the secondary sector have been drives to increase pupil choice and widen the curriculum. Scotland too has suffered particularly from falling rolls in the 16+ population. There is also the problem of rural schools in Highland areas, particularly exacerbated in the Island schools such as those in Orkney and Shetland. The ideal of maintaining pupil choice in areas such as these with an extremely small pupil population and declining staff numbers is extremely problematic.

National Certificate courses and particularly the open learning approach can be especially useful in such situations to maintain pupil choice. As well as providing a sound vocational education, National Certificate programmes allow progress to advanced courses at a higher level. The Certificate may be taken alongside Scottish Certificate of Education Standard 'O' and 'H' grades and meets the requirements for off-the-job learning in the Youth Training Scheme as well as in the Technical and Vocational Education Initiative (TVEI).

The TVEI Open Learning Network sees open learning as providing individual pupil choice within the curriculum. This means providing a diverse menu at 16+ which will both interest and provide new opportunities to this target group. The TVEI open learning modules are seen as being individual components from which different curricula can be assembled in different situations.

The basic format of the delivery system is one of individualized study using structured learning material that is developed centrally and supported by tutorials, in schools or TVEI centres.

The original intention was to produce multi-media packages but this gives rise to major problems:

> 'Packages which consist of videos, tape/slide and audio tape as opposed to print have large cost implications. If delivery was to be truly individualized this would necessitate considerable outlay in audio visual equipment and resources to deliver an individual module to an individual pupil.' (TVEI OL Network first year review).

Most modules that have been produced therefore have been predominantly print based but several have associated software for the BBC microcomputer. For example:

Electronic Systems:	print material, Unilab Alpha Boards
Music Making:	print material, book, electronic keyboard
Keyboarding:	print material, computer disc
Info Tech Office:	print material, computer discs.

Originally the Network operated with seven TVEI projects. Fife TVEI produced and distributed materials to projects located in the East of Scotland and SCET (Scottish Council for Educational Technology) produced and distributed materials to projects located in the West of Scotland. The author's own role within SCET has been the production and distribution of Network materials and supporting the consultancy sessions. Consultancy is offered to all projects by SCET. With the extension of TVEI, production has gradually been devolved from both Fife and SCET to the new TVEI projects together with a cascade of associated skills (eg desk-top publishing experience). The aim has also shifted from production and delivery of packages to support and INSET for teachers.

A possible criticism of the modules produced by the Network may be that the majority of packages were in the microelectronics area and involved a working knowledge of computers. This criticism has been noted and it was partly in an effort to redress this and partly to increase individual choice that modules such as music making, applied science and history of the local area are being produced.

THE PACKAGES

About eight modules are produced each year under Crown Copyright. Around 12 new packages will be available during the summer term of 1988. This will give a total of approximately 25 modules having being produced during the lifetime of the project.

The TVEI open learning packages incorporate several features which make them ideally suited to learning by this method:

- learning is presented in small 'chunks', each module being split up into a number of units of work;
- each unit itself contains a clear statement of objectives at the beginning together with a list of any necessary equipment, an outline of the assessment procedures that must be met and a recommended time for completion;
- each unit utilizes standard icons (Figure 1) highlighting to the learner when they have reached an activity section, self-assessment question or tutor-marked assessment etc; and
- the text is broken up frequently by diagrams, activities and questions so providing maximum feedback and interactivity while minimizing boredom. (An example of a complete page can be seen in Figure 2.)

It is appreciated that many students may be totally new to this learning approach; as an introduction SCET have produced the 'Student's Guide to Open Learning' in the same format as the modules themselves, which introduces students to the icons used, how to contact their tutor etc. This is made available to all TVEI projects in the Network.

Obviously it is not simply the student who may be new to this form of learning and each package therefore contains a detailed 'Manager's Guide' which outlines the contents of each unit of work within the module and clarifies assessment procedures, resource implications etc. This is aimed at the classroom teacher who will be responsible for delivering the module.

MATERIALS PRODUCED

Design, production and printing of packages was initially carried out within the two main production centres (Fife and SCET) by desk-top publishing techniques using Apple Macintosh equipment with Macwrite (for simple wordprocessing), Macdraw (for simple line illustrations) and Pagemaker (the actual page layout program). Shell pages were created, having such features as standard headers and footers and standard icons. By using these throughout all the modules a definitive house style has been established (Figure 1).

When a writer produces material it is keyed into the Macintosh using Macwrite. Page layouts in Macwrite can be set up to give exactly the same dimension as the master pages from Pagemaker and the material is keyed in so as to retain the layout intended by the writer, leaving blank spaces for illustrations which are simply inserted at a later stage by a graphic artist. A hard copy is printed and a cycle of proof reading and amendment by the writer and technical editor, under the guidance of the general editor, takes place. Changes are made to the Macwrite document and eventually an agreed final copy of the text is placed on to pages using Pagemaker together with such illustrations as have been prepared. A final Pagemaker version of the unit is thus produced.

Laser-printed copies of the final Pagemaker documents are distributed to TVEI project coordinators for photocopying and distribution to the learners. By using a laser printer as the final output device, a final print version of extremely high definition can be achieved.

Module Title	Section No. & Title or Sub-head
Unit No. & Title	Page type or Topic Title

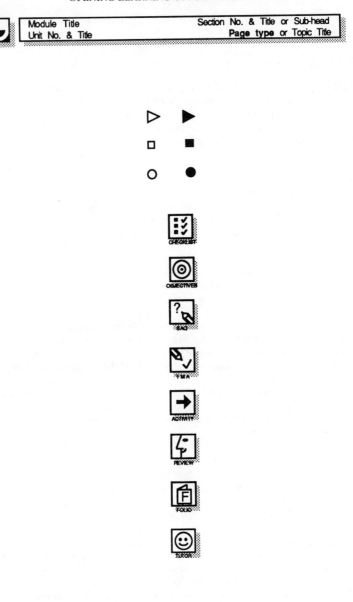

© Crown Copyright 1988   Region   **DRAFT**   1

Figure 1. *Example of standard icons*

Applied Science 2	The Growing and Propagation of Indoor Plants
	Unit 1 Choosing a Plant.

Foliage Plants

In the last group, ,the plants remain alive and attractive all the year round. The great attraction of the plants in this group is the variation and colour of their foliage (leaves). The contrasting colours of their leaves can be most attractive. The plants in this group do not usually flower.

What do you think is the attraction of this group of plants ?

....
....
....
....

The different types of indoor plants

Under the heading "The different groups of indoor plants".

Under each of four groups:-

Write down the names of two plants that you would find in each of these four groups.

1. **Flowering Pot Plants**
2. **Cacti**
3. **Flowering House Plants**
4. **Plants with Variation and Colour in their Foliage (leaves)**

© Crown Copyright 1988   Tayside Region   DRAFT

Figure 2. *Example page*

QUALITY CONTROL

During the initial writing phase there are several checks on quality by team members:

- the general editor provides support and advice on writing in an open learning format;
- the technical editor provides support on the technical issues of the material; and
- the copy editor checks consistency, grammar etc, of the material.

The control of quality is aided by several other factors including the standard design and layout of materials which has been aided by the distribution of standard house-style guidelines and by the provision of a typical format for the materials themselves with clear indications for the placing of self- assessment questions (SAQ), tutor-marked assessments (TMA) etc. The quality of the delivery system and packages is also of prime importance and it is essential that structures are provided to establish support and in-service procedures for staff involved. Much of this support has been provided in the form of consultancy from SCET.

VARIETY OF USE OF PACKAGES

The packages may be delivered in a variety of ways, from one end of the continuum where a class of students will be working through the same modules, to the other extreme where one student will be working through one package individually. The key to delivery is therefore flexibility and adaptability.

CONSULTANCY SESSIONS

The overall aim of the consultancy sessions is to enable TVEI projects to discuss the issues involved in delivering open learning using National Certificate packages developed by the Network. Sessions are tailored to the needs of individual projects and generally are attended by staff who will be managing the delivery of open learning within their individual schools. The consultancy sessions address those issues which will affect staff who embark on providing TVEI Open Learning Network modules to their students.

While both looking at the development of the Network and at packages in detail, as well as examining video case studies, perhaps the most valuable aspect of these sessions is the opportunity afforded to staff to voice their worries and identify problems and benefits which they envisage arising within their own school setting.

While it is difficult to generalize the outcomes of such consultancy sessions, there are certain possible issues identified which tend to worry staff in most schools and colleges thinking about offering the modules. The sessions have therefore helped solve issues such as:

- resources and resource allocation;
- timetabling problems for individualized study;
- suitable space allocation for open learning students and resources;
- supporting the learners and the provision of tutorial support structures; and
- staff development needs and the provision of suitable staff development.

A number of staff development needs have been highlighted through the consultancy sessions, these include:

- raising awareness about open learning systems;

- writing and amending materials;
- becoming familiar with the packages themselves; and
- the importance of computer literacy.

The major resource necessary to underpin all the above needs is, of course, time. When such time is to be made available to staff who are already hard-pressed is an issue that has not been solved.

Some indication of the usefulness of the consultancy sessions may be obtained from an examination of evaluation forms completed by the participants in these sessions. The general consensus would appear to be that the consultancy sessions have been both positive and productive and have fulfilled their aim to raise awareness and solve problems related to the many aspects which must be considered when open learning is to be successfully implemented.

WHAT HAVE BEEN THE OUTCOMES OF THE NETWORK'S ACTIVITIES?

While it is obviously difficult to predict final figures for the actual uptake of Network packages by students in Scottish educational institutions, it is to be hoped that figures for module uptake will be in the hundreds.

Through using self-study materials such as those provided in the Network packages, students will become more actively involved in the learning process and will ultimately assume a greater responsibility for their own learning. In the general world climate that we live in today, people will encounter more and more 'open learning' opportunities when they leave the school setting and enter the workforce. By introducing packages such as these at the senior school level (and indeed throughout all the school years generally) individuals are being presented with an introduction to a 'lifelong education'.

Coupled with this, the 'open learning' type of approach is often associated with increased flexibility in the organization of learning: new patterns for the school day, alternative timetables etc. Such arrangements are increasingly being made for the older pupils, especially in those schools involved in recent initiatives such as TVEI. However, the adoption of open learning/resource-based learning (RBL) schemes should not simply be thought of as being an easy answer to changing conditions within the school setting. Staff must be made fully aware of the thought processes underpinning the whole concept of individualized learning. In-service training must cater for this. Many new skills and techniques are required when working with such an educational medium and in many cases teachers do not find it easy to change their approaches and relationships with their students, let alone introduce new classroom management techniques, become proficient in counselling skills, assessment techniques etc. All this points to the fact that an efficient support structure must exist both at an advisory level prior to the packages being used and within the educational establishment itself both for the staff and the students involved.

CONCLUSION

The TVEI Open Learning Network will, at the end of the project, have made a significant contribution to the delivery of National Certificate packages by open learning.

More important than this, however, is the aspect of support for the deliverers. To provide packages of materials is simply not enough without strong support being offered to the staff who are expected to utilize them.

21. Role and development of continuing education: the response in the East-Midlands

Ted Hutchin, *Nottingham University, UK*

Summary: The aim of this paper is to highlight the need for a structured response to the needs of industry from training and education, and to suggest that the providers of such training, in the area of advanced manufacturing technology, need to employ both traditional and modern methods of delivery and support through the medium of continuing education.

This paper argues that there is a need for a structured response from the traditional providers of training and education whether they be vocationally or academically based. This will involve a flexible approach to such provision comprising the traditional methods of formal courses and training and more modern methods involving the use of open learning material, distance learning and multi-media methods such as interactive video, CBT and expert systems. Training also needs to be more closely linked to skill needs which implies a clear recognition of skill shortages that are evident at the present and also those shortages that are likely to occur through the introduction of advanced manufacturing and related technologies. This further implies that such training will require the close association of industry with the universities and polytechnics. Using the example of the five institutions in the East Midlands the paper addresses these and related issues.

INTRODUCTION

There are three strands in any discussion concerning learning:
- there is the individual and his or her particular needs in terms of learning whether it be a skill or knowledge or a combination of both;
- there is the organization from which the individual comes and its role in determining what training takes place, who should attend such training and the nature of the content; and
- there are the providers of training and education and their role in creating the training courses to meet the needs of industry.

Traditional wisdom has held that people go to one of the providers for training and/or education and that often their organization has helped by paying the bill or by making time available for such activities. In the past the actual learning event has been in the 'normal' mode for such activities (ie chalk and talk, usually evening-based, with little or no attempt to match the event to the actual needs of either the individual or the host organization). The actual merits of such events were rarely called into question, indeed learning was seen by many as an evil to be endured. You didn't pass courses, you survived them! Whether anything of real value was learned was not the central aim, or at least that is what such events seem to suggest. Now, in the economic climate of the eighties, there is a noticeable change in that the old methods, or at least the old practices that surrounded them, are being swept away and learning is now seen in a new light.

When the proposals emanating from the Engineering Council (EC) are also taken into consideration, the whole thrust of adult continuing education takes on a new and vibrant direction. In their booklet 'A call to action' (EC, 1988) the Council state that '..a radical change of attitude towards continuing education and training (CET) is needed'. They then go on to suggest that recent research has indicated that:

- companies that are committed to and practice systematic CET are more successful commercially than those organizations that are not committed to CET;
- most companies adopt a haphazard approach to CET and do not perceive it as a strategic activity to stimulate competitive competence;
- individual engineers and technicians need to be more confident and motivated towards self-learning and they should be more prepared to advance themselves to positions of leadership;
- the engineering profession should introduce required updating for its members;
- the academic and professional institutions, as providers of CET, should market their products more effectively; and
- incentives are need from Government to stimulate action.

Quite clearly the suggestion is that training must not be seen as the first item to drop from the organizational budget in times of hardship, rather the whole process should be given far higher importance within organizations and should be driven from the top.

THE INDIVIDUAL

Perhaps the most important feature about recent developments in learning has been the realization that we are all different with different learning styles and different speeds at which we learn. What works well for one may not work at all for another and if both are put in the same class there is a real risk that effort will be wasted, at least for one, if not both. The work of people such as Kolb and Honey and Mumford has shown that before commencing training events there should be some time spent in the evaluation of the styles of learning that each participant has. Of course this is not to say that there should be a number of separate sessions for each person on the course. What it does imply is that the various styles should be considered when the course is being developed and that this recognition will help ensure that the primary learning events are undertaken in such a way that they are fully understood.

Next, there is a growing realization that individuals should have a degree of responsibility for their own training development. Again, the EC have suggested they should personally maintain their knowledge, skills and understanding for both current and future job roles. This will involve three primary activities:

- making a personal effort and allocating time to update and extend professional competence and competitive knowledge and skills;
- declaring at every performance appraisal, or at other opportunities, personal needs for education and training to improve performance; and
- seizing all the opportunities for CET provided by the employer and elsewhere.

This will involve the individual taking a far higher responsibility for their own training than ever before. It will also have implications for the next group to be considered as part of this equation, the employers.

THE EMPLOYERS

The role of the employers is a crucial one in the development of continuing education. It is they who will have to bear the brunt in terms of resources, people, finance and so on, and therefore they have a major influence on what is going to take place as training. Perhaps here the key theme is that of developing the staff to ensure a keen competitive edge both within the organization and outside. This will involve the creation of training plans that reflect the corporate objectives and the business plan of the company. It also means that the Chief Executive has to be seen to drive the initiative from the top. They must commit themselves and their Board to CET and show the importance of such training to all the workforce. This will involve all managers having a responsibility for the development of CET within their own departments for all engineers so that, through structured performance reviews and so on, the training needs of individuals are properly identified and met.

A major criticism of industry is that it does not support CET (the record over the years in terms of investment being very poor) and where CET is taken up it is often short term and attuned only to immediate needs. Hence the need for top managers to recognize the importance of CET and develop the training plan accordingly (see also Hutchin, 1987). These and other activities outlined in the Engineering Council paper (EC, 1988) show quite clearly the need for continuing education and training, and that the effort involved is more than repaid in the results. However, all this emphasis on CET will be of little value if the providers are not prepared for the demand.

THE PROVIDERS

There is a suspicion that higher education does not understand the needs of industry, that it speaks a different language, and anyway what do university and polytechnic lecturers know about commerce and manufacturing industry? It is often felt, in industry, that the main aim of the higher education sector is to produce high-calibre graduates and post-graduates. The available market for this group is however fairly small when compared to the alternative, namely, the adult population of the country employed in manufacturing, commerce and the service industries. The switch to continuing education will involve the need to understand the changes necessary in the market and to sell products and services to stimulate demand for CET. This will involve these institutions in:

- improving the methods of identifying emerging needs and, where necessary, designing courses appropriately;
- innovating through the introduction of modular courses, distance-learning techniques, distance-learning centres and educational credit schemes;
- collaboration with employers of engineers and technicians, and also with other educational and training organizations (for example, sharing resources);
- encouraging motivation by providing recognition and incentives to staff engaged in CET. Providing key staff with practical insight into industry/commerce by visits and attachments; and
- ensuring regular updating of the technologists within the organization involved in the teaching and training of CET.

This will require a shift in the view of education and its provision as seen by academics. The old practices may have to change to more flexible and adaptive approaches, much more attuned to the needs of industry and the constraints that they have to work under.

At this point it is pertinent to consider the response in the East Midlands where, as a result of discussions between the Vice Chancellors and the two Directors, the five major higher educational establishments in the region set up the Continuing Education in New Technology, East Midlands Programme (CENTEM) with the author as coordinator. (These institutions are: University of Nottingham, University of Leicester, Loughborough University of Technology, Trent Polytechnic and Leicester Polytechnic.)

This is a unique response to the demands for CET for there appears to be no other group such as this operating with such close association between themselves and local industry. The demand for courses of short duration, in this case 30 hours, and addressing the major skill shortage areas within the region was felt to be sufficient to support this activity and the Programme was brought into being. The formal launch of CENTEM was on the 11 May 1988.

The main areas that are being addressed are design, manufacturing technologies such as FMS and CNC, quality, engineering software and microprocessors, materials, production planning and control through the use of philosophies such as HIT and OPT, and so on. These initial modules will be added to in due course through demand and also market research that is being proposed through CENTEM itself, the Engineering Industry Training Board (EITB) and the Engineering Employers Association in the East Midlands. In support of the modules it is intended that there will also be a range of one-day and two-day courses/seminars, executive briefings for CEOs and perhaps, in the future, conferences addressing specialist areas of concern. It is also proposed that open learning material be examined with the view of using it in support of the other training events planned. Therefore there will be a range of activities, each supporting the other, developed and presented to industry to meet the demand for CET. It is not beyond the realms of possibility that in the future other universities and polytechnics will become involved in the process and add to the nature of the programme. Perhaps through initiatives such as the Regional Technology Centre, the provision of training throughout the region will also gain the coordination that is so sadly lacking throughout the UK, let alone the East Midlands.

CENTRE FOR TRAINING AND DEVELOPMENT

The final aspect that is discussed addresses questions concerning the creation and development of a research centre to examine the training and associated developmental activities within companies and educational establishments throughout the UK. Many of the current developments in, for example, educational technology, CAL, CBT and expert systems have involved research but it can be argued that much of this research is fragmented and sporadic.

The idea is to create a research function, at a suitable location in the UK, which would be able to undertake research into the training methods adopted in companies and their suitability for the staff involved bearing in mind such aspects as learning styles, new training methods and so on. It is envisaged that companies and other organizations would contribute to the funding of the Centre, its initial setting up and the provision of staff to carry out research in the field of training and development.

Training in the UK lags behind many of our competitors, the level of investment is far below that of Japan, the USA and even some of our European partners. It is the author's belief that this situation seriously affects the ability of UK industry to match its competitors. The human resource is often overlooked or ignored altogether, even those companies which do invest in training and development often do so in an *ad hoc* fashion resulting in *ad hoc* skill development. There are companies which spend large sums of money on training and they are often the most successful companies in the UK (eg Lucas, Ford and GEC). Yet there is little evaluation of this training with reference to the methods of delivery, the suitability of the training for particular individuals, the development of new training methods such as interactive video and so on. The companies are usually not in a position to evaluate such new methods due to time and other resource restrictions.

Therefore, as there is no recognized centre of training excellence which can evaluate training and development programmes, there is little structured research into the long-term training needs of our major companies, never mind the medium to small companies. The many providers of training, universities, polytechnics and professional institutes such as Ashridge and Henley, all provide high-quality training but with the need to create new methods incorporating continuing education, the development of short course programmes, open and distance learning and others; the methods available to the company training managers are many and varied. Not all are suitable for all people yet the training manager is often ill-equipped to carry out this evaluation.

The creation of the Centre is seen as of paramount importance to meeting the training needs of not just industry but also commerce, banking, insurance and health care. In fact, every sector of the economy would be able to make use of the facilities of the Centre and commission it to carry out research particular to its own needs, which would then become part of the database on training that would be a core feature of the Centre. The Centre would also be able to advise those setting up new training on appropriate methods and technology which would allow those writing new material to concentrate on content rather than the delivery mechanism.

The Centre should not be seen as competition to existing research groups but rather as a focus through which they might be able to reach a wider audience. The promotion of existing research would be a central function of the Centre as would the ability to act as a broker between potential users and existing bodies. Therefore the transfer of such training technology would be greatly aided. So far there have been discussions with one academic institute and also other agencies involved in the provision of training: PICKUP, EITB etc. The support gained so far is encouraging and it is hoped that later in 1988 there will be a conference where potential supporters and providers will be able to meet and discuss the initial formation of the Centre.

CONCLUSIONS

Continuing education and training is the way forward in the alleviation of present skill shortages and the development of existing staff. Individuals themselves have got to take a greater responsibility for their own training and development, and companies should be more ready to support staff in this activity. This is particularly so when companies are becoming increasingly aware of skill shortages and the fact that they have got to train existing staff in order to compete in the market- place. The universities and polytechnics cannot supply sufficient to meet the demand and existing staff will have to be retrained and their skills updated. Hence the need for continuing education.

The challenge is to the individual to take responsibility for their own development and for the companies to set up the infrastructure that allows staff to do just that. It is also up to the suppliers, namely the universities and polytechnics, to meet the challenge of continuing education and develop courses and structures to meet that challenge.

REFERENCES

Engineering Council (1988) *Continuing Education and Training*. Department of Education and Science, London.

Hutchin, C.E. (1987) *Training: The Forgotten Ingredient in the CADCAM Recipe*, Proceedings of CADCAM '87 Conference, 417-422.

Hutchin, C.E. (1988) *The Importance of Training in CAD/CAM Implementation*, Proceedings of CAD/CAM & FEM in Metalworking, Pergamon.

22. Teleconferencing: the Olympus opportunity

Ray Winders, *Plymouth Polytechnic, Plymouth, UK*

Summary: The telephone has been widely used, especially in the USA, to deliver and tutor courses at a distance. Attempts have been made to provide visual support by using compressed forms of video. More recently, satellites have provided broad-band communication of television to multiple sites. The European Space Agency will launch the Olympus satellite in January 1989. There will be no rental charges for approved educational and training initiatives. This is an unparalleled opportunity to develop and evaluate interactive delivery of distance learning.

INTRODUCTION

The problem of presenting information to students without the mediation provided by a face-to-face tutor has been approached in many ways. For half a century the structuring and presentation of material has been a preoccupation of educational technologists. The development from linear programmes on paper rolls to variable programmes on interactive video has been stimulating. More recently, studies in artificial intelligence are bringing us nearer to being able to provide an adaptive tutorial device with some of the qualities of the effective tutor. Parallel with the development of structuring and presentation systems, but only occasionally publicized, is the development of teleconferencing (ie communication using telephone or satellite links to bring the tutor into 'contact' with the students at a distance). Following a brief survey of developments in teleconferencing, the present position is outlined with particular emphasis on the European Olympus Satellite Programme 1989-96.

Teleconferencing is a generic term for a meeting at a distance using electronic communications. At its simplest, three people are linked by telephone so that each can hear and speak to the other two. This may be possible at no additional cost through a modern internal telephone system. At its most complex, groups are linked by television cameras and satellites to participate in live videoconferencing between continents. There is a sharp cut-off point in costs between delivery using a standard telephone line and delivery requiring a broader bandwidth via fibre-optic cables or satellite. The cost to the distant student is a critical factor. Given that the student may have a telephone, a television set and probably a personal computer, what use can be made of these in the delivery of learning at a distance? If home entertainment is to be transformed in the UK by multiple satellite channels captured on a dish of 0.5 metres diameter costing under £200, should education and training providers access this new opportunity to reach potential learners at home or in local study centres?

AUDIOCONFERENCING

Audioconferencing between a large number of participants requires a telephone bridge. This can be a desk-top facility controlled by the conference leader, or a commercial bridging system connecting 20 or more lines using a professional operator. The participant can use a standard telephone handset but a 'hands-free' telephone is more convenient and will allow two or three people to participate on one line. Larger groups will require a loudspeaking telephone which consists of microphones and a loudspeaker all connecting to a standard telephone socket.

The world centre for audioconferencing is the University of Wisconsin Extension at Madison, USA (Parker and Olgren, 1984). Madison is west of Chicago in the corn-belt which is characterized by dispersed farm communities. The University provides 200 loudspeaking telephones located in local schoolrooms, courthouses and even private homes. In addition, individuals use their home telephones. In an average year there are 3,000 hours of audioconferencing including 300 different courses ranging from pigeon keeping to weather for amateur pilots. Some are free-standing courses, others are part of degree or postgraduate courses and a third group is for professionals.

In this third group, is a substantial 'inactive nurse update' programme. In the USA, all nurses, including those not in employment, are required to participate in a regular series of updating courses. For a nurse who, perhaps because of domestic commitments, can only learn at home, audioconferencing provides the means to continuing registration. There are more creative courses. A programme for choir leaders enrolled 226 participants over a three-year period, and 114 organists enrolled for a series in which the professor of music played live over the telephone link and was questioned by participants each able to demonstrate from a local organ.

In the United Kingdom, the Open University (OU) in Scotland has been a regular user of audioconferencing. This has been mainly for tutorial sessions in support of standard OU courses (George, 1979). The University Hospital of Wales at Cardiff uses audioconferencing to tutor medical students on placement in hospitals (Hibbard, 1984). Each group of students is provided with study materials including videos. The tutor conducts a group tutorial over a period of time during which activities take place in each peer group which are then shared and questioned over the telephone link.

In 1984 the Plymouth Audioconferencing Network (PACNET), based at Plymouth Polytechnic, began an evaluation of applications and delivery of a variety of audioconferences for education and training (Winders, 1985). The project, funded by the Manpower Services Commission, focused upon five groups of applications:

- delivery of distance learning;
- courses held on multiple sites;
- students on industrial placement;
- expert contributions from a distance; and
- committee meetings and conferences.

All of these were relatively successful and 326 conferences were held over the two years of the project. A course on acoustics for local government officers was offered from Cornwall College and included participants in Scotland and the Channel Islands. A more innovative use was a phone-in for students on a distance learning BTec course in electronics. They phoned-in with problems from 7pm - 9pm on set evenings, and were able to speak to a tutor and to other members of the course. Several used this as a motivation to stay on the course and to combat the loneliness of the long-distance learner. A main conclusion of the PACNET project was that very careful preparation is needed to create a successful audioconference and that training is needed for all participants, particularly the conference leader.

AUDIOGRAPHIC SYSTEMS

Audioconferencing is usually an adjunct to paper-based study packages. There are, however, systems which enable visuals to be transmitted along a telephone line. The Open

University developed a sophisticated system known as 'Cyclops' (McConnell, 1986). This comprised a screen with touch panels along the bottom. Visuals could be stored on cassette or drawn directly on the screen. All participants saw the build-up of the visual and could add lines or use colour to highlight or underline using their own screen. Though the system was sophisticated, it was difficult for an inexperienced operator to set up and was prone to interference from telephone line noise.

The University of Wisconsin Extension uses 'freeze-frame': television cameras transmit a black and white picture line-by-line along a standard telephone link. The head and shoulders of the lecturer, a view of the class, or images of diagrams and specimens can be transmitted. There has also been experimentation with broadcast teletext. The Israeli Television service broadcast 85 'pages' of text for schools which were changed each week (Chavatidhar, 1986). A section at the bottom of the screen contained questions and answers which were revealed by using the remote control. Viewdata systems, such as Prestel, have been used for the training of travel agents and bank employees. Computer and facsimile links are also used in support of distance learning. The Electronic University Network in San Francisco (Meeks, 1987) acts as a broker for 200 courses based in a variety of colleges and universities. Students receive study disks and are tutored by electronic mail. Assignments sent by electronic mail are returned with comment within 24 hours.

The above systems rely on telephone communication therefore the bandwidth for communication allows only voice or data to be transmitted. Speech/data modems exist which allow data to be transmitted along the same telephone line in the spaces between words. These modems allow the computer to be used by the tutor in a similar manner to an overhead projector. Such modems are not yet available to the public.

SATELLITE DELIVERY

Communication satellites allow transmission of information in the full range from audio to moving colour television. In the UK, satellite television has been used in the public education and training sectors only for prestigious international events. In the USA, some low-cost systems linked to cable TV networks have developed. In Irvine, California, a camera and monitor on a trolley is used to link community centres on two cable channels reserved for conferencing. The system can be linked via satellite to other centres in the USA or anywhere else in the world. Satellite delivery enables Third World countries to leapfrog telephone cable technology and deliver directly to the remotest village. In India and in the Caribbean, large-scale literacy programmes have been delivered by satellite.

A common system, particularly in the USA, is one-way video with audio return. A television studio is linked to satellite to deliver the video, and ordinary telephone lines are used by the participants to talk back to the studio presenters. Large-scale conferences using hotel chains are frequent for in-house business training in the USA. In France the system was used to update hairdressers in seven cities. Top Paris stylists demonstrated new creations. Participants watched the demonstrations then practiced in their own centres. Finally there was a phone-in session in which the Paris stylists answered questions on technique and gave further demonstrations (Carmes, 1984).

Satellite delivery is particularly important in regions where travel is difficult. British Columbia in Canada and neighbouring Alaska both have extensive systems. The British Columbia Knowledge Network has been in operation for over ten years. Education and training programmes are transmitted to 250 community receivers. These form centres for local study groups. In the most remote areas, the television signals are relayed by microwave from the local centres to logging and fishing hamlets. Over 6,000 students are registered on courses ranging from fire-fighters certificate to a degree in child psychology. Telephone return calls to the studio are an important part of the learning process. The presenter greets the caller by name in order to create a 'classroom' atmosphere. The local centres provide study and practical facilities including computer workshops. Two technology buses tour the remote settlements on a regular schedule to provide technical support which includes four computer carrels.

THE OLYMPUS SATELLITE

In British Columbia or Alaska, geography demands delivery by satellite. In Europe, distances rarely totally preclude participation in courses. Delivery systems in Europe have tended to be peripheral to campus systems, except for the Open University in the UK.

Even in the OU, learning depends heavily upon paper-based materials sent through the post. Television broadcasts are seen by many students as optional extras rather than integral units of study. In contrast, business communications are increasingly by electronic methods, particularly in the use of computer-networks and facsimile.

A problem for education and training, which have limited funds particularly for capital equipment, is that considerable investment is required even to undertake a feasibility study of electronic delivery. The European Economic Community, looking forward to the virtual removal of frontiers in 1992, will launch a satellite to promote experimentation in electronic delivery throughout Europe. The satellite, named Olympus, will be launched in January 1989. It will carry two transponders specifically for education and training. The 'special services' transponder will be used to broadcast material throughout Europe. Olympus is a high-powered satellite requiring relatively small receiving dishes of less than one metre in diameter. Current estimates for dish and decoder (television receive only or TVRO) equipment are under £500, and if current plans for entertainment satellites are successful costs could be as low as £200. This means that learners in the most remote settlements throughout Europe can participate live at all levels of education.

The United Kingdom is the main contributor to the costs of launching Olympus and is a leader in utilization plans. The European Space Agency is building mobile uplinks to Olympus which will be stationed at key sites. The Direct Broadcasting (DBS) uplink for the UK will be sited on the London University fibre-optic network 'LIVENET' which connects the London teaching hospitals. This will enable material to be generated at any of the television studios in the network. A major use will be medical education. New techniques can be demonstrated even from an operating theatre and transmitted to teaching hospitals throughout Europe. The London uplink will also be used by other organizations which need to reach large numbers of sites; these include a network for the clergy, the British Universities Film Council, language teaching groups and technical education. Encryption facilities will be used for 'confidential' broadcasts, particularly in medicine.

The special services uplink will be located at Plymouth Polytechnic and will be connected direct to the Polytechnic's television studio. There will be return audio links to facilitate one-way video with audio return. As a result of a feasibility study prepared for the Polytechnic by Brian Champness of Communication Studies and Planning Ltd, the Polytechnic will provide facilities for a number of educational and training organizations and has at present an allocation of two hours daily for teleconferencing. The Training Agency (formerly MSC) is taking a lead in this initiative. In order to evaluate the potential of satellites for training, the Polytechnic will produce for the Agency two series of programmes designed for live presentation.

The first series will exploit the immediacy of satellite by demonstrating the latest techniques of information technology in engineering. The second series will exploit interactivity by creating situations in the studio which can be modified by comments from the audience of managers of small to medium businesses. A job interview will be shown and, following comments from the participants who could be anywhere in the UK, the interview will be improved. There are a large number of other users. A project to use uplinks in other countries, to link children live across Europe, is an exciting prospect. The Olympus satellite can carry five simultaneous language channels so that children could describe their life in Paris, in French, illustrated by video inserts. Other children would either receive in French or in their own language. Experiments for in-house industrial training across Europe will also take place. Successful firms will then transfer to commercial satellites having evaluated their initial attempts on Olympus.

CONCLUSION

Research into artificial intelligence, the development of computer-driven simulation and video, and new opportunities in teleconferencing, will transform distance learning over the next decade. Towards the end of the decade we may see a shift in emphasis to learner-centred delivery both on and off campus. It is important that educators in all guises, including educational technologists, are at the heart of these developments. Too often, innovation has been equipment-led. Many institutions have bought sophisticated hardware only to find that relevant software is not obtainable. The European Space Agency has provided a unique opportunity on a continental scale. If the educational community does not seize this opportunity the large corporations will move in. It is an opportunity to devise new applications in audio, data and video communication in collaboration with colleagues throughout Europe.

REFERENCES

Carmes, P. (1984) Telecom hair. *Le Bulletin de l'Idate, Montpellier,* **19,** 233-237.
Chavatidhar, D. (1986) Exploring teletext for instruction and education: the Israeli experience. *Media in Education and Development,* **19,** 4, 150-153.
George, J. (1979) Tutorials at home, a growing trend. *Teaching at a Distance,* **14,** 19-24.
Hibbard, B.M. (1984) The Linked Tutorial. University Hospital of Wales (videotape).
McConnell, D. (1986) The impact of Cyclops shared screen conferencing in distance education. *British Journal of Educational Technology,* **17,** 1, 41-74.
Meeks, N.B. (1987) The quiet revolution. *Byte,* **12,** 2, 183-190.
Parker, L. and Olgren, G.H. (1984) *The teleconferencing resource book.* North Holland, Amsterdam.
Sanker, H.C. (1985) Satellite conferencing in the Caribbean, *Educational Media International,* **4,** 12-20.
Winders, R. (1985) Teleconferencing - student interaction by telephone - the PACNET experience. *Programmed Learning and Educational Technology,* **20,** 4, 126-132.

23. Meeting INSET needs through distance learning video packages

Peter Stubbington, *INSET Open Learning Unit, Cosham, UK*

Summary: Recent educational legislation in the UK has promoted the systematic and purposeful planning of INSET for teachers. Financial support has changed and Local Education Authorities have to maximize the effectiveness of available resources, seeking to meet identified INSET needs and using means which will be acceptable to, and received with, enthusiasm by teachers. As part of its scheme to achieve these objectives, Hampshire Education Authority has established the INSET Open Learning Unit which produces distance learning video packages for use by its teachers. The packages are intended to be non-threatening and to bring intimacy to INSET, drawing upon the substantial talents and initiative within Hampshire.

FROM TRIST TO INSET OPEN LEARNING UNIT

During 1985, Hampshire Education Authority made a submission for consideration by the Manpower Services Commission (MSC) for funding as part of TRIST (Technical and Vocational Education Initiative Related In-Service Training). The submission was accepted, and in January 1986, Hampshire Mobile Production Unit came into being, funded under TRIST for five terms with three staff; the general editor and director of the Unit (also the then County Adviser for educational technology who had conceived and piloted the idea of INSET video packages) and two specially appointed producers (secondary teachers seconded for five terms). The Unit's aim was to support Hampshire teachers with distance learning INSET video packages which explore aspects of current educational practice in Hampshire schools.

The producers were charged with producing 30 distance learning INSET video packages during their secondment. Each package was to be commissioned by a member of the education advisory service. The INSET potential of a video package is greater than that which an individual can achieve by more time-honoured means. The commissioner can, given the same amount of planning and preparation as for a weekend course, engage thousands of teachers, enabling them to see what is going on in other schools and stimulating them to reflect upon their own practice.

Submissions for commissions were vetted by the general editor of the Unit, whose other responsibilities included:

- oversight of the setting up, equipping and running of the Unit;
- induction of the two producers; and
- approving the edited video and editing the package notes.

The Unit is now the Hampshire Education 'INSET Open Learning Unit' and is run by the two pilot producers who are on permanent contracts to Hampshire Education Authority and have responsibility for all aspects of the Unit's operation, generally alternatively producing packages with the other producer in the role of production assistant.

INSET NEEDS IN HAMPSHIRE

Video packages are part of the Authority's scheme to provide INSET for its teaching staff, some 11,600 teachers in the 4+ to 16+ sector. The substantial demand for INSET necessitates approaches which are materials-led. Under current legislation, each teacher is to have five days per annum of INSET in addition to GRIST (Grant Related In-Service Training). GRIST funding varies according to whether proposed training falls within national (70 per cent of funding) or local (50 per cent of funding) curriculum priority areas or outside of these (nil funding). Distance learning INSET video packages are part of the strategy to maximize the effective distribution of available resources, both human and material.

VIDEO PACKAGES

Each video package comprises two parts:

- a VHS video recording with a target running time of 15 minutes; and
- notes on approximately four sides of A4 (a copy to be kept by each teacher on the return of the video to the Unit's library) which:
  - offer guidance on how to use the package;
  - explain and extend ideas developed in the video; and
  - raise discussion points designed to stimulate further activity.

These packages have the advantage that they are tailor-made to meet local INSET needs, identifying and advocating good policy. Each package links the user with local, accessible 'experts', often class teachers like themselves with whom they can identify. Formative evaluation has enabled evolutionary improvements of the materials produced and the Unit's operation.

FACILITIES

Initially, the Unit was conceived as mobile and was based in a vehicle which housed all of the audio and video recording equipment, edit suite and wordprocessing facility. Besides the mobile Unit, there are now land-based facilities, a second edit suite and desk-top publishing equipment.

Portable VHS recording equipment and ambient lighting are used, minimizing intrusion, to support a 'fly on the wall' brief which can only be achieved with thorough planning from which the producer behind the camera is able to identify and capture the essential audio and video elements. Radio microphones are used to capture audio; although these are expensive to buy, they are imperative when recording in such active locations as classrooms.

The initial recording is made, this is then edited on to a fresh tape and the copies for the library shelf are copied from that edited version. The playback quality achieved is good, certainly adequate to the purpose.

PRODUCTION SEQUENCE

Phase one: initial planning

Initial briefing: the producer contacts the commissioner to discuss requirements, advise on production procedure and arrange a date for the production planning meeting(s).

Preliminary meeting: (at least two weeks prior to production week, but preferably long before this) the commissioner briefs and consults *all* of those who will be involved in the production and others who may be affected.

Draft Notes: following the preliminary meeting, the commissioner is in a position to develop the first draft of the package notes. Since the Unit has no clerical staff, the commissioner is required to deliver these to the producer on floppy disk, via electronic mail or as a file on one of the Unit's portable text processors.

Production planning meeting: (at least one week prior to production week) this final, on-site planning session brings together the producer, the commissioner and all those actively involved in the production. The purpose is to develop an outline shooting schedule based on the draft notes and taking into account the peculiarities of both the recording environment and administrative constraints. The producer subsequently finalizes the schedule in time for the production week while the commissioner finalizes the notes.

Phase two: production week

Monday/Tuesday: shooting takes place at one or possibly two sites and the commissioner is present for consultation.

Tuesday/Wednesday to Friday: the commissioner must be available for post-production editorial consultation during the process of video and audio editing which is completed during the production week. Commissioners can lose all sense of urgency, regarding completion, once the cameras have been on location, it is therefore most important to minimize loose ends at the end of phase two.

Phase three: completion

The producer edits the text (further editorial consultation with the commissioner may be needed; this depends on the quality of text supplied, its compliance with house style, copyright clearance etc). Five copies of the video are made for the library (further copies are produced subsequently if demand requires this). One hundred copies of the notes are held at any time with on-demand printing when the photocopying equipment will allow.

COMMISSIONING PACKAGES

Those who commission packages usually have a responsibility for INSET delivery and the packages are to complement or supplant the taught component, increasing the scope of the commissioner. The best commissioners are committed to the package and plan it thoroughly, enthusiastic commissioners having a sense of ownership. Some have delegated package planning to others, such as headteachers and advisory teachers, but the effectiveness of such delegation is very variable; there can be a substantial gap between the commissioner's original conception and the product. Information gaps between commissioners and those to whom they delegate consultant responsibility, or between themselves and the school featured in terms of what is actually going on in that school, often cause packages to founder.

The commissioner must identify:

- the purpose of the finished package (not merely to gratify the commissioner in achieving some short-term objective, eg showing the video at the next conference);
- those who will use it;
- how they will use it;
- what they will gain as a consequence of using it;
- what information, in the form of pictures, sound and text the package will contain;
- the school to be featured in the production (being certain of a high correlation between perceptions of the school and what actually takes place there);
- the staff to be involved (clearing all arrangements with the headteacher);

- that good educational practice is demonstrated both in the action to be focused upon and that which may seem to be incidental, eg other children at work, displays etc (poor practice, incidental to the package, can prove distracting and destroy the integrity of the package); and
- that health and safety regulations are adhered to.

Video is a charismatic medium, it is sometimes necessary to persuade the commissioner that pointing a video camera and recording can achieve little that is worth while unless it is part of a structured programme of investigation or exposition. Commissioners vary considerably in their perceptions of production. It creates problems when the commissioner insists that the notes can only be written after the video has been edited! The producer aims to produce a structured learning package and the 'permanence' of the text is important relative to the transient experience which the video offers. The video component of the packages can enjoy too great an emphasis, consideration of the text content being eclipsed; if the video is of greater importance to the commissioner this can lead to production of the notes being delayed (sometimes for substantial periods). The commissioner may be tempted to delegate the notes or part of these to someone else (a class teacher usually produces these with admirable speed but the quality of notes can be very variable).

The package, in part or as a whole, should not be made available until the editorial processes are completed. The usual copyright conditions apply to these packages. Commissioners may make representations to the effect that they need the package for an imminent course/conference etc and suggest that the video be made available to them before the notes have been printed, others suggest that they copy the tape/notes themselves so that they have them to hand. The integrity of the package is destroyed if the video is seen without the notes; in most packages the video lacks continuity and is not intended to stand alone. The production of 'pirate' copies results in the Unit being unable to monitor the use of the package for purposes of evaluation and the video (or perhaps the notes) being seen out of context. These create 'wrong' perceptions of the Unit's purpose and productions in terms of the learning it is sought to achieve and the quality of reproduction it is sought to maintain.

The amount of time required of a commissioner in producing a video package is considerable; the Unit argues that a properly produced package will provide an ample return in terms of the gains mentioned previously and through time saved as the package is used and the commissioner is released to do other work or, as a consequence of the experience gained by teachers using the package, to provide INSET at a higher level.

LEARNERS HAVE CONTROL

Video playback facilities are available in most schools and the UK has one of the highest levels of domestic video facility in the world. All Hampshire teachers have access to the Unit's products by writing to or telephoning the Unit's librarian to borrow the package(s) they want to use; these are sent to them by post or courier, no charge being made for the service.

Individual teachers say that they are impressed and grateful that they have such easy access to the packages. Teachers are enabled to take charge of INSET, choosing the time and place of study, working with colleagues or alone, borrowing packages related to their own curriculum responsibilities and the age group they teach or examining cross-curricular issues and aspects of other groups' contributions to the education process.

In conclusion, the Unit is fully booked and the volume of accessions continues to rise; both are due to the intimacy and accessibility of its products which, commissioned by those able to identify local INSET needs they are responsible for satisfying, are supported by a readily available network of advisory teachers and local experts.

24. The provision of graphic materials on the online NERIS database

Andrew Lancaster, *Faculty of Education and Design, Brunel University, UK*

Summary: In providing information about any subject pure text is often sufficient in order to convey the meaning, however the addition of a graphic image may be of value in order to clarify or enhance the material concerned. In some cases a picture or diagram may be the only vehicle through which all of the necessary information may be comprehended.

Many 'information providers' have forwarded materials containing both text and graphic images to be included in the NERIS (National Educational Resources Information Service) online database. In recent months, development work has been undertaken at NERIS to provide the necessary system requirements to enable such materials to be both uploaded and downloaded from the database. Two specific areas of this work have been undertaken at Brunel University, namely:

- a software evaluation to discover a suitable vector computer- aided design software package to process the graphic images; and
- the provision of guidelines to enable information providers who have limited graphic or computer-aided design experience to format the graphic materials prior to them being sent to NERIS.

This paper seeks to outline the potential of the NERIS database in providing online graphic materials, together with some of the issues which have arisen during the development work.

A BRIEF BACKGROUND TO NERIS

'The National Educational Resources Information Service (NERIS) is a computerized online educational database of curriculum materials and information. The idea of the development stems from a two-fold desire to provide teachers with a single point of reference that will enable them to identify learning materials located in a multitude of sources and, secondly, from a concern to create a system capable of delivering up-to-date or little- known materials directly into schools. The initial development phases are funded by the Industry/Education Unit of the Department of Trade and Industry whose interest started with a concern to provide industry-related teaching materials in the areas of mathematics and science in secondary schools. The NERIS development team is based in Woburn on the edge of Milton Keynes within easy reach of the Open University where the mainframe computer that holds the NERIS database is located.' (Taken from *NERIS an Introduction*, 1987)

NERIS, GRAPHICS AND BRUNEL UNIVERSITY

Although the type of resources which are stored on the NERIS online database vary in terms of physical size and copyright restrictions, a large proportion are available in their entirety to be directly downloaded by users. Such resources may comprise purely text or, in a growing number of cases, may provide graphics or computer software. The initial launch of NERIS provided a service known as NERIS Level One, an easy-to-use viewdata format accessed through a microcomputer/modem arrangement via Prestel or The Times

Network System (TTNS) to the records held on a mainframe computer at the Open University.

Users were able to combine a maximum of two interest areas together with the required age phase and media to initiate a search. The required information could be saved to the user's computer disc drive to be printed out offline, thus saving telephone costs. In the case of large resources or those to be purchased, the information retrieved would comprise mainly details concerning availability, while smaller resources (typically about four to five sheets of A4 paper in size) could be downloaded completely. At this stage of the development work the downloading procedure could only support textual items. Information providers wishing to include graphic items in a resource were therefore forced either to create them somewhat crudely using characters such as dots and dashes available on the standard keyboard, or in many cases had to exclude them from the resource.

At the time NERIS Level One was launched, the development work was already well on the way to providing NERIS Level Two, a service which not only enabled greater flexibility in search strategies but also the facility to upload and download graphics and computer software from the system. At the current time Level Two has already been trialled and is shortly to be released for general access via the same routes as Level One together with 'direct access' facility enabling a connection without having to pass through Prestel or TTNS. The development work which has been specifically undertaken to enable graphic materials to be supported on the database can be divided into the following areas:

- system requirements to enable the graphic materials to be encoded on to the database and decoded at the user's computer;
- the provision of software to enable the paper-based graphic images forwarded by the various information providers to be processed into computer files prior to the encoding procedure; and
- the provision of guidelines and support for a limited number of people, most probably drawn from existing information providers, to undertake the graphic formatting duties when the development work is complete.

The development work concerning the system requirements has been carried out by the NERIS Development Team together with some external programming input from a company named 'Resource', who have been responsible for the production of the necessary decoding software for the user.

When consideration was given to the type of software needed to format the drawings it was evident that the types of graphic images fell into two main types:

- images comprising 'vectors' such as lines and shapes; and
- images which could not be easily produced by the type of software which would be used for the production of the vector images or by a conventional keyboard – for instance, symbols such as Greek characters often used in a mathematics or science context.

The Faculty of Education and Design at Brunel University was approached by NERIS to assist with two particular areas of the graphics development work, namely the choice of software suitable for processing the vector images (liaising with another party working on the character graphics) and the provision of guidelines for those who would be responsible for processing the graphic images in the long term.

THE CHOICE OF A SUITABLE SOFTWARE PACKAGE FOR PRODUCING VECTOR IMAGES

Before an analysis of potential vector computer-aided design packages could be undertaken it was necessary to establish criteria by which the potential use of the software could be judged. This 'brief' was largely fixed by the system requirements which had already been laid down concerning what type of graphics could be supported at the encoding and decoding stages. As a result the following criteria formed the basis for the software analysis. The chosen package should:

- run on microcomputers typically found in educational establishments;
- be capable of producing simple vector graphics such as lines, circles, polygons and arcs;
- be user friendly bearing in mind that potential users may have little computer-aided design experience;
- include a text facility for inclusion in the graphic images;
- include a block fill or shade facility to provide basic enhancement;
- drive a plotter in order to generate the necessary commands to enable the drawing file to be encoded and decoded from the database; and
- be within a realistic price range for educational use.

Having established the stated criteria it was possible to carry out a broad review of computer-aided design software culminating in the production of a comprehensive list of packages produced for the educational market. Literature and specifications were obtained for the software in order to assess which had specific vector applications and an attempt was made to gain actual experience of using the software which potentially fulfilled the NERIS brief.

The actual process of gaining hands-on experience of the 18 respective packages which emerged from the literature survey proved to be more difficult than was first imagined. Some of the software was already available within the Faculty and a limited number of publishers were willing to loan packages for evaluation purposes, however the majority had to be reviewed away from the University at either teachers' centres or at schools. The process of tracing the software and then travelling to undertake the evaluation proved time-consuming but in many cases enabled invaluable comments from 'seasoned' users to be noted.

The actual evaluation process was undertaken by means of an elimination process based largely on how well the various packages fulfilled the specified brief. For this purpose the initial criteria were rationalized and ranked into the following areas of importance:

- how comprehensively the packages performed the necessary vector functions;
- cost;
- user friendliness; and
- the type of microcomputer and related hardware required to run the package.

In addition to these criteria, miscellaneous features were also noted which could have a bearing on the final choice. These included factors such as the potential of the system for building a library of subject-based 'components' (for example, experimental apparatus) which the user could create and draw upon at a later date. The evaluation process resulted in three software packages emerging as most suited to the needs of NERIS and in the final analysis one package stood out from the others because of its greater user friendliness and the fact that it was cheaper than its counterparts.

WHO WILL FORMAT THE GRAPHICS MATERIAL FORWARDED TO NERIS?

The graphics development work has not only involved the process of setting up the necessary structure to create, encode and decode information from the database but also to assess who would be best suited to undertake the graphic formatting duties once the system is up and running. At the current time NERIS gathers and disseminates information through a series of subject 'node points' who are able to comment on both the educational and technical validity of any resource submitted for inclusion on the database. It therefore seemed sensible that a selected number of personnel at these node points would be the most logical choice for the graphic formatting responsibilities because of the subject specialism they possessed. If it were left simply to a remote group of computer-aided design specialists to create the graphic files, their lack of subject-related technical knowledge could lead to inaccuracies in drawings to the extent that the finished illustrations may not fulfill their role in supporting or enhancing the text.

The fact that subject specialists would be responsible for creating graphic files does, however, create the problem of finding people who have had some experience of making decisions about the best method of presenting any given item of graphic information, as well as ideally having some experience of using a simple computer-aided design package. In reality, few people can offer all of these skills, therefore the choice of a user-friendly software package and provision of some form of support proved to be of great importance. It would be impossible directly to support all of the graphic formatters due to geographical factors, therefore it has been necessary to write a series of self-instructional guidelines to enable the subject specialists to make valid decisions concerning the graphic presentation of materials and overcome the common problems which occur when using the software.

THE PRODUCTION OF GUIDELINES FOR GRAPHIC FORMATTERS

It was found that during the survey of computer-aided design software that many of the user manuals were badly produced making the task of getting used to the software that much more difficult. Fortunately, the documentation provided with the actual software selected for use in formatting the graphic records was one of the best of those encountered. Guidelines, therefore, only had to be written to assist the subject specialists to make decisions concerning whether the vector or character software is most applicable for formatting particular images or which type of graphic presentation is best employed for a given situation.

The major problem in writing such guidelines was determining the actual base level of computing and graphic knowledge of those undertaking the formatting. Due to the probable range of knowledge of the potential formatters, it was decided that guidelines provided in a linear format, to be read from cover to cover, would not be an efficient format for self-instruction as some readers would inevitably need more help than others. After several different instructional formats had been considered, it was decided that the guidelines would be best written in a reference-form accessed by algorithms used to assist with decision-making processes. It would be inevitable that each user would have unique needs and would therefore only need to refer to certain passages for help. Instead, a diagram outlining the various stages which need to be undertaken in the production of a graphic file, as shown in Figure 1, together with three algorithms concerning the choice of software and the selection of the most appropriate type of presentation and enhancement, were provided to aid the decision-making process.

Using the procedural diagrams and algorithms as a guide, the formatter could create the drawing, being given the option to be re-routed to more detailed background information within the reference section of the booklet if applicable.

The reference materials, algorithms and case studies of some drawings which had already been formatted were assembled in discrete sections indexed by a series of symbols, as shown in Figure 2, to provide the user with visual cues to their location.

These symbols were also used in the re-routing process by including them in a box together with a specific page number to provide clear guidance as to the location of the

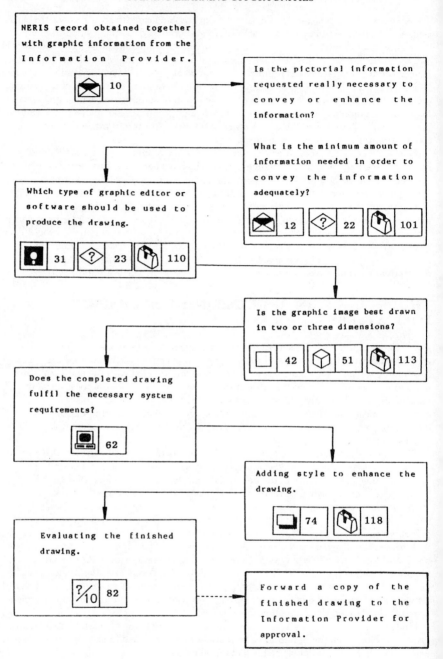

Figure 1. *Stages in producing a drawing to be included in a NERIS record*

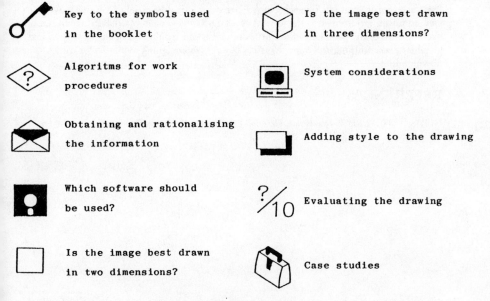

Key to the symbols used in the booklet

Is the image best drawn in three dimensions?

Algoritms for work procedures

System considerations

Obtaining and rationalising the information

Adding style to the drawing

Which software should be used?

Evaluating the drawing

Is the image best drawn in two dimensions?

Case studies

Figure 2. *Index of symbols used*

relevant supporting information. This is illustrated in Figure 3 which shows how the user would be re-routed to page 50 of the case study section.

Figure 3. *Symbol re-routeing user*

The guidelines having been compiled are shortly due for distribution to a limited number of information providers for evaluation and comment prior to them being released when the network of graphic formatters is established in the near future.

FUTURE PROSPECTS FOR GRAPHIC MATERIALS FROM NERIS

There is no doubt that the addition of graphic materials to the resources currently held on the NERIS database will be of immense value, not only to support textual items but in some cases to give users access to resources which so far have been impossible to carry on the online service. It may well be that the amount of time taken in resource centres within schools to produce teaching materials by wordprocessing and cut and paste techniques, will be greatly reduced when teachers discover the availability of relevant resources, teaching packs and worksheets that are available in a matter of minutes from the printer. Interest is already growing among information providers concerning the added range of materials which can now be forwarded to NERIS due to the development which has allowed both graphic and computer software to be delivered.

The major restriction on delivering materials via the online service is the size which can realistically be downloaded. This is mainly due to the time it would take to transfer the whole file to the user's disc drive, and in practice the indications are that files in excess of

25k (or larger than about five sides of A4) are impracticable to deliver in this way. With a view to future requirements, the advent of a CD-ROM version of NERIS would not only overcome all of the problems of online search costs but would also open the way to text, graphics and computer software resources of any size becoming available for direct downloading.

REFERENCES

NERIS (1987) *NERIS an Introduction*. National Educational Resources Information Service.

25. China's television universities: the future

David Hawkridge, *Institute of Educational Technology, The Open University, Milton Keynes, UK*

Summary: This paper complements and updates a paper published in the British Journal of Educational Technology in 1983 ('China's Television Universities' by David Hawkridge and Bob McCormick). The television university system in China is now expanding and modernizing with help from a World Bank loan, yet there are potential problems of staffing, dependence on television, urban bias and academic standing. The Bank has high expectations of the system and there are agreed performance indicators, listed in the paper, against which it will be judged. Beyond 1990, will the student body of the television universities change in size and nature? Will the universities offer different courses? Will they change the media they use to reach students? Will these universities ever die because they are not needed? This paper offers answers to these important questions.

INTRODUCTION

The Chinese Television Universities (TVUs) were founded in 1979 as a federal system of 28 provincial institutions plus one central validating and course-producing unit. They now teach about a million students through textbooks and through television programmes produced mainly by the central unit and broadcast during the day by the national television network and, since 1987, by a satellite channel. The students chiefly belong to work units and are released to study full time, six hours a day, six days a week, for three years, usually in classes located at their place of work but also in special study centres. Hawkridge and McCormick (1983) provide a detailed account.

The Chinese Ministry of Education (now upgraded to the State Education Commission) decided in 1981 to invest the equivalent of about $100 million in the TVUs, and to seek in addition a World Bank loan of about $80 million for expanding and modernizing them. As a member of the Preparation Mission for the World Bank project in October 1982, I assisted in drawing up plans for this expansion and modernization. As Chairman of the International Advisory Panel for the project, appointed in 1984 by the Minister of Education, I have been able to observe and advise on developments.

POTENTIAL PROBLEMS

During the Preparation Mission, I noted several possible problems, none of which has yet been solved satisfactorily (Hawkridge and McCormick, 1983). Those problems are as follows:

Staffing

I forecast a shortage of trained technical staff for the TVUs and of trained tutors for the workstations and study centres. In fact, the technical training programme has proceeded quite slowly, for several reasons. Planning, erection and refurbishment of buildings, essential before new imported computers and television production and transmission equipment could be installed, took longer than expected and is still not finished in all provinces. The number of national workshops and seminars that can be organized each year in a country the size of China is limited by resources. The few suitably qualified staff cannot always be spared to send for training and the plans for sending staff to be trained overseas could not be carried through without intensive language training, not widely or speedily available. Recently, the Chinese authorities agreed to extend the training programme in an attempt to ensure that sufficient technical staff would be available in the system. There is also a dearth of trained tutors in many regions because such people are greatly in demand for other courses. Instead, many rather poorly qualified tutors struggle with the content of the televised courses and textbooks, sometimes only a little ahead of their students.

Dependence on television

I foresaw difficulties for students, and staff, in moving from the kind of televised backboard lessons used at first (mainly 'talking blackboard') to the kind of television that uses the full range of powerful presentation techniques. As yet, this is not a serious problem for the students because few programmes of the latter variety have been made, but TVU students depend more on TV, and less on print, than British Open University students. So it is important to help TVU students to learn well from television. As for the television production staff, they occupy inferior positions in the system, working for teachers, and those producers who wish to experiment with 'new' kinds of programme will battle to persuade many of the teachers that a different approach can be valuable.

Urban bias

I suggested that the TVUs would serve best the urban students for many years to come, even if a satellite were used. In a country like China equity is important, and the State Education Commission wants to reduce urban bias as soon as it can, while recognizing the economies that stem from teaching first those in densely populated areas. Despite Intelsat's help in renting to China an additional channel, now carrying television university broadcasts for 36 hours a week, and despite the erection of large numbers of Chinese-made six-metre receiving dishes in towns, urban bias continues.

Academic standing

I forecast that there would be difficulty in persuading employers and graduates that the degrees granted by TVUs were of good quality. Transfer of credit would be difficult to obtain. Academic staff of the TVUs would have problems in maintaining their academic standing. On the first of these issues data are coming in. There is no transfer of credit yet in China, so it may take a decade or more for the quality of the television universities' degrees to be tested in this way. So far, there is only anecdotal evidence on the third point.

THE WORLD BANK'S EXPECTATIONS

The World Bank, in 1983, noted that 69 per cent of the first intake of 110,000 students in 1979 had graduated with a college degree three years later. This was the kind of expectation on which the loan was based. The Bank recognized that the TVUs lacked TV production and transmission capacity, with the result that they could not admit enough students, that they lacked teaching space and scientific equipment, and that their staff needed training. The loan was expected to change the situation, with the Chinese government paying for buildings, Chinese-made equipment and training by Chinese experts, the loan paying for foreign equipment, including computers, and staff training by foreign experts in China and overseas.

The Bank expected that:

- The CRTVU would have its own production centre, for broadcast television, equipped with the loan money. Similarly, CRTVU would have computers, laboratories and a printing plant. Each of the nine major TVUs would also have a production centre for broadcast television, a transmission centre, computers and laboratories on the same basis. Each of the 19 minor TVUs would have a video production centre, computers and laboratories on the same basis. Staff of all the TVUs would be trained in a large training programme, for which Chinese and foreign experts would do the teaching.
- The TVU system would extend its coverage to offer its courses to more of the population, including people in rural areas, and that student numbers would increase greatly, from 280,000 in 1983 to 1,300,000 in 1990 and to 2,000,000 in 2000. The Bank predicted that more middle-school leavers would become TVU students (rising from 6 per cent in 1983 to 30 per cent by 1990) and fewer employed workers. It also foresaw that the proportion of part-time students would remain roughly one-third up to 1990.
- The system would offer a wider range of courses by using videocassettes where there was not sufficient air time. For example, the CRTVU would increase the number of its courses from 50 in 1983 to 170 by 1990, introducing subjects such as civil and architectural engineering, light industrial management, industrial chemistry, accounting, political science and law. CRTVU TV programme production would increase from 300 a year to 700. In the major PTVUs, total production of programmes would rise to 1,350 a year with a further 1,900 programmes a year being produced in the minor PTVUs.
- The physical facilities of 85 study centres would be improved to contain laboratories, audiovisual equipment and classrooms, covering a total area of about 300,000 square metres, about three-quarters being new construction. The percentage of experiments that students would be able to complete was expected to rise from 20-30 per cent to 80 per cent.
- Management of the TVUs would be improved through installation of mainframe computers and microcomputers. These would be used to establish records of all students and their achievements, to facilitate record-keeping in libraries and stores, to schedule classes, students and staff and to aid the financial management of each TVU and its branches.
- Training, which the Bank saw as essential if good use was to be made of the equipment installed with Chinese and Bank funds, would be provided through a technical assistance programme that brought foreign trainers and consultants to China, and sent Chinese staff members overseas.

THE AGREED PERFORMANCE INDICATORS

Based on these expectations, China and the Bank agreed a list of performance indicators, in the same way as indicators are agreed for other World Bank projects. These will become an important part of the evaluation of the success of the project. Besides these performance indicators, the Bank agreed with China that it would be important to undertake tracer studies that would explore what had happened to the graduates of the television universities. Pilot studies of this nature have been complete and written up (Ma, 1987), and now the major sampling studies are under way in selected provinces.

An evaluation report will be compiled in 1989, based on the tracer studies and the agreed performance indicators. Data collection plans have been laid, and all 28 institutions will participate. There will also be an opportunity to review the training programme, although its impact is hard to determine accurately. By the time the project ends formally

Performance Indicator	1983	1986	1990
Full time students enrolled	240,000	400,000	900,000
Part time students enrolled	130,000	150,000	400,000
Total students enrolled	370,000	550,000	1,300,000
Percent who are recently from middle school	6	15-20	30-40
No.of courses taught only by face-to-face method	Many	Few	None
No.of courses developed by CRTVU			
Science and engineering	28	35	60
Social science and humanities	22	90	110
No.of courses developed by each PTVU			
Science and engineering	4-8	12	20
Social science and humanities	3-7	30	35
No.of fields of study developed by CRTVU			
Science and engineering	4	6	10-12
Social science and humanities	1	10	11-12
No of programmes produced each year			
CRTVU	300	500	700
All major TVUs		800	1350
All minor TVUs		1000	1900
Percent of experiments performed	20-3	30-40	70-90
Percent of students able to perform experiments	50-60	60-70	80-100

Table 1. *Performance Indicators for the Chinese Television Universities*

in 1990, a verdict should be in, although the longer-term effects will be of even more vital interest.

THE FUTURE BEYOND 1990

Many questions can be asked about the future of the television universities beyond 1990. I shall try to answer four that seem vitally important.

Will the student body change in size and nature?

Yes, it seems very likely indeed that the student body will continue to expand for at least a decade. The upper limit will be reached when resources can no longer be found to pay students' fees and wages. Work units are already exercising selectivity in that they choose only their best candidates to be students, but there are signs in some provinces that employers are not increasing the size or number of their classes. Units do not want to release a higher proportion of people from regular work, and they cannot stand the cost.

The student body is also beginning to change its nature and seems very likely to go on doing so. The percentage of school-leavers, unassigned as yet to jobs, as opposed to mature workers aged 25-35, is rising from its initially very low level. But the number of part-time students who follow the courses in their own time, outside any framework of work unit or study centre classes, is rising fast. They often pay for themselves, just like Open University students. These two trends have implications for the success rate of students: until recently, the pass rate was very high indeed, but it may show a decline over the next few years, because school-leavers may not be as motivated as mature workers, and part-time students without tutor support have much more difficulty than full-timers in preparing for examinations.

Will the TVUs change the kinds of courses they offer?

Yes, here too change seems likely, but mainly in the sense that new lines will be added. The highly vocational nature of the courses will not change, as the Chinese authorities take a utilitarian view of the TVUs and do not intend to offer a general liberal arts education through them. In the summer of 1987 the TVUs agreed to decentralize course production to a greater extent, with up to 40 per cent of the courses being produced in the provinces, sometimes by regional consortia of TVUs. This new policy is also likely to lead to greater diversity.

Will the TVUs change the media they use to reach students?

Possibly. Television seems likely to continue as a delivery medium for at least a decade, particularly as the Chinese are planning to have more satellite channels devoted entirely to education, perhaps even a dedicated satellite. Use of television is likely to change, as I have suggested, away from the 'talking blackboard' that represents a first stage of transition from traditional Chinese teaching methods to those that make full use of the medium. Videocassettes are already being used widely in the TVUs as an alternative medium, but little or no attempt has been made to exploit this medium by adapting the educational message to it. Instead, the cassettes simply carry copies of television broadcasts. Computers have come on the scene as part of the modernization, but chiefly for teaching programming and computing, not for computer-assisted learning of other subjects. Software is extremely scarce and seems likely to be so for at least a decade. The biggest changes could occur in the print medium. Another World Bank project being planned will, if it is implemented, lead to modernization of the 6,000 university textbooks in China. This process is likely to benefit TVU students in particular as the books will become more suited to independent learning (in this case learning without a well-qualified tutor available).

Will they ever die because they are no longer needed?

Not for a long time. China's secondary schools are slowly improving their age participation rate. The tertiary sector cannot expand fast enough, without the help of TVUs, to meet demands for higher education in a country of a billion people in which hardly any graduates were produced during the ten tumultuous years of the Cultural Revolution (1966-76). It is true that the TVUs turn out graduates with a college degree, not equivalent to that of Beijing University, but it seems clear that the national need for qualified people at that level cannot be satisfied for many years to come (see McCormick, 1985). It is safe to predict that the TVUs will operate in the 21st century, though they may have different students, different courses and use media differently.

REFERENCES

Hawkridge, D. and McCormick, B. (1983) China's television universities. *British Journal of Educational Technology*, **14**, 3.

Ma, Weixiang (1987) The graduates of China's television universities: two pilot studies. *International Journal of Educational Development*, **7**, 4.

McCormick, B. (1985) The radio and television universities and the development of higher education in China, *China Quarterly*.

Section 4:
Learning and the learner

26. Improving learning: a three-sided campaign

Dr Phil Race, *Polytechnic of Wales, UK*

Summary:

'You can't teach a man to teach. You can, however, help him see how his students' learning may be improved.' (after Galileo!)

We can't do our students' learning for them, we can only try to help facilitate their progress. Improved learning is not just about increased subject knowledge or skills, it is also about improved *capability*. This paper describes three ways in which I try to ensure that students' capability is improved.

First, students can benefit from help aimed at improving their learning skills. I will outline a study-skills development programme which aims to help students become more capable managers of their learning.

Second, well-designed learning materials can enhance the quality of students' learning. I will discuss some criteria for determining the quality of learning materials, particularly materials which can be used in open-learning mode.

Thirdly, teaching and learning processes need to be regarded as more important than the content of study programmes. I will explore an educational development course for teaching staff, aiming to raise their awareness of process options they can employ to facilitate student learning.

Although the order above may seem logical, I will actually explore these issues in reverse order in this paper, for reasons which will (I hope) become apparent!

CAPABILITY versus CONTENT

The biggest fault with higher education (and maybe all education?) is that we concentrate on the *content* of our courses and programmes. The content grows and grows. We try to fill every available minute with *delivering* the content. We often deliver much more content than our students can ever get to grips with.

Then, we tend to measure students on *how much they can remember*. Would it not be far better to measure them on *what they could do?*

Recent initiatives have highlighted the importance of developing students' capability. The Royal Society of Arts published a 'manifesto' with the title 'Education for Capability' in 1980, listing nine important criteria for developing learners' skills. The British Government's thinking on 'Enterprise', currently being encouraged in higher education through the Manpower Services Commission (now the Training Agency), is a further example.

It is much more important that we turn out capable students than merely knowledgeable ones. 'Capability' does not just involve helping our students become effective at using their subject knowledge and skills. Capability also involves helping our students become effective learners. They are going to be learning and re-learning throughout their careers, as technological advances render past content obsolete. So we need to devote far more time to assisting students to develop their learning skills. Most of their learning (in the context of a lifetime or a career) will be done under their own steam.

WHY A THREE-SIDED CAMPAIGN?

In any teaching institution, you will find three kinds of people:

- *Interested/dedicated people:* they are probably good at what they do, but is what they do enough for the real needs of their students?
- *Curious/opportunist people:* these are the experimenters. These are the people who will try out different approaches and will try to measure how well each approach works. These are the people who come along to Educational Technology International Conferences.
- *Traditionalist/obstructionist people:* Have you met them? Are you one of them? Notice I put the two words together! 'I've managed alright for years doing so-and-so, why should I change now?' 'What I do is based on years of experience.'

Why a 'campaign'?

Is it war? I'd say so! The 'enemy' is the traditional approach. The enemy is the 'I transmit, you receive' approach. ('Transmitters' may enjoy transmitting, but how good is 'reception'? 'Receivers' may become good at receiving, but that has little to do with developing their capability to do all sorts of much more important things!)

Why three-sided?

Mainly because it isn't enough to simply try to stop transmitters transmitting! If you suggest that a lecturer vastly reduce the lecturing content of a course, he or she may well feel threatened and rebel against the idea. So, in addition to attempts to develop teachers so that they are real learning facilitators, what else can we do? What can we do that is less threatening to the traditionalists?

Learner-centred approaches: the central premise

It is less threatening (for teachers) to look at the learner's side of the teaching-learning process. All three sides of the 'campaign' spill over into issues of learner-centredness. Much more attention is being given these days to *how* learners learn (eg Entwistle and Ramsden, 1983).

EDUCATIONAL DEVELOPMENT PROVISION

A thorough recent review of the principles of educational development was provided by Main (1985). The words 'educational development' are often seen as rather less threatening than 'staff development' (even where the purposes may coincide). Educational development may be seen as being about the development of improved learning resources. The covert side of educational development is the focus on processes. No-one feels threatened by explorations of students' learning processes. However, teaching processes need ultimately to respond to students' ways of learning.

Courses, seminars or workshops?

All sorts of factors make it difficult to organize a coherent course of educational development for practising teachers in higher education. Timetable commitments, departmental meetings, visits, conferences, all mean that most staff can only come to some parts of such a course.

Seminars are very good for learning about what someone else has done. However, even after seminars which include lively discussions, there is a tendency for most people to go away and continue more or less as they would have if they hadn't attended the seminar.

My own feeling is that workshops provide the most efficient means of causing teaching staff to develop their skills. That said, I'm referring to 'real' workshops, not dressed-up seminars! In a genuine workshop, the processes are participant-centred. The conductor of the event is a facilitator, and occasionally a resource. The conductor designs a framework where participants can discover things for themselves. Participants then leave the workshop with *ownership* of the new ideas concerned. They are then far more likely to go away and try them out for themselves.

At the Polytechnic of Wales, I conduct a fortnightly series of educational development workshops. These are intended for new staff who wish to develop their teaching processes 'from scratch', but also for experienced staff who wish to re-examine the structure of their teaching strategies. The content of the workshop programme has 'student-centredness' running right through it. Here are some titles of two-hour workshop sessions which have proved useful:

- Making learning objectives useful to students;
- Designing self-assessment exercises;
- Designing and using student feedback questionnaires;
- Writing self-study modules;
- Editing self-study modules;
- Designing assignment questions and marking schemes;
- Sharing assessment criteria with students; and
- Interactive handouts: turning lectures into learning experiences.
  (see also Race, 1988a)

You will probably notice that most of the ingredients I have mentioned above have direct relevance to open-learning materials; more about that later.

Preaching to the converted?

The staff who choose to come along to an educational development event tend to be the ones who are already doing their job well. Because they don't have a guilty conscience about their performance, they don't feel threatened by exploration of other ways of doing things. They are then likely to try out new techniques and are willing to report back their findings in due course.

But what about the staff who most need to be developed? How can they be persuaded to participate in staff development activities? It is of course possible to make attendance mandatory (for example, for newly-appointed staff). But mandatory attendance often causes resentment and even hostility to the topics involved in the programme.

Direct staff development may therefore be regarded as something which will work for a relatively small number of teaching staff: the already-good, and to some extent the 'new and willing to listen'. We therefore need some less threatening vehicles for change.

NEUTRAL TERRITORY: LEARNING RESOURCES

'Learning resources' can be taken to include all sorts of things: open learning modules, computer-based training packages, study guides, even things so basic as handout material and visual aids. There is no shortage of expert advice regarding the production and usage of excellent learning resources materials. Harris (1979) analysed the use of educational materials in the context of detailed discussion of processes and modes of learning. Harris and Bell (1986) extended the analysis to match assessment processes to learners' needs. The production of resource materials has been explored by Clarke (1982).

We'll come back to open-learning resource materials later, meanwhile let's stay with the sorts of resource materials which can be used as part of 'traditional' teaching/learning situations. 'Let me help you to produce some new learning resources for your students' is much more digestible than 'let me convince you that the way you teach needs to be adjusted dramatically towards meeting your learners' needs'. The student-centred side of learning can be taken on board in the design of learning resources without the threat to traditional teaching processes being quite so overt. Once convinced of the benefits of a student-centred approach, the dedicated teacher will spontaneously begin to adjust teaching processes so as to enhance learning productivity.

Some criteria for learning resources materials

As you'll already have guessed, I would hope that learning resource materials will not simply provide the student with subject matter, but will actively develop his or her learning of the subject. I list below a few checklist questions which may help to distinguish those resource materials that promote active learning. In the checklist I use the word 'it' for the resource; 'it' may be anything from a handout, a self-study module, a computer-based-learning programme, a study guide, and so on.

- Is it clear what the learner should be able to do after having used it? (eg are objectives spelled out clearly?)
- What does the learner *do* with it?
- Has the learner freedom of pace when using it?
- Is it full of questions and activities, rather than content?
- Can the learner tell how well he or she is getting on with it? (eg are there self-assessment questions and responses?)
- Can the learner use it as a revision aid when preparing for formal assessment?
- Can learners benefit from group sessions after having used it on their own?

STUDY-SKILLS DEVELOPMENT

Increasingly in higher and further education, time and resources are being given to assisting students to develop their learning skills. Much has happened since I presented an account of my own efforts in this field to the ETIC Conference in 1981 (Race, 1981). It is now clear that students' needs are not just in the high-profile areas of exam technique and revision strategy. They need help in taking on the responsibility for being effective *managers* of their own learning. They need help in time management and effort management. They don't need prescriptions for how it should be done! What they do need is help in measuring how well (or otherwise) they are getting on. Once they know something is wrong, most students will actively do something about it. The trouble is that they so often don't know that they've got problems.

My present thinking on study skills development is centred around helping learners find out the details of the criteria they are eventually to be measured by. This applies equally to criteria relating to marking schemes that will be used on students' exam performance, and also to broader criteria relating to the overall assessment processes and structures. Students are readily 'switched on' by attention to things relating to how they are going to be assessed. They often learn more from the criteria themselves than from the mere subject matter! What matters is that they do learn, and in a way directed towards being able to prove that they've learned.

Sadly, for too long, assessment criteria such as exam-marking schemes have tended to be closely guarded secrets. A national examining board for which I've marked over the last decade instructs examiners to destroy all marking schemes and model answers immediately after the paper has been marked. Why? It is because there is fear that if the criteria were published, the board would come into disrepute? This fear is unfounded (in my opinion) as the criteria have already to be so refined that any member of a team of 30 examiners is able to mark a given script to within 1 or 2 per cent.

I have certainly found with my own students over the years that they have learned very 'thirstily' when given the chance to apply detailed marking schemes to their own efforts, particularly in private.

A lot can indeed be done to help students develop learning skills by providing study-skills seminars and workshops. Students can be helped to examine their methods and strategies and can learn much from each other. However, to change one's behaviour from something that has after all worked all right so far, to something untried as yet, takes courage! That is why my most recent study-skills work (Race, 1988b) tends to use open-learning format so that students can think through their existing strategies in private, and also experiment with new ideas in private, *before* adding the benefits of group discussion to their toolkits.

OPEN LEARNING

Where does open learning fit into the three-sided campaign? Everywhere! Open learning involves learners taking responsibility in managing their own learning. It involves the creation and use of specially designed resource materials. Above all, it requires from the 'teacher' a role that is much more overtly along the lines of facilitator.

Increasing numbers of teaching staff are getting involved in open learning in one way or another. Many become tutors on a distance basis. Some are writing open learning materials of their own. Others are adapting existing open-learning materials to make them suitable for use by their students.

In open learning, the learner has much more control of learning processes. The learner is in charge of the pace of learning. The learner may take control of the times and places where he or she does the learning. The 'teacher' becomes the learning materials. Those supporting open learners don't do the 'transmitting'. They may still do things like counselling, assessing, and dealing with learners' individual problems. I have further explored the principles and practices of open learning (Race, 1987), and also analysed how they can be embedded within more traditional teaching-learning systems. The open learner may also need direct help to maximize his or her skills in the new responsibilities faced; I have recently addressed this need (Race, 1986) in a study-skills guidebook specifically for new open learners.

The most common reaction from those who have become involved in open learning is 'it's changed the way I do things with my ordinary students'. Open learning therefore provides a valuable staff- development tool. Since venturing into open learning is perceived as a new direction by most traditionalist teachers, they don't regard it as a threat to their normal way of teaching. When they begin to translate the learner-centred approach to their normal teaching, it is felt as a natural and spontaneous development, not something occurring 'on command'.

One of the strengths of open learning is that the learner has much more 'ownership' of the newly gained knowledge and skills than if he or she had been taught traditionally. Similarly, teaching staff who become more learner-centred as a result of involvement with open learning feel that they can take all the credit for their improved teaching performance.

CONCLUSIONS

There are several tools that can be used for the purpose of improving learning. The most successful strategies are those which involve resource materials, particularly open-learning materials, which automatically make learning more student-centred. Although the disadvantages of the 'transmit-receive' model are well known, it will probably be an uphill campaign to persuade many of the 'transmitters' that they are not doing their learners justice.

REFERENCES

Clarke, J. (1982) *Resource-based Learning for Higher and Continuing Education*. Croom Helm, London.

Entwistle, N. and Ramsden, P. (1983) *Understanding Student Learning*. Croom Helm, London.

Harris, D. (1979) *Preparing Educational Materials*. Croom Helm, London.

Harris, D. and Bell, C. (1986) *Evaluating and Assessing for Learning*. Kogan Page, London.

Main, A. (1985) *Educational Staff Development*. Croom Helm, London.

Race, P. (1981) Help yourself to success: improving polytechnic students' study skills. In Percival, F. and Ellington, H. (eds) *Aspects of Educational Technology XV*. Kogan Page, London.

Race, P. (1986) *How to Win as an Open Learner*. Council for Educational Technology, London.

Race, P. (1987) *Flexible Approaches to Training*. Council for Educational Technology, London.

Race, P. (1988a) Interactive handouts: turning lectures into learning experiences, *CICED Series 2*, No 10, Scottish Central Institutions Committee for Educational Development, Dundee.

Race, P. (1988b) *CICED Series 3: Study Skills Booklets*, Scottish Central Institutions Committee for Educational Development, Dundee.

27. Problem-based learning in education and training

Henry I Ellington, *Robert Gordon's Institute of Technology, Aberdeen, UK*

INTRODUCTION

Ladies and gentlemen, when I received the original publicity material for ETIC 88 I was very pleased to see that the overall theme of the Conference was to be 'Improving Learning'. This, after all, is what educational and training technology should be all about: helping learners to learn more effectively. I was even more pleased when Chris Bell asked me to give the opening keynote address, a singular honour under any circumstances, and speak on this main theme.

Now anyone giving the opening keynote address at a conference such as this can do one of two things. The first is to attempt to give the delegates a broad review of the area to be covered by the conference, thus providing a sort of 'advance organizer' that prepares the way for more detailed treatment of specific aspects in the various papers and workshops that are to follow. The second is to present a case or argument relating to the conference theme, thus providing the delegates with food for thought or mental stimulation (hopefully both!). Because of the virtually all-embracing nature of the main theme of this Conference, I felt that it would be almost impossible to do it any sort of justice in a 'review type' keynote address and decided to adopt the second course. I therefore propose to spend the next 45 minutes or so trying to convince you that increasing the amount of problem-based learning that takes place in our various educational and training establishments would greatly improve the quality of the learning that takes place therein.

Following the example of Martin Luther, I will present my argument in the form of a series of theses. Delegates will no doubt be relieved to learn that I propose to present slightly fewer than him, three as opposed to 95. Also I hope that the conference organizers are duly appreciative of the fact that I have decided to display them using the overhead projector rather than nailing them to the door of the lecture hall! Once I have presented my three theses I will illustrate and support my argument by means of four case studies - case studies that will show how it is possible to adopt a problem-based approach to learning in all sectors of education and also in industrial training.

MY THREE THESES

As I have indicated, I will present my argument in favour of more widespread use of problem-based learning in the form of three theses. Here is the first of these.

First thesis

Our educational system is, to a large extent, failing to produce the sort of people that modern industry and commerce want. If you work in industry or commerce you probably need no convincing of the truth of this assertion. If, on the other hand, you work in education, it may come as a bit of a surprise to you, although it should not since industry and commerce have been telling us educationalists as much for many years now.

Let me cite two pieces of evidence in support of this first thesis. The first comes from a fact- finding tour that my colleague Eric Addinall and I made of Unilever's Port Sunlight Research Laboratories back in 1980 as part of a consultancy job. One of the main purposes of our tour was to find out what Unilever's senior scientists and administrators were looking for in the physics graduates that came to them from our universities and polytechnics. The results came as something of a surprise to us for the Unilever staff were virtually unanimous in telling us that the things they most looked for were:

- the ability to tackle and solve novel problems by employing an open-minded, cross-disciplinary approach;
- the ability to work across traditional disciplinary boundaries both within physics and between physics and other disciplines such as chemistry, biology, engineering and economics; and
- the ability to think laterally and open-endedly rather than simply apply standard techniques and procedures.

They were also virtually unanimous in indicting Britain's colleges and universities for not producing people of this type. Instead (they maintained) most of them were simply producing subject-based specialists, the sort of people who spend their graduate and post-graduate careers learning 'more and more about less and less until they eventually know everything about nothing' to quote one anonymous cynic.

My second piece of evidence comes from a paper that was given at ETIC 82, at Bulmershe College in Reading (Lewin, 1983). In this paper on 'Industry-education initiatives: the key to our future', Ron Lewin, a consultant for technology with Berkshire Local Education Authority, cited some of the findings of a research programme that had been carried out in Buckinghamshire and Berkshire during the previous five years. His words are worth quoting at some length, as they make my present case perfectly:

'The team's observations confirmed what has been said by many people before: that on the one hand the present educational system stresses the importance of analysis, criticism and the acquisition of knowledge; while, on the other hand, it neglects the formulation of solutions to problems, planning, organization and preparing, in fact constructive and creative activities of all kinds. Yet the future of this country is largely dependent on the education system encouraging, recognizing and producing people who have this broad range of talent.'

I could, without difficulty, go on citing similar evidence for the remainder of the time available to me, but in the hope that I have now made my point will instead proceed to my second thesis.

Second thesis

One of the main reasons for this failure of the education system is the fact that our present educational system places far too much emphasis on *content* and not nearly enough on *process*.

Here I imagine that it is the educationalists who are nodding their heads in agreement since this imbalance between content and process in our educational system has become increasingly widely recognized in recent years. The problem of course arises from the fact that our educational system becomes almost entirely subject-based after the end of the primary stage. Until then pupils are taught by generalists who are, as a result, usually able to provide them with a fairly broad, cross-disciplinary perspective. In addition, the considerable freedom for curricular variation and innovation that has existed in British primary schools since they were liberated from the inhibiting shackles of the 11+ examination, means that teachers can, if they so wish, devote a considerable proportion of their time to helping their pupils to broaden their minds and develop the process- centred skills that will be so useful to them in later life. Nearly all of them do.

Unfortunately, all this stops once our pupils move on to secondary school where, to paraphrase Wordsworth, shades of the prison house begin to close upon the growing boy. To put it bluntly, education generally ceases to be enjoyable once a pupil moves on to secondary school. First, virtually all the teaching is rigidly subject-based with each subject being taught by a subject specialist who, however great his mastery may be of his own discipline, all too often lacks the background or ability to teach in a stimulating, cross-disciplinary way. Indeed, subject specialist are seldom encouraged to teach in such a way. Second, the curriculum is intensive and (by general consensus) grossly overcrowded leaving little room for innovation or experiment. Third, teaching is dominated by the need to prepare pupils for examinations, thus virtually forcing teachers to spend nearly all their time concentrating on the content of their subjects at the expense of helping their pupils to develop wider skills. As I have said, the resulting educational experience is all too seldom enjoyed by the children who are subjected to it.

Nor do things get very much better once our pupils move on to tertiary education where, if anything, the subject dominance and concentration on content at the expense of process become even more pronounced. This fact has been pointed out, and deplored, by many authors: see, for example, *Education After School* by Tyrrell Burgess (Burgess, 1977). Indeed, Burgess felt so strongly about the lack of process-based learning in our educational system that he subsequently got together with a group of like-minded people and founded the 'Education for capability' movement that is currently doing so much to promote its wider use (Burgess, 1985).

The limitations of content-dominated learning were also highlighted by John Cowan in the highly stimulating opening keynote address that he gave at ETIC 86 in Edinburgh (Cowan, 1987). In a section of his talk entitled 'Subject-specific learning tends to be narrow and of restricted utility' (a powerful statement in its own right!) he made the following telling point:

'As the knowledge explosion progresses, the world increasingly requires knowledge- handling abilities and interdisciplinary perspectives rather than the storage and mastery of knowledge however specialized. Indeed narrow specialized knowledge, which so rapidly becomes an anachronism, is in itself of little more than fleeting value.'

If we accept the definition of true education as 'what is left when the facts have been forgotten' (Ellington and Percival, 1977), Cowan's indictment of the domination of education by content becomes even more damning.

As with my first thesis, I could go on producing supporting evidence of this type virtually indefinitely but feel that it is now time to present the third and final leg of my argument.

Third thesis

More widespread use of problem- based learning could help improve the situation.

At this point I think that I should explain exactly what I mean by 'problem-based learning' since the term is a comparatively new one, even though the activity that it describes is not. Indeed, when I first came across the term I felt a little bit like Molière's 'Bourgeois Gentilhomme' who was surprised and delighted to discover that he had been speaking prose all his life without realizing the fact. In a similar way I realized that I and my colleagues at RGIT had, for many years, been using problem- based learning in many of our gaming and simulation exercises without being aware of it!

In essence, problem-based learning is a form of project-based learning, traditionally one of the most commonly used student- centred learning methods in virtually all disciplines. Morgan (1983) describes project-based learning as:

'an activity in which students develop an understanding of a topic through some kind of involvement in an actual (or simulated) real life problem or issue and in which they have some degree of responsibility for designing their learning activities'.

Thus, the essential characteristics of project-based learning are that it is *based on a problem* and involves *student responsibility for learning.*

According to David Boud (1985) who was largely responsible for bringing the term into common use, problem-based learning has one important additional characteristic, namely that:

'the starting point for learning should be a problem, a query or a puzzle that the learner wishes to solve. Organized forms of knowledge, academic disciplines, are only introduced when the demands of the problem require them.'

In other words, problem-based learning is essentially a process- based activity *only bringing in content as and when it is required.*

In Australia, where David Boud works, a number of higher education establishments have gone so far as to base entire courses on problem-based learning. Swinburne Institute of Technology in Melbourne, for example, which I visited last summer runs highly rated problem-based courses in both civil engineering and medicine. One feature of these courses is that the students spend much of their time working in cooperative groups thus adding the undoubted benefits of peer interaction and peer teaching to the other benefits of problem-based learning. I and my colleagues at RGIT have always believed that multi-disciplinary problems of the type that we build into many of our simulation/games are best tackled by groups rather than by individuals, indeed all four of the case studies that I will shortly be describing have this feature. For this reason I would add a fourth desirable characteristic to problem-based learning: *group cooperation.*

As I stated in my third thesis, I believe that more widespread use of the sort of problem based learning that I have just described could go a long way towards redressing the present imbalance between content and process in our educational system, and would thus help to produce the sort of people that the employment market requires. Furthermore I believe that such problem-based learning could play a useful role in virtually all sectors of education and training. I think that I can best convince you of the truth of these assertions by looking at specific examples of the use of problem-based learning in actual educational and training situations, so I will now move on to the second part of my talk, the four illustrative case studies.

MY FOUR CASE STUDIES

My four case studies will demonstrate the versatility of the problem-based approach to learning by showing how it can be used in industrial training, in tertiary education, in secondary education and in primary education.

First case study: Use of problem- based learning in industrial training

During the last 15 years I and my colleagues at RGIT have made extensive use of the problem-based approach in devising training exercises for industry and commerce. The one that I am about to describe is typical.

In 1983 my colleague Eric Addinall and I were asked to help design a one-week inservice course for middle managers working at the United Kingdom Atomic Energy Authority's Nuclear Power Development Establishment at Dounreay in Caithness. The subject areas to be covered had already been identified and we were asked to build an element of experiential learning into the course structure by developing a series of simulation exercises relevant to the work situation at Dounreay. How we did this was described in detail in a paper given at ETIC 84 in Bradford (Ellington and Addinall, 1985).

The pivotal feature of the course that we developed was a whole- day simulation exercise based on the sort of problem that staff at Dounreay might well be confronted with in their actual job situations. It was built round a scenario in which the 16 course participants, working as a single cooperative group, had to respond to a major policy decision that had implications for all the various divisions into which Dounreay is divided. This was presented to the participants in the form of a 'memorandum from the directorate' telling them that it had been decided to make Dounreay much more self-sufficient, the object of the exercise being to consider the implications of the memorandum and establish an agreed overall policy for its implementation throughout Dounreay. The participants (who represented all sections of Dounreay and had a wide range of disciplinary backgrounds) were told that they could organize themselves in any way they liked and could have access to any information that they required but that they had to be ready to present their joint report to the deputy director by 3.00pm. Like the prospect of being hanged first thing in the morning, this concentrated their minds wonderfully!

Delegates will recognize that this exercise had all the characteristics of problem-based learning that I have just described since it was *based on a real-life problem*, required the participants *to bring in only such 'content' as they felt they needed* and could only be completed satisfactorily if the participants *worked as an effective cooperative group*. The exercise proved an outstanding success, the main complaint from the participants being that they did not have time to do it full justice. They all felt that it had provided them with a unique and invaluable learning experience that could only make them more effective managers.

Since it was first run in 1984 the exercise has been used in four subsequent courses always with a different scenario. The time allocated to the exercise has also been progressively increased and now takes up two full days of the course. Indeed the entire course has now been effectively built around the exercise with the early components being largely designed to prepare the participants to take part in it.

Second case study: Use of problem based learning in tertiary education

My second case study shows how it is possible to build problem- based learning into an otherwise conventional degree course, in this case the BSc in mathematical sciences that is run at my own college.

An effective consultant mathematical scientist working in industry or commerce must possess both mathematical modelling skills (the ability to apply mathematical techniques to the solution of real-life problems) and interpersonal and communication skills (the ability to work as an effective component of a professional team and to relate to, and communicate with, non-mathematicians). In order to help their students to develop these various skills, staff of RGIT's School of Mathematical Sciences and Computer Studies have collaborated with the Institute's communication studies and educational technology staff in developing a highly innovative 'Mathematical models and methods' course within the above degree (Usher and Earl, 1987). This combines basic instruction in mathematical modelling and communication studies with a systematic programme of group modelling exercises in which the students have to put what they have learned into practice. The latter incorporate all the features of problem-based learning that I described earlier.

In each group modelling exercise the students (working in small cooperative groups of three to five) take the role of teams of 'consultants' who have been brought in to help their 'clients' solve real-life problems by applying the principles of mathematical modelling. These problems vary enormously in nature, for example: 'helping a dental practice optimize its appointment system'; 'predicting the overall reliability of the inspection schedule for a paper production line'; 'determining the optimum shape of the battens used in racing skiffs', being three of the many that have been used so far.

In each case the team is assigned a member of staff as a client, a client who, for the purpose of the exercise, is assumed not to be a mathematical scientist. The team has to establish the nature of the problem together with any constraints within which they have to operate, decide how to tackle it, allocate tasks (including in most cases carrying out research in areas thrown up by the problem), agree on a recommended solution, give an oral presentation of this solution to their client and other members of staff, answer any questions asked and prepare a written report. They are assessed by a battery of techniques including continuous assessment by the client, assessment of their oral presentation and written report, and peer assessment.

The above system is now in its fourth year of use and all the indications are that it is proving extremely successful, particularly in terms of preparing students to cope more effectively with working in the outside world and making them more attractive to prospective employers. This, after all, is why it was developed in the first place.

Third case study: Use of problem-based learning in secondary education

Since 1973 I and my colleagues at RGIT have been involved in the development of a large number of gaming and simulation exercises for use in secondary schools. Many of these have been multi- disciplinary exercises that incorporated a large element of problem-based learning, the one that I am going to describe, the 'Project Scotia' Competition, being possibly the best example of this particular genre.

'Project Scotia' was a national competition for secondary schools that was run jointly by the Institution of Electrical Engineers, the British Broadcasting Corporation and the Independent Television Authority in collaboration with RGIT over the winter of 1978-79 (Ellington, Addinall and Hately, 1980). It involved cross-disciplinary teams of senior pupils trying to design the best possible UHF television broadcasting network for the hypothetical 'Scotia' region supposedly located somewhere off the West Coast of Scotland (and fiendishly designed to pose just about every type of problem with which television engineers could possibly be confronted!). The teams had to achieve set coverage targets and work within strict technical and economic constraints and, once they had planned their scheme, had to describe and justify it in a written 'consultants' report'. They also had to produce a multi-media presentation of their scheme using models, drawings etc. The project was of a highly demanding nature, and was designed to foster effective interdepartmental and cross disciplinary cooperation. It required the pupils to carry out detailed calculations of a highly technical nature and also to take full account of all relevant economic, geographical, social and environmental factors. It also provided an ideal vehicle for them to develop and display their literary and artistic skills.

Like the other exercises described so far, the 'Project Scotia' competition contained all the elements of problem-based learning that I listed earlier. The original competition proved extremely successful, culminating in a 'live final' held in the IEE's London headquarters in September 1979. Here the five finalists first set up their multi-media presentations and then described their schemes to the judges before taking part in a 'Young Scientist of the Year' type question-and-answer session before an invited audience. The competition was subsequently rerun on a local basis in the South West of Scotland during 1980 where it formed a model for similar competitions that have been run every year since. The IEE has also used it as a model for further national competitions.

Fourth case study: Use of problem-based learning in primary education

My fourth and final case study deals with a highly ambitious project that was carried out in Scotland's Grampian Region during the 1986-87 school year, an attempt to introduce problem-based learning into the curricula of primary schools throughout the Region. The project will be described in detail in a separate paper (Ellington, Addinall and McNaughton, 1989) so I will only outline its main features here.

At the start of the 1986 Autumn Term all primary schools in Grampian Region were invited to participate in a science study which would involve teams of pupils tackling problems chosen by their class teacher. Twenty-six teams from 21 different schools accepted the invitation and each of these was assigned two advisers, one from RGIT and one from Grampian Education Authority. Each team was also given £75 by Goodfellow Associates, a Firm of Offshore Oil Consultants who had offered to sponsor the project. The projects tackled by the pupils varied enormously in character and scope, everything from designing a fox-proof pen for young pheasants to devising a method for de-ballasting and siting a model oil production platform! Each team was visited an average of four times by its two advisers who provided advice, help and technical and logistical support as and when required. The project reached its climax in May 1987 when the participating teams displayed the products of their efforts at a 'show day' held in RGIT.

The science study was universally acknowledged to have been a great success and has since been used as a vehicle for promoting the even more widespread use of problem-based learning in Grampian's schools. I and my colleagues hope that it will encourage other Educational Authorities to do likewise.

CONCLUSION

Ladies and gentlemen, I have now shown you how it is possible to make effective use of problem-based learning in all sectors of our educational system, from primary through to tertiary, and also in industrial training. I hope that I have also convinced you that the more widespread use of such an approach could make a valuable contribution to the education of our future citizens. I now rest my case and hope that you all have an extremely stimulating and enjoyable conference. Thank you for your courtesy and attention.

REFERENCES

Boud, D.J. (1985) Problem based learning in perspective. In Boud, D.J. (ed) *Problem based Learning in Education for the Professions*. Higher Education Research and Development Society of Australasia, Sydney, pp 13-18.

Burgess, T. (1977) *Education After School*. Penguin Books, Harmondsworth.

Burgess, T. (1985) *Education for Capability*. NFER-Nelson, Windsor.

Cowan, J. (1987) Learner-centred learning: the key issues (or seven deadly sins which frustrate facilitation). In Percival, F., Craig, D. and Buglass, D. (eds) *Aspects of Educational Technology XX*. Kogan Page, London.

Ellington, H.I. and Addinall, E. (1985) Building experiential learning into an inservice training course for middle managers. In Alloway, B.S. and Mills, G.M. (eds) *Aspects of Educational Technology XVIII*. Kogan Page, London.

Ellington, H.I., Addinall, E. and Hately, M.C. (1980) The Project Scotia Competition. *Physics Education*, **15**, 220-222.

Ellington, H.I., Addinall, E. and McNaughton, B. (1989) Introducing problem based learning into the primary school: a major initiative in Grampian Region. In Bell, C., Winders, R. and Davies, J. (eds) *Aspects of Educational Technology XXII*. Kogan Page, London.

Ellington, H.I. and Percival, F. (1977) Educating 'through' science using multi disciplinary simulation/games. *Programmed Learning and Educational Technology*, **14**, 2, 117-126.

Lewin, R.H. (1983) Industry-education initiatives: the key to th e future. In Trott, A., Strongman, H. and Giddins, L. (eds) *Aspects of Educational Technology XVI*. Kogan Page, London.

Morgan, A. (1983) Theoretical aspects of project based learning in higher education. *British Journal of Education Technology*, **14**, 1, 66-78.

Usher, J.R. and Earl, S.E. (1987) Group modelling and communication. In Berry, J.S., Burghes, D.N., Huntley, I.D., James, D.J.G. and Moscardini, A.O. (eds) *Mathematical Modelling Courses*. Ellis Horwood, Chichester.

28. The effects on understanding of teaching 14-year-old comprehensive pupils about approaches to learning

C F Buckle and G D Cotterill, *Faculty of Education, University of Birmingham, UK*

Summary: This paper describes an experiment which was aimed at increasing the level of understanding of 14-year-old pupils in a city comprehensive school. The introduction of the new examination at 16, the General Certificate of Secondary Education, has placed more stress on the importance of examining in ways which encourage pupils to explore and apply ideas rather than concentrating on the recall of information.

The experiment aimed to bring together two aspects of learning design, one of which has been widely adopted while the other does not appear to have been applied in this way. The contributions of Robert Gagné have had a major influence in the field and his learning hierarchy technique was used. The work of Ference Marton on the approaches which students use when learning from text, although carried out mainly in higher education, provided the basis for the other key aspect of the design of the learning experience. The results showed a significant increase in the level of understanding when these factors were incorporated into the design.

The implications for classroom design are discussed.

THE GCSE

In introducing the new General Certificate of Secondary Education in 1984, the Secretaries of State for England and Wales expressed the hope that the use of national criteria would make a real contribution to the improvement not only of examining but also of teaching and learning processes in schools and colleges.

The examination was intended to be suitable for the great majority of the school population at 16. Differentiated examinations would be used to enable candidates across the ability range to demonstrate their knowledge, abilities and achievements (GCSE National Criteria 1985).

A set of specific criteria, initially covering 20 subject areas, were published at the same time. These were expressed in terms of aims and related assessment objectives. The criteria for science contained ten aims which included: the provision of a worthwhile educational experience for all pupils which will enable them to acquire sufficient understanding and knowledge; to become confident citizens in a technological world; and to recognize the usefulness and limitations of the scientific method and appreciate its applicability in other disciplines in everyday life.

There are 21 assessment objectives which include:
'The skills and abilities to:

- translate information from one form to another;
- extract from available information data relevant to a particular context;

  – use experimental data, recognize patterns in such data, hypothesize and deduce relationships.' (GCSE National Criteria Science 1985)

Objectives such as these clearly require types of learning which are meaningful rather than rote and teaching methods which encourage students to think about the ways in which they learn.

PROMOTING MEANINGFUL LEARNING

Ausubel proposed a useful way of distinguishing between rote and meaningful learning. The distinction was based on the idea of the learner's cognitive structure which he defined as,

'The total content and organization of a given individual's ideas, or the content and organization of his ideas in a particular area of knowledge.' (Ausubel and Robinson, 1971)

The degree to which the new learning is related to the individual's existing cognitive structure determines whether it is rote or meaningful in character. Ausubel's model involved higher order (ie more abstract or general ideas) acting as subsumers for related lower-order ideas and factual information.

It has been the subject of a good deal of research by studies using advanced organizers, the findings of which were not clear cut but revealed the importance of taking into account the effects of the interactions with other factors (Mayer, 1979). His views have, however, had a substantial influence on thinking about teaching and learning in recent years. The need to treat the learner as an individual whose understanding of new materials depends on the extent to which he or she can relate these to his or her prior knowledge, understanding and experiences is now more widely recognized.

Detailed guidance on structuring learning materials was provided by Gagné's work on intellectual skills (Gagné and Briggs, 1974). With topics in science and mathematics his learning hierarchy model has been particularly useful for this purpose. The theoretical basis has been in information processing models of memory (Gagné and White, 1978), and in a further development known as the productive learning hierarchy, White and Mayer (1980) provide a technique for identifying the declarative knowledge associated with the intellectual skills identified in the ordinary learning hierarchy.

When designing learning materials Gagné's work suggests that if the learner's attention is drawn to the relationship between the new intellectual skills and relevant aspects of his or her cognitive structure, the likelihood of learning which is meaningful should be greatly increased.

Another aspect of meaningful learning relates to the way in which the individual studies the learning materials. Marton and Saljo (1976) investigated the approaches adopted by undergraduates studying text. They identified two contrasting approaches, which they regarded as two levels of information processing, deep and surface. In the surface approach the individual was interested in being able to recall information and adopted a rote-learning strategy. Those using the deep approach were concerned with understanding the arguments. The student's approach was shown to be related to the learning outcome. Although the original evidence for these approaches to learning was found in studies using undergraduates, more recent work (eg Biggs, 1985) and the experiment reported here suggest the existence of analogous process in 14-year-olds.

The other factor involved in the present study relates to the use of a meta-cognitive strategy.

'Meta cognition refers to one's knowledge concerning one's own cognitive processes and products or anything related to them, eg the learning-relevant properties of information or data.' (Flavell, 1976)

In the same article Flavell draws attention to the value of studying and encouraging the use of external sources of information rather than placing excessive emphasis on the individual's memory. With the expansion of information technology this is a very important aspect of learning.

Biggs (1985) proposed the term meta learning to refer to students' awareness of their learning intentions and their control over the strategies which they adopt to achieve those. This experiment investigated the extent to which 14-year-old pupils of average ability could modify their approach to the learning of a scientific topic after they had been made aware of the existence and nature of deep and surface approaches to learning. Because these approaches were rather abstract notions care was taken to explain to them in the context of a recent learning experience. A set of learning materials on a topic in mechanics was used for this purpose.

EXPERIMENTAL DESIGN

The experiment involved three sets of learning materials – two on science topics and an explanation of deep and surface approaches to learning. The design is given in Figure 1.

Session 1	Learning materials on mechanics
Session 2	Post test on mechanics
Session 3	Learning materials on deep and surface approaches to learning
Session 4	Initial evaluation of optics materials
Session 5	Learning materials on optics
Session 5 (a)	Students approach questionnaire
Session 6	Post test on optics materials
Session 7	Post test on optics given as retention test (3 weeks later)

Figure 1. *The design of the experiment*

The learners

The learners were third-year pupils, mean age 14.2 years, at a Birmingham Comprehensive School. The mean scores for the group on the AH2 test of intellectual ability were not significantly different from the C band of the National Scores indicating they were of average ability.

They had all studied science in their previous two years at the school. The learning materials and the tests were presented during science lessons on their normal timetable.

The learning materials

Figure 1 shows that there were three sets of learning materials with associated tests.

The first set took the form of worksheets which included information, explanations and directions for practical activities on the topic of Hooke's Law about the relationship between extension and load on a spring. The structure and content of these learning materials were based on the text-books used in the school.

The second set was novel for the pupils. It comprised an explanation of the different approaches to human learning as 'deep' and 'surface'. The former was described as being concerned with thinking about the idea of the principle involved and the ways in which this could be used to explain the observations in the experiment, while the latter involved concentrating on remembering facts and information (eg learning the law by heart).

The third set of materials was carefully designed with objectives based on an analysis of the intellectual skills involved. A learning hierarchy, Figure 2, was derived for this purpose. The lowest levels were treated as prerequisites and checked by initial evaluation. The results from the pupils who lacked these prerequisites are not included in the analysis of the data.

The tests

The post-tests contained more items designed to test understanding than is often the case at this age. Additional questions involving factual recall were also included to make the test appear more familiar and to give the pupils confidence. The scores from these questions were not included in the analysis.

To minimize the effects of learning styles many of the questions required the use of information presented visually. The maximum mark for each of the post-tests was 17.

The other test was designed to categorize the approach which the pupil had adopted when studying the optics materials. It consisted of a seven-item questionnaire, each containing two alternatives, for example:

- I made a special effort to remember the Law of Reflections.
- I used the Law of Reflection to check if I had measured the angle of reflection carefully.
- I used different values for the incident angle to give me more points for my graph.
- I looked at the booklet to see how many readings to take.

The maximum possible deep approach score, therefore, was seven marks.

RESULTS

The Post-tests

The analysis was based on the scores for items which tested understanding.

Table 1 shows that there was a substantial improvement in performance between tests, the scores on the optics test representing a high level of understanding.

The mean score on the deep alternatives to the seven questions on the approach test was 3.77 with a standard deviation 1.36.

The correlation between the deep approach score and the optics post-test score was r=+0.523, which was highly significant at p<0.001.

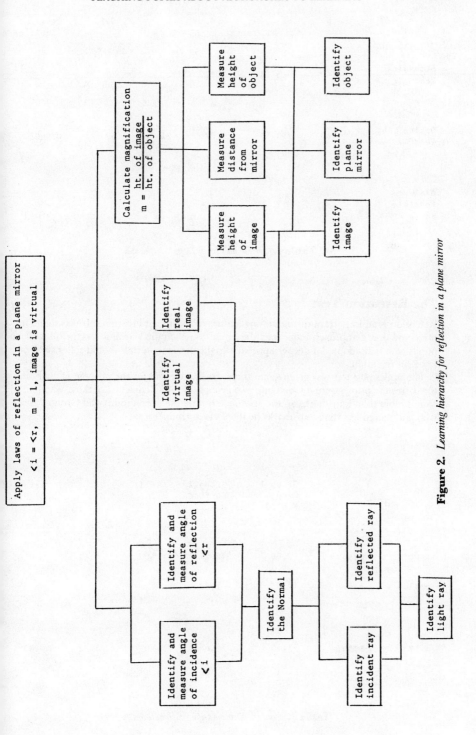

Figure 2. *Learning hierarchy for reflection in a plane mirror*

	N	$\bar{x}$	s.d.	t	d.f.	level of significance
Mechanics Test	60	5.13	1.72			
Optics Test	60	13.50	2.22	22.7	59	0.0005
Maximum Possible Score	-	17	-			

Table 1. *Differences between post-test scores*

The Retention Test

Retention is an important distinguishing feature of meaningful learning. It was therefore predicted that if approach influenced the extent to which the learning was meaningful, the pupils who had adopted a deeper approach to the optics materials should suffer smaller losses on retention.

The optics post-test was given again three weeks later and for the purpose of analysing the scores the pupils were divided into two groups. Group 1 consisted of those who had scored more than four marks on the approach test (ie the deep group) and Group 2 those who had scored less than four marks (ie the surface group).

		Group 1 Deep N = 20	Group 2 Surface N = 22	d.f.	t	level of significance
Loss On	mean	2.00	5.27	40	5.62	0.0005
Retention	s.d.	1.95	1.83			
Ability	mean	71.15	74.64	40	1.72	0.05
AH2	s.d.	6.21	6.88			

Table 2. *Loss on retention, approach and ability*

DISCUSSION

The results indicate that the pupils understood the idea of deep and surface approaches to learning, recognized these in their own studies and it appears that some of them modified their approach between studying the mechanics and the optics materials. Direct evidence on the this point was not obtained in the experiment but the level of performance substantially increased. This result is in line with the findings of Biggs (1985), using public examination results for a sample of over 300 from a similar age group, and Marton and Saljo (1976) with undergraduates.

The high level of performance on the optics post-test (a group mean of 79 per cent with all the questions testing understanding) was, no doubt, partly due to the use of a learning hierarchy in the design of the materials. These materials, however, did not contain formative evaluation items and appropriate remedial work to ensure mastery of each intellectual skill before proceeding to the next one. It therefore seems reasonable to attribute a substantial part of the pupils' performance to the approach which they adopted for the learning task. This assumption is supported by the evidence from the retention test.

The effect of the approach on retention was more important than the effect of ability. In this case the more able sub-group appeared to have been influenced to a greater degree by those aspects of teaching and examining in secondary school which encourage verbatim learning.

It would appear that the effects of deep and surface approaches to learning are factors which the learning designer should take into account. If accuracy of detail on recall is required then a surface approach may be the most appropriate. If understanding transfer and the ability to relate new ideas to the ideas and information already present in the learner's cognitive structure are the intended outcomes, then a deep approach would seem to be essential.

Implications for educational technology

The principles and practice of educational technology have had a substantial influence on educational thinking over the last 30 years. Bloom's taxonomy of cognitive domain objectives, especially the lower levels, has formed the basis of the work by many Examination Boards, thus helping the process of linking course objectives to summative evaluation. This process was taken a step further with the introduction of the GCSE, where the syllabuses contain assessment objectives and grade criteria. The importance of systematic initial and formative evaluation is now recognized.

Educational technology also represents the combination of learning theory with appropriate equipment to provide the opportunities for learning. It is not only the technology which has changed. Behavioural learning theories which were the basis of most of the early work have been developed and balanced by a recognition that the cognitive perspective cannot be ignored. The crucial role of prior knowledge and experience in meaningful learning has been established with learners from a wide age range lending support to Ausubel's arguments about cognitive structure.

Other factors have emerged from research into information processing models of learning including the existence of styles of learning. Entwistle (1981) suggests ways in which these styles are related to memory structures and processes. To accommodate certain styles the learning experiences must be made available with the emphasis on different forms of presentation. Riding and Dyer (1980) and Ridding and Banner (1986), for example, have shown that extraverts prefer verbal material while introverts prefer images. These styles are probably not under the learners' control and may not be susceptible to change so it is advantageous to provide a variety of learning materials to enable the individual to choose those to which they are best suited.

The modern hard-disc microcomputer with its vast storage capacity and fast processing capabilities combined with interactive video and CD-ROM provide the opportunity for materials to be presented in a manner which suits a variety of learning styles (Riding and Buckle, 1987).

The processing and storage power of this technology can also be used to ensure that the structuring of the learning experiences, as well as the modes of presentation, encourage meaningful learning. To this end the learning designer should ensure that a deep approach is not only possible but is facilitated.

REFERENCES

Ausubel, D.P. and Robinson, F.G. (1971) *School Learning*. Holt, Reinhart and Winston, London.
Biggs, J.B. (1985) The role of meta learning in study processes. *British Journal of Educational Psychology*, **55**, 185-212.
Department of Education and Science (1985) *General Certificate in Education: National Criteria, Science Criteria*. HMSO, London.
Entwistle, N. (1981) *Styles of Learning Teaching*. Wiley, Chichester.
Flavell, J.H. (1976) Meta cognitive aspects of problem solving. In Resnick, L.B. (ed) *The Nature of Intelligence*. LEA, New Jersey.
Gagné, R.M. and Briggs, L.J. (1974) *Principles of Instructional Design*. Holt, Rinehart and Winston, New York.
Gagné, R.M. and White, R.T. (1978) Memory structures and learning outcomes. *Review of Educational Research*, **48**, 2, 187-222.
Marton, F. and Saljo, R. (1976) On qualitative differences in learning. *British Journal of Educational Psychology*, **46**, 4-11.
Mayer, R.E. (1979) Twenty years of research on advance organizers. *Instructional Science*, **8**, 133-167.
Riding, R.J. and Banner, G.E. (1986) Sex and personality differences in second language performance in secondary school pupils. *British Journal of Educational Psychology*, **56**, 366-370.
Riding, R.J. and Buckle, C.F. (1987) Computer developments and educational psychology. *Educational Psychology*, **7**, 1, 5-11.
Riding, R.J. and Dyer, V.A. (1980) The relationship between extraverson and verbal-imagery learning style in twelve-year-old children. *Personality and Individual Differences*, **1**, 273-299.
White, R.T. and Mayer, R.E. (1980) Understanding intellectual skills. *Instructional Science*, **9**, 101-127.

29. Introducing problem-based learning into the primary school: a major initiative in Grampian Region

H I C Ellington, E Addinall and B McNaughton, *Robert Gordon's Institute of Technology, Aberdeen, UK*

Summary: This paper describes a unique experiment that took place in Scotland's Grampian Region during 1986-87: an attempt to introduce problem-based science teaching into the primary school curriculum. The project was jointly sponsored by Goodfellow Associates Ltd (a firm of offshore oil consultants), Robert Gordon's Institute of Technology (RGIT: one of Scotland's largest polytechnic higher education establishments) and Grampian Education Authority. It thus represented a major collaboration between industry, tertiary education and the school sector, being carried out as part of the 'Industry Year' programmes of the participating organizations. It involved 21 primary schools, spread throughout Grampian Region, tackling highly demanding projects over the winter of 1986-87 and then displaying their work at a show day held in RGIT in May 1987. The paper describes how the project originated, how it was organized, how it was evaluated, and how it was subsequently used to promote the widespread use of problem-based learning in Grampian schools.

THE ORIGINS OF THE PROJECT

The idea for the project was conceived in 1985, in the course of an after-dinner conversation between one of the authors (Prof McNaughton) and Mr Ron Goodfellow, Managing Director of Goodfellow Associates Ltd, a firm of Offshore and Subsea Technology Consultants. Mr Goodfellow indicated that his organization would like to help education in some way, and, after exploring a number of possibilities, the idea of Goodfellow Associates sponsoring an educational project in Grampian schools, with the help of Robert Gordon's Institute of Technology (RGIT), was developed.

Following lengthy discussions between Goodfellow Associates, RGIT and Grampian Education Authority, it was decided to target the project at primary schools rather than at secondary schools because of the greater scope for curricular innovation in the former. It was also decided to run the project over the spring and summer terms of 1986. Unfortunately, these plans had to be abandoned because of the industrial action that was then taking place in Scottish schools over the teachers' long-standing pay claim. In anticipation of a settlement being reached during the summer, it was decided to take a gamble and make detailed arrangements for running the project over the winter of 1986-87. This work was carried out by a team of RGIT and Grampian Education Department staff led by the Vice Principal of RGIT, Mr Gavin Ross, with Goodfellow Associates being consulted at all stages. Fortunately, the teachers' dispute was settled during the summer, and the project was able to go ahead as planned.

HOW THE PROJECT WAS ORGANIZED

At the end of August 1986, Grampian Education Authority sent a letter to all the primary schools in the Region giving them advance notice of the project. This told them the aim of the project, to encourage a problem-based approach to primary science teaching, and outlined the proposed structure. This would involve class teams of pupils tackling projects involving practical investigation during the winter and spring of 1986-87 as part of their normal curricular work, and then displaying the outcomes at a 'show day' to be held in RGIT during the summer term. A month later, the schools were sent more detailed information together with an application form whereby they could enroll for the project and outline the work they proposed to tackle. In the event, 26 teams from 21 different schools covering all parts of Grampian Region decided to participate.

Stage 1 of the project: the work carried out in the schools

Once the deadline for enrolment in the project (November 15) had passed, each participating team was assigned two advisers, one from RGIT and one from Grampian Region. These had the responsibility of visiting the teams at regular intervals and giving them any advice, help and material or logistical support that they required. On average, each team was visited four times by their two advisers during the following six months. Three people from RGIT were involved in this work (the three authors of this paper) together with six people from Grampian Education Authority (five Primary Advisers and the Schools/Industry Liaison Officer). Each team was also given 5 by Goodfellow Associates in order to help meet any costs involved (buying materials or equipment, carrying out visits etc).

The choice of project was left entirely to the class teacher in charge of each team, and the final list of problems tackled was both impressive and diverse. Some were largely science-based (looking at motion, energy, water purification etc), others were based on some aspect of technology (eg designing bridges, preventing storm damage to cranes or positioning a model oil production platform on the seabed), while others were concerned with human or environmental problems such as designing aids for the handicapped, protecting their school from vandals or building a predator-proof pen for young pheasants. Two of the projects are described in more detail below.

The project tackled by Arduthie Primary School, Stonehaven

Here, a P7 class (age 11-12) investigated the problems that are faced by Third World countries in supplying their people with pure drinking water. This led them to an in-depth study of the various impurities that may be present in untreated water and what can be done to remove them. This work involved a wide range of experiments, including filtration, distillation, carrying out chemical tests and so on (see Figure 1). They also looked at their own local water supply system and made a visit to a water plant, as well as carrying out a wide range of general work on water, the weather, etc.

The Project carried out by Towie Primary School

In this small country school, a mixed class of P5-P7 (age 9-12) looked at how they might meet their local energy needs by exploiting the various natural sources of energy at their disposal. One group concentrated on water power, damming a nearby burn and building a number of water-wheel systems, one of which was used to drive a pebble-polishing device. Another group concentrated on wind power, building several wind generators of different types, including the one shown in Figure 2. The pupils also carried out a wide range of related work, including holding simulated 'Council Meetings' on energy policy and building several models.

Stage 2 of the project: the show day

The second stage of the project involved the different teams preparing exhibits of their

Figure 1. *Pupils at Arduthie Primary School, Stonehaven finding out what impurities are present in different samples of water*

work for display at the 'show day'. Once they had done this, the material that they had produced was collected by staff of Grampian's Teachers' Resources Centre, who then prepared and set up the final exhibits.

The show day took place on May 27 1987, and involved two parallel sets of activities. The first (the actual exhibition) involved part of the team from each participating school manning their exhibit and describing their work to the various visitors and invited guests (see Figure 3).

The other set of activities that took place at the show day consisted of further problem-solving work carried out by the various pupils who were not involved in manning the exhibits. This involved tackling two groups of problems. The first, carried out by the younger pupils, involved building the highest possible towers out of tubes of paper and trying to devise methods of making plasticene models float. The second, carried out by the older pupils, involved devising timing devices capable of controlling scaled-down versions of the different stages of raising a diver's decompression chamber from the seabed to the surface. The timing devices were tested at the end of the show day, with a model decompression chamber constructed by RGIT's School of Mechanical and Offshore Engineering being raised to the roof of the hall during the process. This formed the climax of the day, and, indeed, of the whole project.

HOW THE PROJECT WAS EVALUATED

During the latter stages of the project, a large-scale formal evaluation was planned and administered by the Educational Technology Unit at RGIT. This was based on the use of

Figure 2. *Pupils at Towie Primary School working on one of the wind generators that they built*

four questionnaires, designed to elicit information on virtually all aspects of the project, including its organizational efficiency, educational value, and cost-effectiveness. The first of these four questionnaires (all of which employed a mix of complementary open and closed questions) was issued to all the class teachers who had supervised projects, the second to all participating pupils, the third to the Grampian Education Authority advisers and the fourth to the RGIT advisers. The response rate was very high, with questionnaires being returned by 24 of the 25 teachers who saw the project through to the show day, by virtually all of the participating pupils in their classes (a total of 425), by five of the six Grampian advisers and by all three of the RGIT advisers.

It is impossible to do more than touch upon the most important features of the evaluation here.

The organizational efficiency of the project

Feedback on the project's organizational efficiency was sought mainly from the participating class teachers, who were asked to complete four-point Likert scales rating 12 different organizational aspects of the project from 'completely satisfactory' to 'not at all satisfactory' and back up their responses with open comments.

The responses indicated that there were no serious flaws in the organization, with the 12 different aspects of the organization being rated 'completely satisfactory' by 54 per cent of the 24 respondees and 'reasonably satisfactory' by a further (37 per cent). None of the 12 aspects were rated 'not very satisfactory' or 'not at all satisfactory' by more than six respondees. The responses did, however, identify a number of areas in which the organization could be improved, information that will be extremely useful when future projects are being planned.

Figure 3. *Part of the exhibition mounted at the 'show-day'*

The educational value of the project

Here, the responses were uniformly positive. The class teachers and Grampian Education Authority advisers, for example, gave the 12 stated educational objectives of the project average achievement ratings of 8.3 and 8.0 on a 0-10 scale, the respective ranges for the two groups being 7.2-9.2 and 7.0-9.3. In both cases, the objectives with the highest achievement ratings were 'Encouraging pupils to use imagination, initiative and flexibility' and 'Enhancing pupils' enjoyment'.

The teachers also gave the five main educational aspects of the project an average usefulness rating of 8.5 on a 0-10 scale, with 'Participating in the exhibition at the show day' being given the highest rating (9.3) and 'Preparation of material for the show- day exhibition' the lowest (7.7).

Equally encouraging, no less then 95 per cent of the participating pupils admitted to having learned 'an awful lot' or 'quite a lot' from the project! The quality of work carried out by the pupils was also given extremely high ratings by both the Grampian Region and the RGIT advisers, who were asked to give their professional assessment of its quality. Finally, when asked whether they would like to take part in another project of similar type, the response from both teachers and pupils was overwhelmingly positive, as the following table shows:

The cost-effectiveness of the project

This part of the evaluation was mainly for the benefit of the sponsoring organizations, particularly RGIT and Grampian Region. Goodfellow Associates were already satisfied that they had got everything they wanted from the project and that it had given them

	definitely	probably	undecided	probably not	definitely not
teachers	17	6	1	0	0
pupils	210	138	62	5	5

Table 1. *Responses to possible participation in a future project*

extremely good 'value for money', and had, indeed, already expressed an interest in being involved in further projects of a similar nature. What RGIT and Grampian Region wanted to know was whether the extremely large commitments that they had made to the project in terms of money, staff time, etc, represented a worthwhile use of these limited resources. Here again, the results of the evaluation were extremely positive, with all of the RGIT and Grampian Region staff surveyed believing both that their own commitment to the project could be justified and that their respective organizations had benefited greatly from their involvement. They were also unanimous in wanting to see similar projects run in Grampian Region in future years.

HOW THE SUCCESS OF THE PROJECT WAS EXPLOITED

It was always hoped that the project described above would not only constitute a valuable educational exercise in its own right but would also act as a catalyst for the spread of problem-based science teaching throughout Grampian Region. Following the outstanding success of the show day, it was decided to take a number of steps to help ensure that this happened.

Putting the show-day exhibition on tour

Because the project show day had been an 'invitation only' affair, it was decided to give a much larger number of people an opportunity to see the exhibition by putting it on tour at the start of the 1987 autumn term. During September and October, the exhibition was put on display in three secondary schools (Elgin Academy, Peterhead Academy and Powis Academy, Aberdeen) with children from the schools who had taken part in the project manning the stands. At each venue, the exhibition was visited by pupils and teachers from local primary and secondary schools, parents, local people, local councillors, etc, and in all cases proved a great success. It aroused particular interest among pupils from the lower years of secondary schools and teachers who will be teaching the new Standard Grade science syllabus, which encourages the use of problem-based methods.

Mounting workshops for teachers

In conjunction with the touring exhibition, the Department of Science and Technology of the Northern College of Education mounted a programme of workshops on the organization of problem-based learning. These were designed for promoted teachers, who it was hoped would then promote problem-based learning in their own schools. The workshops were heavily over-subscribed, with over 200 teachers taking part. Indeed, Northern College of Education had to run an additional workshop to cope with the overspill. It later ran a series of follow-up workshops for entire schools. To back-up the workshops, a Teacher's Guide on the organization of problem-based science teaching was produced by Grampian Education Authority and the Northern College; this is now being widely used in schools throughout Grampian Region.

Producing a video for use in staff development

Using the video record of the project that was made by RGIT's Educational Technology Unit, Grampian Education Authority and RGIT have collaborated in the production of a video that will be used for staff development purposes throughout the Region. Copies are being made available to individual schools who are interested in introducing problem-based science teaching into their curricula.

CONCLUSION

From the point of view of the end user, Grampian Education Authority, there is no doubt that the project has been an outstanding success, not only in its own right but also as a vehicle for promoting problem-based science teaching in Grampian schools. Not only has it helped a large number of teachers (especially primary teachers with little or no experience of science teaching) to gain confidence in carrying out this type of work, but it has also provided the Region with a pool of experienced advisers and administrators who can help promote and support further developments in this important area. The authors hope that this paper will help encourage similar developments elsewhere.

ACKNOWLEDGEMENTS

The authors wish to acknowledge the contributions made to the project by all the many people who were involved, both at the planning and at the operational stage.

30. Curing learning skills ailments by diagnosis and open surgery

Andrew Taylor and Phil Race, *The Polytechnic of Wales, Pontypridd, UK*

Summary: Few would doubt that students often do not perform in examinations as well as their teachers would wish. The reasons for this are, to say the least, difficult to pin-point. If there was a single identifiable reason, it is certain that by now it would have been found and a cure effected. There are, of course, a multiplicity of reasons why students do not maximize their performance. Williams (1985) points to the trend of considering a 'matrix of variables' which affect academic performance, and this is a sensible approach. This paper, accordingly, takes just one aspect of studying (study habits) and describes the authors' attempts to establish which students need help and then describes some support measures for those individuals in need.

WHERE DOES IT HURT?

There is no lack of evidence to indicate that students are not maximizing their efficiency when studying.

Gibbs (1981) states that some students are aware that their method of taking notes is ridiculous but that they lack the confidence to change, and so continue in a highly inefficient and unproductive way.

First-year graduate students coming to college from an A level or indeed from a BTec background should, as Wright (1982) holds, reappraise their study techniques because the requirements for study at higher education will, or should be, different from their previous experience.

To conduct such a review often needs help, unfortunately both Wright and Gibbs (1980) make the point that 'learning to learn' workshops are often attended by over-anxious, high achievers with reasonably good study habits. Those in need of support in order to facilitate change are usually less keen to attend.

Ample evidence therefore exists to support the notion that many students would benefit enormously from a reappraisal of their study practices.

DO YOU THINK I NEED AN OPERATION, DOCTOR?

The first-year intake in the Department of Estate Management and Quantity Surveying at the Polytechnic of Wales (approximately 90 students) were asked to complete a questionnaire devised by Taylor (1987). Certain of the questions are intended to be diagnostic in that they are indicative of, but not an infallible pointer to, examination performance at the end of the first year. The questionnaire was administered in early February when a pattern of study is established and while there is still time to initiate change prior to the year-end assessments.

The questionnaire was intended to be partly qualitative and partly quantitative in that not only was the time spent studying felt to be indicative of performance, but also the quality of the time spent was considered to be important.

Table 1 shows a précis of the diagnostic elements of the questionnaire, together with the

REF:	PRÉCIS OF QUESTION	N = 48 EM	N = 40 QS	"AT RISK" RESPONSE
B.4	Review of previous week's study	15	8	"Never"
B.5	Number of days spent studying each week	13	4	$\leqslant 3$ days
B.6	Contentment with present study method	22	10	"not content" and "very discontent"
B.7	Length of most effective study session	2	4	$\geqslant 4$ hours
B.9	Work with other students to pool knowledge	6	2	"Never"
B.10	Free time/leisure activities guilt or enjoyment	7	3	"usually guilty" and "always guilty"
B.11	Facilities at usual place of study	7	5	"poor" and "very poor"
B.12	Optimum or ideal study hours	6	0	$\leqslant 9$ hours
B.13	Study skills course in induction week	23	1	"Didn't attend" and "waste of time"
B.16	Typical study hours each week	20	8	$\leqslant 9$ hours
B.17	Motivation to succeed on chosen course	6	5	"Slightly motivated" and "unmotivated"
B.18	Time management	24	13	"poor" and "very poor"
B.19	Student's responsibility for learning	2	2	"occasionally" and "never"

Table 1. *Diagnostic elements of questionnaire 1987/88*

'at risk' response and the numbers of estate management (EM) and quantity surveying (QS) undergraduates who made the response.

The extent to which the responses to the diagnostic questions were indicative of performance in examinations is reported by Taylor as inevitably variable but when viewed as one indicator in a matrix of others it is a useful predicative tool.

Several studies have been undertaken, Entwistle and Entwistle (1970), McKay (1978) and the Hale Report (1964), which show that total hours per week spent in private study and class contact are typically between 35 and 40. These figures compare less favourably with those found by Taylor in the analysis of the 1986/7 intake of first-year undergraduate quantity surveying and estate management students, who scored a mean of 12.8 and 11.3 hours/week respectively for private study. These figures, when added to the class contact hours/week for the two groups, produce figures of 29.8 for quantity surveying students and 25.8 for estate management students and are significantly less than those reported by several other workers in the field.

The diagnostic question, B16 (see Table 1), asks students to state their typical study hours each week and the arbitrary 'single figure' response of <9 is taken to be an 'at risk' response.

It may well be that the low hours in response to this particular diagnostic question are of more significance as a predictor than a more qualitatively orientated question such as B6, which asks students to state their views on their degree of contentment with their present study methods from a range of very content, content, not content and very discontent

Taken as a whole, the diagnostic questions do form a picture of an individual's study practices from which it is clear that a reappraisal, at least, of current study may be indicated.

An analysis was undertaken to determine the individual students who were in the 'at risk' category on four or more occasions. The results of this analysis showed that 19 estate management and eight quantity surveying students were in the 'four and over' category.

I'M AFRAID IT'S GOT TO BE SURGERY!

The extent to which the reported study practices gave cause for concern varied from those with the minimum four 'at risk' responses to some individuals with as many as ten. However, for the purposes of identification of students with learning problems, no distinction was made as to the severity of the risk.

The 28 students thus identified were invited to attend an initial seminar/workshop at which it was explained to them how they had been identified. Some 68 per cent of the identified students attended the first voluntary session at which the authors took pains to appear non-threatening and supportive.

Anecdotally, many students showed little surprise that they had been selected and several seemed relieved that support measures aimed at change had been instigated.

PREPARING FOR SURGERY: THE PRE-MED

Although most students were not surprised to have been diagnosed to be 'at risk', it became apparent that their predicament had sharpened their minds regarding improving their positions.

We gave them the opportunity once again to respond to the questionnaire items which had been used to diagnose their weaknesses. This time, however, we immediately put them into groups and charged each group with deciding what would be a good answer to each of the selected questionnaire items. This allowed each student to see where their personal answer fell short of a desirable answer. It also allowed members of the group to sympathize with each other and share their perceptions of the difficulties they faced in matching their study performance with their own suggestions regarding desirable practice.

Why bother to seek a cure?

The students were asked, 'Why are you a student, what's in it for you?' Their responses were discussed in terms of their career expectations and also their expectations of the Polytechnic. It became apparent (not to our surprise) that many of the students had not adjusted their expectations since schooldays. They still expected to be 'taught'. They expected to be prodded and coaxed. They expected pressure to be applied to them. They expected lots of assessment and feedback well before any formal examination of their performance.

We explained to the group that in higher education, students were expected to be much more responsible for their own learning strategies and standards. Yes, they would indeed be examined in due course, but part of the purpose of such examination was to determine to what extent they were each successful in taking responsibility for managing their own performance as learners, not just in terms of the amount of subject material they had memorized.

How to make things better?

The students were then asked to brainstorm (on acetate slips) completions of the statement: 'Things would be much better if only I .....' Some typical completions are listed below:

- '.. wasn't so lazy.'
- '.. got out of bed in the mornings.'
- '.. organized myself better.'
- '.. disciplined myself.'
- '.. watched less TV.'
- '.. got into a routine.'
- '.. wasn't so easily distracted.'
- '.. arranged my time better.'
- '.. didn't have a TV.'
- '.. did more studying.'
- '.. managed the work better.'
- '.. found the subject more interesting.'
- '.. had more set work.'
- '.. didn't have a pub nearby.'
- '.. had more will-power.'
- '.. had more intense concentration.'
- '.. was more motivated.'
- '.. wasn't such a lazy fathead!'
- '.. didn't find lectures so boring (not Andy Taylor's).'
- '.. bothered to work.'
- '.. was not distracted.'
- '.. had more books.'
- '.. had regular sleeping patterns.'
- '.. didn't leave it till the last minute.'
- '.. didn't play so much sport.'

From these completions, it is clear that most students know more or less what they need to do to improve things! The problem remains to get them to do something actively about such problems.

Feedback Questionnaire

"Improve Your Study Skills" Series

Please complete and return to Dr. Phil Race, Room
Polytechnic of Wales, Pontypridd, CF37 1DL.

Please answer these questions honestly: your answers will he
improve these self-study modules on Study Skills aspects.

---

1.   Please write the Title of the module you're giv
comments on:

. . . .

---

2.   Please circle the words below which you think descri
the style of the material.

informal	formal	chatty	interesti
boring	stimulating	patronising	motivating
readable	longwinded	irritating	pleasant

---

3.   How did you use the Self-Analysis Questions (honestly
Please tick one of the options below.

    * I had a go (in writing) at each SAQ then I consult
      the Response.

    * I skipped the SAQs!

    * I **thought about** the SAQs then looked at the response

---

4.   How useful did you find the Responses to the SAQs?

    very useful   quite useful   not useful

---

5.   Was the material suitable for you to work through it
your own time, at your own pace?

    Yes   Mostly   No

Figure 1. *Example of a feedback questionnaire*

6.   Please list below the most useful parts of the material you used:

*

*

*

7.   Please list below the parts you found least useful:

*

*

*

8.   Please explain how the material helped you most:

The material helped me personally as follows:

9.   I am developing several other similar modules covering various aspects of study-skills development. Please list any topic you would like included in the series:

*

*

*

10.   Please indicate whether you would like me to supply you with other modules in this series in return for further feedback comments:

        Yes   Maybe   No

11.   Any other comments, reactions, criticisms:

Name (please print)....................................

Department...............Course...........Date..........

OPEN SURGERY

Two open-learning modules, Race (1988), were issued to the students to allow them to tackle some of the issues they had raised. The open-learning materials allow each student to explore in privacy ways of actively tackling some of the problems they had identified. One of the advantages is that the students can use them several times if necessary.

Each module has short lists of objectives (the things the user should be better able to do after completing the module). Each module has also some self-assessment questions. Each of these asks the user to pick an option, make a decision or make a plan. Each of the self-analysis questions is backed by a response so that the student can compare what they did with suggestions and advice from the author.

The first module 'Organizing your studies' is about getting down to structured work, taking on the responsibility involved and balancing the amount of time and effort devoted to various kinds of work (in the light of the relative value of different kinds of work regarding preparing for formal assessment).

The second module contains three separate (but related) sections, 'Active reading', 'Getting started' (particularly concerned with getting started on essay-type answers, both for coursework and exams), and 'Writing essays' (concerned with the structure of essays).

Each student was provided with a feedback questionnaire for each module (see Figure 1). The purpose of this questionnaire is not only to gain feedback about the effectiveness of the modules, but also to cause each student to reflect on the things they have gained from the modules.

POST OPEN-SURGERY RECOVERY

The feedback gathered at the time of writing is not sufficient to treat statistically. We will also need to compare feedback with actual exam performance in due course. However, typical responses to Question 8 on the questionnaire are encouraging, and are listed below.

The material helped me personally as follows:

- by suggesting new approaches to studying not based on long periods at routine times.
- by showing me where I could improve and where I had been going wrong in the past.
- by forcing me into reassessing my attitude towards work.
- I actually wrote down what was wrong and did some self analysis.
- by bringing to light various points which had not occurred to me.
- by focusing my attention on a newly developed idea of essay-writing and readability.
- by helping me differentiate between WORK and work (ie important work versus routine work).
- by using up regular small spaces of time, eg, on train.
- in planning.

Most of the small sample analysed, reported that the SAQ responses had been very useful or quite useful. All reported that the material was suitable for them to work through in their own time at their own pace.

CONCLUSIONS

We believe that it is very useful for 'at risk' students to be identified, even if the diagnosis causes them some discomfort. A cure for study-skills weaknesses has to come from within each student, but the use of open-learning study-skills development materials can facilitate the processes of students exploring strategies which will help overcome the problems. The advantage of the open-learning pathway is that students suffering learning 'pains' have the comfort of privacy while they reflect and adjust their learning strategies.

REFERENCES

Entwistle, N.J. and Entwistle, D. (1970) The relationships between personality, study methods and academic performance. *British Journal of Educational Psychology*, **41,** 132-141.

Gibbs, G. (1980) Can students be taught how to study. *Higher Education Bulletin*, **5,** 2, 107-108.

Gibbs, G. (1981) *Teaching Students to Learn: A Student-centred Approach.* Open University Press, Milton Keynes.

Hale Report (University Grants Committee) (1964) *Committee on University Teaching Methods.* HMSO, London.

McKay, R. (1978) Effectiveness of learning: the place of study. In Piper, D.W. (ed) *The Efficiency and Effectiveness of Teaching in Higher Education.* University of London teaching Methods Unit, Cavendish Press, Leicester.

Race, P. (1988) *Improve Your Study Skills Modules.* CICED Series 3, Central Institutions Committee for Educational Development, Dundee.

Taylor, A.P. (1987) An investigation into the study habits and learning styles of first-year undergraduates in the department of Estate Management and Quantity Surveying at the Polytechnic of Wales. Unpublished MEd dissertation, University College, Cardiff.

Williams, E. (1985) An examination of study habits and learning strategies in polytechnic students. Unpublished thesis, CNAA.

Wright, J. (1982) *Learning to Learn in Higher Education.* Croom Helm, London.

31. Strategies for effective listening: a CBT-centred approach

M D Vinegrad, *Goldsmiths College, London, UK*

Summary: Listening is a core communication skill yet it tends to receive little attention in the training literature. Part of the reason may be that people are apt to take listening for granted. After all, everyone knows how to listen. A considerable body of evidence, however, suggests that listening is a complex skill, or rather band of skills, many of which can be improved by training.

FREQUENCY OF LISTENING

Compared to other forms of communication, listening may be more important than is realized. A number of studies have looked at the degree to which we use listening, speaking, reading and writing. Although the studies have spanned a period of years from 1929 onwards and have involved different groups of individuals, the results have been surprisingly consistent. A representative set of results for a 'typical working day' might be:

- listening 45 per cent
- speaking 30 per cent
- reading 16 per cent
- writing 9 per cent

While results necessarily vary according to the nature of people's work, listening emerges as the leading communication channel. Although listening may be the most used, it is almost certainly the least taught of communication skills.

In recent years interest in listening as a teachable skill has increased. Two leading American companies, Sperry Corporation and Xerox, have introduced listening courses as an element of staff development (Steil et al, 1983). In these, considerable emphasis is placed upon the importance of listening in the work situation. In this country the current 1988 BACIE brochure on Training Courses and Workshops lists a few similar developments.

Steil et al have described three main foci for training:

- understanding the nature of the listening process;
- assessing listening habits and abilities; and
- improving component skills.

UNDERSTANDING THE NATURE OF THE LISTENING PROCESS

The literature on listening strongly reflects the influence of Nichols, a pioneer worker in the field. Beginning with a doctoral study in 1948 and extending through a series of articles and books, Nichols explored the dos and don'ts of effective listening. In one form or another the type of rules listed by Nichols have become almost the stock in trade of writers on listening (for example Nichols and Lewis, 1954; Nichols and Stevens, 1957; Wolff et al, 1983). The following list of listening problems based on Barker (1971) provides an example of this approach:

- viewing a topic as uninteresting;
- criticising a speaker's delivery instead of the message;
- getting overstimulated or emotionally involved;
- listening only for facts and neglecting ideas;
- preparing to answer questions or points before having heard the speaker out;
- wasting the advantages of the speed of thought over the speed at which the message can be delivered (ie you can think faster than someone can speak);
- trying to outline everything;
- tolerating or failing to adjust to distractions;
- pretending to attend to someone who is speaking;
- listening only when something is easy to understand;
- allowing emotionally laden words to interfere with listening; and
- allowing personal prejudices and convictions to interfere with attention and comprehension.

Types of listening

Another approach to understanding the listening process consists of differentiating between different types and levels of listening activity. Among levels that can be distinguished are:

- *Serious listening:* this is close to the classroom or lecture situation. The primary purpose is to pick out and encapsulate salient points.
- *Critical listening:* the listener attempts to analyse the message in some way. This may be to pick out factual statements and to differentiate these from opinions or to be on the alert for bias, propaganda or advertising.
- *Courteous listening:* this occurs in a variety of settings. For example, listening to someone's troubles, serving as a sounding board for someone's ideas or listening simply because the social relationship requires it. Closely related to this is listening to give encouragement or support (eg an adult listening to a child). Since listening is a way of paying attention to people, not listening can be disparaging and discouraging.
- *Conversational listening:* good conversationalists are usually good listeners. Conversational listening probably involves elements of most types of listening.

One can of course only loosely differentiate between types of listening. There is considerable overlap between the above categories. Also, while listening in one mode, one may suddenly become alert to the significance of what is being said and so switch to another type or level of listening.

Listening as a perceptual process

Another approach to understanding the nature of listening is to consider the process itself. Listening is like any perceptual process in that it is highly selective. We perceive what we expect to perceive and remember what fits in with our prevailing interests and ideas.

The nature of the listening process has been summarized by Steil et al (1983) in the form of a four-stage listening model. This is termed SIER (sensing, interpreting, evaluating, responding). Among other things the model is intended to emphasize the difference between listening and hearing. Hearing may be largely passive, 'words go into one ear and out the other'. Listening, on the other hand, implies an active process. When we listen we do more than passively register a stream of words, we react, interpret, think about and store ideas for future recall.

I will return to this model a little later when discussing methods of listening training.

ASSESSING LISTENING HABITS AND ABILITIES

A second major training objective consists of getting people to think about their own listening habits. There are a number of standardized tests of listening but these are probably of limited value. This is because there is no evidence that the tests are actually measuring anything beyond general factors of intelligence and memory.

Informal inventories and questionnaires provide a more direct approach. Here participants are asked to rate themselves and other people on a variety of scales. Steil et al provide one such example. Once again I will return to this topic shortly under the section on listening training.

IMPROVEMENT OF COMPONENT SKILLS

The third main focus for training involves the improvement of component skills.

While training courses are becoming more available they are probably still the exception rather than the rule. Because of this the design of self-instructional materials would appear desirable both as a means of filling a gap and as a potential stimulant to further development. CBT and related methods would seem an appropriate approach. Interactive video and interactive audio clearly have much to offer in a field of this type.

I would like to discuss two applications which I have been exploring in what I have termed a 'CBT-centred approach'.

Listening to discussion groups

The first of these applications is designed to focus the attention of the learner upon listening as a perceptual process. The listening situation is that of the 'discussion group'.

There are, of course, many forms of discussion group, for example committees, boards of directors, management worker panels, tutorial groups and so on. Being a participant in such a group involves both listening and speaking. What I want to discuss is one approach to how one might become a more effective listener in such a situation.

How individuals interact in face-to-face discussion groups has been intensively studied from a number of points of view. Among these is the work of Bales (1970) who devised a set of categories for recording and rating what goes on in groups. I have tried, experimentally, to adapt this method for the purpose of listening training. (I should hasten to add that Bales was interested in studying social structure not listening training.)

The scheme devised by Bales was essentially as shown in Figure 1.

The categories are intended to be exhaustive in the sense that everything that is said (or done) can be fitted into one of the slots. To use the scales an observer or group member ticks appropriate categories as interactions occur. One of the simplest ways of keeping track is by assigning code letters to the categories and keeping a record of these along with individual identities. To use the scales a little preliminary training is usually necessary. Before pursuing this, however, one might ask how engaging in such categorizing activity might contribute towards listening training.

Using the categories clearly entails listening in a rather special way. The scheme forces one to attend to the structure or pattern of communication within the group. In this way it imposes a kind of cognitive framework upon the listener. When making the ratings one is doing something more than just attending to the content of what is being said, one is also attending to a higher-order structural variable.

However, as soon as one starts to use the scheme it becomes obvious that it can be quite difficult to decide upon the categories. What people say doesn't fit neatly into just one slot.

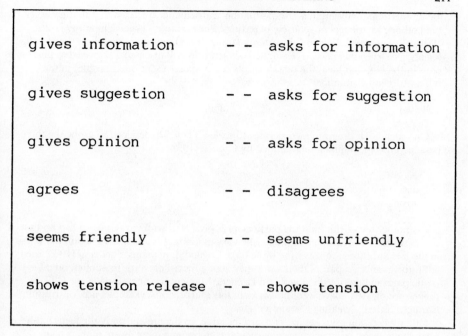

gives information	– –	asks for information
gives suggestion	– –	asks for suggestion
gives opinion	– –	asks for opinion
agrees	– –	disagrees
seems friendly	– –	seems unfriendly
shows tension release	– –	shows tension

Figure 1. *Bales' rating categories*

The rater must interpret and evaluate in order to make the decisions. It is for this reason that I believe the procedure has potential for listening training. All listening involves interpretation and evaluation. Although the Bales scales are limited in scope they can nonetheless be useful for explicitly focusing attention upon the interpretative and evaluative nature of the listening process. Most people agree that the exercise provides a new and interesting listening experience.

A CBT-centred approach

The experience of using the scales can be particularly productive when two or more people discuss and compare their ratings. A 'CBT-centred approach' is one such method. A BBC microcomputer is linked to a Tandberg TCCR programmable tape recorder. The audio track contains some form of group discussion while the computer is programmed to provide synchronized exercises involving the rating scales. A number of arrangements are possible. For example, as the tape plays, ratings are displayed on the screen. The computer may be programmed to provide a choice of such ratings (different 'observers'). These may be displayed either separately or simultaneously. One advantage of using the Tandberg TCCR is that it allows a student to skip back and forth through the tape thus facilitating study of the material. In addition, a student may also input their own ratings and these may be stored for comparison with the computer's and those of other students.

The method is 'CBT-centred' in so far as it is intended to serve as a stimulus for discussion in a group setting.

Self appraisal scales

As mentioned earlier, self-appraisal of listening abilities has been defined as a training goal.

I would like to describe briefly how CBT may also be applied in this area as a technique for stimulating discussion in a group situation. Participants are asked to rate themselves (and others) as listeners in a variety of settings. For example, 'When I'm at my best', 'When I'm at work', 'When I'm with my family' etc. One technique utilizes the so-called semantic differential scale. An example is shown below. Participants are asked to place a cross in the box that gives the best description of themselves (or other people) in the relevant listening situation:

Biased   Fair

One such CBT program incorporates 13 scales. These are designed to probe the three basic psychological dimensions defined by Osgood (1952):

- good-bad;
- active-passive; and
- strong-weak.

In another test of this kind the participant is presented with various word lists and asked to choose those words which best describe various kinds of listener. Once again the words in the lists are chosen to cover the three basic Osgood dimensions. Steil et al (1983) used self-rating scales. As part of their work they kept a record of words most often used by participants to describe good and bad listeners. Many of the items used in the CBT program indicated above were drawn from this source. Some examples are 'distrustful', 'caring', 'listless', 'yielding', 'attentive' etc.

Other self-rating exercises are of course possible. In the present study the focus has been upon scales designed to encourage participants to become more aware of their own listening habits and of the qualities of good and poor listeners.

LISTENING TRAINING AND THE ROLE OF CBT

In this brief paper I have attempted to indicate some of the ways in which listening training may be approached. Listening is a broad subject and I have done no more than scratch the surface of one or two aspects. I have tried to suggest that CBT may have a role as a stimulant for discussion and interaction in a workshop setting. This does not of course preclude the use of CBT for self-instruction on an individual basis. In a field where courses are not common there would seem to be considerable potential for such development using modern techniques of interactive audio and video.

REFERENCES

Bales, R.F. (1970) *Personality and Interpersonal Behaviour*. Holt, Rinehart and Winston Inc, New York.
Barker, L.L. (1971) *Listening Behaviour*. Prentice-Hall, Englewood Cliffs.
Nichols, R. (1948) Factors accounting for differences in comprehension of materials presented orally in the classroom. Unpublished doctoral dissertation, State University of Iowa, Iowa City.
Nichols, R. and Lewis, T. (1954) *Listening and Speaking*. William C.Brown, Dubuque, Iowa.
Nichols, R. and Stevens, L. (1957) *Are You Listening?* McGraw Hill, New York.
Osgood, C.E. (1952) The nature and measurement of meaning. *Psychological Bulletin*, **49,** 197-237.
Steil, L.K., Summerfield, J. and de Mare, G. (1983) *Listening: It Can Change Your Life*. John Wiley & Sons.
Wolff, F.I., Marsnik, N.C., Tacey, W.B. and Nichols, R.G. (1983) *Perceptive Listening*. Holt, Rinehart & Winston Inc, New York.

32. Peer tutoring in higher education: an experiment

Nancy Falchikov, *Napier College, Edinburgh, UK*
and Carol Fitz-Gibbon, *University of Newcastle Upon Tyne, UK*

Summary: What are the consequences of assigning students to tutor other students? Is this use of peer tutoring effective and justifiable in higher education? These questions were explored by a controlled field experiment. Students were randomly assigned to be tutors, tutees or to study alone. The effects on achievement and attitudes were assessed and compared with those from the far more extensive body of literature on peer tutoring among school-age pupils.

INTRODUCTION

In learning-by-tutoring projects, a major aim is that the tutors will learn the work that they are tutoring. If, by tutoring, they learn work at least as well as they would by alternative activities, such as independent study, then this justifies using tutoring as a teaching technique (ie it justifies assigning students to act as tutors rather than asking for volunteers). Tutoring becomes a method of instruction selected by the lecturer or teacher as an appropriate method. But what is the empirical evidence: do tutors learn at least as well from being tutors as from other activities? There is, of course, valuable experiential learning associated with taking on the role of a tutor: learning about communicating, organizing material, interpersonal skills and reflection on the subject (Goodlad, 1979). But do tutors also learn the instructional topic? Obviously they are supposed to 'learn' it enough to teach it, but do they in consequence learn it as well as or even better than by spending the same time in independent study?

Answers to such empirical questions require controlled field experiments, preferably 'true' experiments, in which randomly equivalent groups are assigned to the different methods of learning. (The term 'true experiment' derives from the noted text by Campbell and Stanley, 1966.)

Such experiments have been conducted in large numbers with school populations. Some evidence, and considerable amounts of analysis and valuable speculation, were collected in *Children as Teachers* (Allen, 1976). Since then, the advent of meta analysis (introduced by Glass, McGaw and Smith, 1981) as a technique for research synthesis, has provided an ideal method for summarizing the growing body of data on peer tutoring. Cohen, Kulik and Kulik (1982) provided a meta analysis on the educational outcomes, synthesizing data from 65 experiments on tutoring. These experiments were all concerned with school populations, however, and generalization to the college level can neither be assumed nor ruled out. It is worth noting that tutoring programs were considered, overall, to be an effective means of raising achievement for both tutors and tutees.

Meta analyses are useful in providing evidence of the size of the effects which one might expect to find. Effects of different 'treatments' are usually reported as an effect size which is a standardized mean difference (ie effect size = the treatment group mean minus the control group mean/the pooled standard deviation). For example, if the effect size were 1.00 this would indicate that the treatment group's mean score was a standard deviation higher than that of the control group. Such an effect size is large, and those found in practice are generally much smaller that 1.00. The work of Cohen, Kulik and Kulik (1982) indicated that projects involving tutoring in mathematics had an average effect size of about 0.60, whereas effect sizes were considerably smaller when reading was the area tutored: 0.29 for tutees and 0.21 for tutors.

The use of peer tutoring in higher education described here involved a topic which was more verbal than mathematical, and it may be that the effect sizes to be expected would be closer to those for reading than for mathematics.

Another aspect of the project described is that the tutors and tutees were of about the same age (ie the project was same-age rather than cross-age peer tutoring). In the analyses conducted by Cohen, Kulik and Kulik, effect sizes were 0.29 for the same-age and 0.35 for cross-age among tutees. A similar difference pertained for tutors: 0.28 and 0.35 for same-age and cross-age respectively. In a sense, the project to be described started with two counts against it: use of a verbal topic and use of same-age rather than cross-age tutoring.

There is other evidence for the lesser effectiveness of same-age tutoring. Posen (1983) working with young offenders, found that while tutors were happy with their role, tutees expressed many reservations and in some cases hostility: 'Why should he be a tutor?' Fitz-Gibbon (1980) reporting five projects, of which two were same-age projects, noted that 'cross-age tutoring is more promising than same-age tutoring'. In same-age tutoring, as many as 50 per cent of the tutors appeared to teachers not to have taken on the tutoring role properly and, as in the Posen study, there was some dissatisfaction from tutees who did not like their assigned role. Furthermore, pupils who had been assigned to independent study, scored significantly higher on the post-test than either tutors or tutees, a finding out-of-line with the vast majority of studies of cross-age tutoring.

However, college students can be expected to be more mature than school pupils and they have chosen to be at college. Their motivational characteristics can be expected to differ from those of school pupils and perhaps same-age tutoring can work with these students even though it has not appeared promising in school pupils.

METHOD

First-year students studying psychology as part of a four-year degree in catering and accommodation studies at Napier College, Edinburgh, acted as tutors, tutees or independent study students. Students were randomly allocated to the three groups.

In November, a video film of a lecture on alcohol and alcoholism given by an experienced lecturer was viewed by members of the tutor and independent study groups. At a mutually convenient time, tutors then gave a one-to-one tutorial to their tutees. After finishing the exercise, all participants completed a feedback questionnaire in which questions relating to the scheme in general were answered. A short test was administered three weeks after the tutoring had taken place. The test comprised two kinds of items: multiple-choice items requiring simple recognition, and short essay questions which required higher-level cognitive skills.

BEST-LIKED FEATURES OF THE SCHEME

Students were asked 'What did you like best about this scheme?'

For the *tutor* group, nearly half the comments made fell into the 'personal and study skills' category, with 'one-to-one relation benefits' being the second most frequently mentioned feature.

For the *tutee* and *independent study* groups, however, 'flexibility' was the most frequently mentioned best-liked feature of the scheme. In common with the tutor group, the tutee group also appeared to like the 'one-to-one relation benefits'. The independence afforded the independent study group was second most frequently cited best-liked feature of the scheme.

LEAST-LIKED FEATURE OF THE SCHEME

As with best-liked features, least-liked feature ratings differed according to group. The *tutor* group listed 'time' as the least- desirable feature. This finding was in accord with responses to a subsequent item on the questionnaire concerning the amount of time they spent on the topic. For tutors, this was between two and three hours, whereas the tutees and the independent study groups reported between one and two hours on average.

For the *tutee* group 'lack of confidence in partner' was the least- liked feature, echoing some of the problems reported in the literature. The tutees' lack of confidence in their partner was echoed by a degree of lack of self-confidence in the tutor group.

For the *independent study* group 'lack of contact' was the least- liked feature. Learning is a sociable experience and arrangements which do not provide a social dimension appear to suffer negative attitudes and a high drop-out rate (see for example Robin, 1976).

SEMANTIC DIFFERENTIAL MEASURES

In a manner similar to that employed in semantic differential measures (as developed by Osgood, Suci and Tannenbaum, 1957), students were asked to respond to a series of a bipolar adjectives following the statement: 'The scheme of tutoring/being tutored by a peer/studying independently makes you . . .'. They responded according to the method of studying to which they had been assigned.

While the overall pattern of responses suggested that all groups perceived the scheme to be beneficial, there were marked differences in emphasis according to group membership. To a greater extent than for any other group, the tutor group perceived that the scheme made them think more, learn more, and become more critical, structured and confident.

Those assigned to the independent study group, not surprisingly perceived the scheme to confer the quality of independence.

Both responses to another set of bipolar adjectives following the statement: 'The scheme of tutoring/being tutored by a peer/studying independently is . . .' also showed differences according to the groups. Both tutor and tutee groups rated the scheme as time-consuming yet they found it enjoyable and challenging. The independent study group also rated the scheme as challenging, but differed from the other two groups in perceiving it to be time-saving. However, this group appeared to enjoy the experience to a lesser extent than their peers.

TEST RESULTS

As already noted, there were two types of items used in the post-test. There were ten multiple-choice and two short essay questions. In addition to these locally constructed measures, there was some indication of ability by reference to the grades obtained on Highers prior to entry to the course. A scale for Highers was constructed by counting 20 points for a grade A, 15 points for a B and 10 points for a C.

The immediate post-test

Approximately 84 per cent of the class attended the post-test which took place during normal lesson time, this total being made up of 100 per cent of the tutor group, 84.6 per cent of the independent study group, and only 62 per cent of the tutee group. The unfortunate attrition in the tutee group made their performance difficult to interpret.

The tutor group had the highest scores on both parts of the post-test. Its performance was superior to that of the other two groups.

Using Highers as a covariate, the overall F-test for the three group means was $F(2,32) = 0.75$ (p=0.47). One way to interpret this finding would be to note that all students, no matter to what group they were assigned, achieved about what would be expected on the basis of knowledge of their academic ability as indicated by Highers. If that interpretation is accepted, then the decision as to which method of instruction to use would rest on considerations other than cognitive achievement. The finding that 62 per cent of tutors and tutees reported the scheme as 'enjoyable' as opposed to only 38 per cent of the independent study group, would thus be a good reason for using peer tutoring.

However, lack of statistically significant differences at the 0.05 level should not deter us from examining the pattern in the data (as well argued by Carver, 1978) and, in particular, it is of interest to look at effect sizes for the purpose of comparing the present results with others in the literature. One-way analyses of variance were conducted on the scores of the 16 tutors, 10 tutees and 10 independent study persons for whom there was a score on Highers and on the post-test.

Regarding the independent study group as the control group and using the square root of MSwithin (mean square within) to give the standard deviation, the tutor group's effect size on Highers was -0.05, that is the tutor group mean was very slightly lower than the independent study group mean. At post-test, the effect size was, however, 0.34 showing that tutors had, on average, learned more than the independent study group. The figure of 0.34 is rather better than the effect sizes of about 0.20 expected on the basis of the Cohen, Kulik and Kulik analyses discussed earlier.

The tutees as a group had a lower mean score on Highers than the independent study group, with an effect size of -0.89. Thus they were apparently a less-able group to begin with. On the post-test the effect size for tutees was -0.37, indicating that the gap between them and the control group had closed quite considerably. However, it is difficult to interpret this finding given the high absenteeism in the tutee group.

Previous work has suggested that well-structured work lends itself better to peer tutoring than more discursive or open-minded topics (cf Fitz-Gibbon, 1980). If we examine only the multiple-choice scores, we find that both the tutors and the tutees out-performed the independent study group, with effect sizes of 0.70 for tutors and 0.36 for tutees. The overall F-test for the multiple-choice scores using an analysis of covariance (with Highers as the covariate) was $F(2,32) = 1.82$ (p=0.17). Thus, as one might expect with such small numbers, the conventional level of 0.05 for 'statistical significance' was not achieved. However, the effect sizes were far from trivial and in line with the positive effects often reported in the literature.

Other evidence of the effects of tutoring

As noted above, there was some expectation that having to teach a subject would lead to a better understanding of it. Knowing something really well after teaching it is a frequently remarked-upon experience. In response to the statement 'My grasp of this subject now is: . .', none of the tutors chose the response 'poor' or worse, and half chose 'good' or 'very good'. The differences between mean the responses on this item from the tutor, tutee and study-alone groups were statistically significant at the 0.02 level: $F(2,33) = 4.53$. This finding was also consistent with their report that being a tutor made them think more.

Thus there were strong indications that the phenomenon of learning-by-tutoring had been experienced by the tutors. These self-report measures were considered important findings both because the short cognitive tests could not be sensitive to all the learning which had occurred and because the subjective experience of the learner is important, especially when it is consistent with the test data, as it is here.

One source of the better learning might have been that the tutors reported having spent more time on the project but this was, in itself, an indication of the motivational impact of being assigned to tutor.

SUMMARY AND DISCUSSION

A same-age tutoring project was implemented as a true experiment with three randomly assigned groups: tutors, tutees and (as a 'control' group) independent study. The findings supported to some extent the warning signals in the literature with regard to the negative impact of being assigned a tutee role, although interpretation was not clear due to attrition in this group.

The findings for tutors were in the line with the positive effects generally noted in the school population literature for cross-age as opposed to same-age tutoring. Possibly the greater maturity of the college students in this same-age project led them to take the tutoring role seriously. Indeed, they reported spending more time than other groups in preparation, deriving benefits in the realm of personal skills and study skills, being made to think more and feeling they had a better grasp of the material. They had the highest average scores on post-tests.

Clearly many more experiments are needed with college-age students to elucidate further the way in which peer tutoring produces its fairly consistently found benefits for tutors, and ways in which the experience can be as beneficial for the tutees. Changes of role or the use of cross-age designs in college populations will be needed.

REFERENCES

Allen, V. (ed) (1976) *Children as Teachers: Theory and Research on Tutoring*. Academic Press, New York.

Campbell, D.T. and Stanley, J.C. (1966) *Experimental and Quasi-experimental Designs for Research*. Rand McNally, Chicago.

Carver, R.P. (1978) The case against statistical significance testing. *Harvard Educational Review*, **48**, 3, 378-399.

Cohen, P.A., Kulik, J.A. and Kulik, C.L. (1982) Educational outcomes of tutoring: a meta-analysis of findings, *American Educational Research Journal*, **19**, 2, 237-248.

Fitz-Gibbon, C.T. (1978) *Setting-up and Evaluating Tutoring Projects*. Centre for the Study of Evaluation, Los Angeles. (Available from the Education Library, University of Newcastle.)

Fitz-Gibbon, C.T. (1980) *Measuring Time-use and Evaluating Peer Tutoring in Urban Secondary Schools*. Final Report for the Social Science Research Council.

Glass, G.V. McGaw, B. and Smith, M.L. (1981) *Meta-analysis in Social Research*. Sage Publications, Beverly Hills.

Goodlad, S. (1979) *Learning by Teaching: An Introduction to Tutoring*. Community Service Volunteers.

Karweit, N. (1985) Should we lengthen the school term? *Educational Researcher*, **14**, 6, 9-14.

Osgood, C.E., Suci, G.J. and Tannenbaum, P.H. (1957) *The Measurement of Meaning*. University of Illinois, Urbana.

Posen, B. (1983) Peer tutoring among young offenders: two experiments. MEd Thesis, University of Newcastle Upon Tyne.

Robin, A.L. (1976) Behavioural instruction in the college classroom. *Review of Educational Research*, **46**, 3, 313-354.

33. Self and peer assessment and the negotiated curriculum: experience on the District Nurse Practical Work Teachers' Certificate Course

Stephen M Cox, *Coventry Polytechnic, Coventry, UK*

Summary: This paper describes the design and operation of a course for experienced, mature district nurses who wish to become qualified to supervise district nurse students on their practical work placements. Because of the nature of the course members, the changing national scene in nurse training and education, and the applied nature of the course itself, the course team decided to abandon many of the elements of a normal course. Instead they substituted self and peer assessment, groupwork and group problem-solving exercises, and elements of negotiation of the curriculum. The course was evaluated at interim and final stages, using Likert scale questionnaires based on course members' own perceptions.

BACKGROUND

A variety of changing circumstances at national level indicate that, particularly on vocational courses such as this one, a new approach to the processes of curriculum design and operation is appropriate. Specifically, the proposals contained in documents such as 'Project 2000', (UKCC, 1986), 'Transferable Skills in Higher Education' (NAB, 1986), and various statements on education for capability from Professor Charles Handy and the Royal Society of Arts, make it clear that traditional approaches to producing traditional students and graduates are no longer appropriate. Moreover, those in the vanguard of advocating changes in the ways in which we help our students to learn (Gibbs, 1981; Boud, 1986; and Ramsden, 1985), emphasize that the importance of students' involvement in the choice of what and how they study is an important factor in their success and satisfaction. (For a more detailed treatment of this matter, see Cox, 1987).

COURSE STRUCTURE

The course is organised into three blocks:

- Block 1	12 Days
- Inter block period	12 Weeks
- Block 2	13 Days
- Inter block period	12 Weeks
- Block 3	10 Days

The inter-block periods allow course members to put some of what they have learned into practice by tutoring the student district nurses who accompany them on placement.

The course comprises a number of elements:

– the adult learner	24 hours
– study skills	8 hours
– management of learning	40 hours
– context of practical work teaching	24 hours
– current developments in nursing and the Health Service	16 hours
– personal and professional development	16 hours

In addition, it is a requirement of the English National Board for Nursing, Midwifery and Health Visiting (ENB), that each student produces four pieces of work for assessment during the course, each of which must be of a pass standard.

SELECTION PROCEDURE

Each candidate for the course was told that not only were they being appraised on their academic and professional qualifications for the course, but also they were informed about its unconventional nature and invited to judge whether or not it might be suitable for them. The philosophy and rationale behind the course were clearly explained and each applicant was given the opportunity to withdraw if she felt doubtful.

EARLY STAGES OF THE COURSE

Adult learners very often come to higher education in a very anxious and apprehensive state. Our first task as a course team is to try to overcome some of these feelings and, particularly because of the short timescale of each full-time block, to begin to generate a good working atmosphere as soon as possible.

The first activity was a conventional 'icebreaker' in which each member of the group, including the tutors, interviewed one another, and then introduced each other to the group. This exercise has a number of advantages:

- each person makes an early contribution to the group proceedings;
- everyone has at least one person she knows in the group when it comes to breaktime; and
- and everyone learns something about everyone else in the group at an early stage.

After standard enrollment procedures, and before a detailed examination of the syllabus, course members were asked to reflect individually upon the qualities and attributes required in an excellent practical work teacher (PWT). Next, they were asked to share their ideas in pairs and then in groups of four to design an overhead projector transparency which summarized their views. These were then presented to the whole course by each group in turn. In parallel with this, course members were taken through a personal reflection and career-planning exercise, and asked to set goals for their personal and professional development for the duration of the course and beyond.

Having undertaken these preliminary exercises, the course members were then better equipped to confront the syllabus, and to make their requirements for changes and alterations known at this early stage. In the event, the changes in the course which they felt able to ask for at this early stage were relatively minor and it was only later in the course at the negotiation sessions at the beginning of the second and third blocks that planning to meet the students' expressed needs came into its own.

SELF AND PEER ASSESSMENT

Because the course was designed to produce effective teachers of practical work to district nurse students, the course team felt that it was very important to develop the skills of assessment in the course members from the earliest moment. Therefore, it was agreed that the first assignment would be completed before the end of the first block. Preparation for this task took the form of a modified and extended version of the essay-marking exercise devised by Gibbs (1981), and also used by Falchikov (1986) in her work with psychology undergraduates.

To begin with, course members were given two brief essays on the same subject to mark, as if they were tutors. They were encouraged to write comments in the margin and to write advice to the authors at the end. Then in pairs they discussed and compared their perceptions of the two essays. In groups of four with a scribe/rapporteur, they were asked to identify the strengths and weaknesses of the two essays. These were then collected orally by the tutor, one item in turn from each group, and placed as a list on the OHP screen until all the items were exhausted. This list formed the basis of the next stage which was for groups to weight the items to form a marking scheme. After a period of negotiation and discussion in plenary, the group as a whole agreed on a common marking scheme for the first assignment (see Appendix 1 for the agreed scheme). Before they used it for their own work, the group were asked to apply it to a pair of exam essays on the same question, to give course members the opportunity further to practice and extend their assessment skills. Course members were then asked to write their first assignment and to assess their own work and that of two colleagues before the end of the block. The three tutors associated with the course each marked one third of the assignments, with self, peer and tutor marks each carrying equal weight for the final score.

For some of the course members the whole process of self and peer assessment was very difficult, superimposed upon the already taxing task of writing an academic essay, often for the first time in many years. On receiving their marks and the comments from tutors and peers, some members were upset and needed support and time to come to terms with the difference between their own and others' perceptions about their work.

In the later stages of the course, members became much more familiar and comfortable with the process, and the 'hand-back' sessions when work was retuned and comments made on one another's performance, were very noisy and lively, with much productive discussion going on all round the room.

The final assignment was a video role play. The problems of peer, tutor and self assessment are compounded in such circumstances by the threat posed by the imminent replay of performances, warts and all. One or two members of the course had suffered very unfortunate experiences of the use of video for this sort of event; a compromise was reached by which course members elected to work in private groups, alone with the recording equipment, performing role plays the substance of which had been agreed beforehand. Only after all recording was over were tutors allowed to view the videos with the groups and to help to assess them on the basis of criteria drawn up by the whole group beforehand. The recordings of those people who so wished were erased. The others were kept securely by the course tutor for the external examiner to view.

TASK-BASED GROUPWORK

As the course progressed, the course members became more assertive over the nature and scope of the activities which they wished to pursue. In the sessions on the management of learning, and the adult learner in particular, this resulted in group projects becoming the main vehicle of the course, with teams of four or five designing a one-day course on AIDS for local health care personnel, complete with objectives, timetables and costings; an induction programme for an auxiliary worker joining the health centre, and the production of a student feedback questionnaire to assist in evaluating the quality of the student's practical work experience. In all cases, each group presented its work to the others using the OHP and other aids, and photocopies of each group's work were made available to the others.

COURSE MONITORING AND EVALUATION

Because the course was innovative and because the tutors frequently consulted course members on the progress of the course, course evaluation questionnaires were used at the end of each block. To ensure that they addressed the issues which the course members themselves thought important, they were devised as Likert Scale attitude questionnaires. Each person was asked to write down what were for her the three or four most important issues or feelings about the course. These were then collected and read out preceded by a question number, and each course member indicated by a pencil mark on a pre-printed form whether she agreed strongly, agreed, neither agreed nor disagreed, disagreed or disagreed strongly with each statement. These were then processed through an optical mark reader and the results made known to the students and staff associated with the course before the commencement of the inter-block period. (For the final questionnaire and results see Appendix 2.)

HOW SUCCESSFUL WAS THE COURSE?

The course received a strongly positive evaluation from its members, in particular it is worth noticing the unanimous view that the course promoted a high standard of group learning (Q10) and that the course was stimulating and enjoyable (Q4). Similar consensus was found in the view that the group work had been a very useful method of learning (Q6), that the peer group had been very supportive and understanding, and (fortunately) that the course had improved individuals' teaching and learning skills (Q59).

The responses on self and peer assessment also make interesting reading. One effect seems to have been to sensitize course members to the likely reactions to criticism of their own students (Q56). There was some, but not total, agreement that it was difficult (Q31 and Q45), and similarly that it was invaluable (Q44). There was very little support for the view that it might devalue a course (Q51).

REFERENCES

Boud, D. (1986) Facilitating learning in continuing education: some important sources. *Studies in Higher Education*, **11**, 3, 237-243.
Cox, S. (1987) Peer and self assessment. *Nursing Times*, **83**, 33, 62-64.
Falchikov, N. (1986) Product comparisons and process benefits of collaborative peer group and self-assessments. *Assessment and Evaluation in Higher Education*, 146-166.
Gibbs, G. (1981) *Teaching Students to Learn.* Open University Press, London.
Ramsden, P. (1985) Student learning research; retrospective and prospect, *Higher Education Research and Development*, **41, 59-69.**

APPENDIX 1

COVENTRY POLYTECHNIC: DEPARTMENT OF APPLIED SOCIAL STUDIES/LEARNING SYSTEMS DEVELOPMENT

Essay-writing criteria

Introduction	concise, well-structured definite statement of intent	10
Content	stimulating and relevant reasoning/argument supported by evidence/precise expression of knowledge	15
Answers the question	reference back to question	15
Structure	logical development (intro; central argument and summary conclusion)	15
Quote sources	accurately in context using bibliography	5
Style	appropriate level and language; authoritative use of technical language	5
Presentation	legibility, grammar, punctuation, spelling	5

APPENDIX 2

QUESTIONNAIRE AND RESULTS

	Agree Strongly	Agree	Neither Agree or disagree	Disagree	Disagree Strongly	No Reply
1. The group was very supportive during self and peer assessment.	10	3	1			
2. Information was not always imparted in correct order for our assignments.	3	10	1			
3. I found the video assignments stressful.	2	7	1	1	3	
4. I found the course stimulating and enjoyable.	8	6				
5. I found the peer group very supportive and understanding.	11	2	1			
6. The group work has been a very useful method of learning.	11	3				
7. The course has made me feel more confident and assertive.	4	10				
8. I have gained a lot of knowledge from plans designed by the groups and from the seminars.	6	7				1
9. Once the nerves had settled, the video was a very good learning tool.	4	6	4			
10. Management are not aware of the nature of this course.	7	7				
11. This course has promoted a high standard of group learning.	7	7				
12. Peer group support has made us a cohesive course group.	7	5	1	1		
13. I found the video film making was very hard.	1	4	3	5	1	
14. It took me a long time to adjust to a novel learning situation.	2	3	5	3	1	
15. The peer assessments did have a valid use, once we became adjusted to the idea.	4	8		2		
16. I was amazed at the standard of work we were able to produce.	6	5	3			
17. Peer and self assessment is a good way of learning.	2	8	3	1		
18. The assignments were hard work at first, but easier as each one was achieved.		8	2	4		
19. I have enjoyed working with my peer group.	11	3				
20. I needed more work on computers.	1	5	4	2	2	
21. My P.W.T mentor was not absolutely sure of her role.	5	5		3	1	
22. I have learnt a lot.	5	9				
23. I feel I can cope with my professional responsibilities in a more progressive way.	5	9				
24. The counselling sessions were very useful.	4	8	1	1		
25. I feel totally confident in my ability to prepare for a student of any sort.	1	5	6	2		
26. Because I had built up a relationship with my peers, I found it very difficult to point out their weaknesses when assessing them.	2	5	3	4		
27. The presentations of seminars on current developments, research and Microteaching should have been better spaced (so that some peope did not have 3 presentations to do in 1 block).	3	10	1			
28. I found I enjoyed and learned more doing group work than from "lectures".	7	7				
29. I was relieved that the course did not overload us with extra reading.	3	10	1			
30. I wish that the last block could have been organised so that we all could have seen each others research.	7	5	2			

	Agree Strongly	Agree	Neither Agree or disagree	Disagree	Disagree Strongly
31. I found (peer and self assessment) difficult to do originally.	2	10	1	1	
32. I feel confident to plan a students practical experience course.	1	13			
33. By planning a students p.e. course I will use material and ideas from my colleagues.	4	10			
34. The video assignment was less stressful that I had expected.	1	7	4	1	1
35. I feel I have a clear understanding of my role as a P.W.T.	4	10			
36. I benefited more when working in small groups.	5	6	3		
37. I would like to have presented the research assignment during Block 2.	1	5	6	2	
38. Perhaps we could have used 2 or 3 mornings to present research assignments as I feel there was too much information to pack into 1 day.	2	10	2		
39. I enjoyed the supportive feeling that the group demonstrated.	10	2	2		
40. I found that watching myself on video created some 'self image' problems.	3	8	1	2	
41. I feel I have gained in confidence as a result of the course.	4	9	1		
42. Collecting information for seminar work was very beneficial.	6	7	1		
43. Being a recipient of other's seminar work was very beneficial.	9	5			
44. Peer group work and assessment was invaluable.	2	8	2	2	
45. Peer group assessment was often difficult.	2	9	1	1	
46. Sometimes I would have liked more tutor direction/particiption in assignments.	2	7	3	2	
47. Sometimes I would have liked more tutor participation in assessments.	3	5	5	1	
48. The third block was the most stressful to me.	1	5	2	5	
49. I should have liked either the pre-assignments or video assignment in block 2.	3	7	3	1	
50. Working in small groups and sharing results was a most constructive format.	8	6			
51. I think that peer assessment may devalue a course.	1	1	1	1	8
52. I feel tutors need to be present at all presentations.	2	4	4	4	
53. I feel confident to evaluate a student's work.	2	12			
54. I think some course members were not always constructive.	1	9	2	2	
55. I feel I could attempt a counselling session with confidence.	2	5	6	1	
56. Self and peer assessment made me aware of possible student reaction to criticism.	8	6			
57. I feel that this course has stretched my personal and professional capabilities .	3	10	1		
58. I now feel that I have more confidence when handling difficult situations.	2	11	1		
59. The course has improved my teaching and learning skills.	7	7			

	Agree Strongly	Agree	Neither Agree Nor Disagree	Disagree	Disagree Strongly	No Reply
60. The course has made me aware of my professional responsibilities	4	10				
61. After my nerves had subsided, I enjoyed the video and its outcome as a teaching tool.	2	10	2			
62. I am more aware of the necessity of being aware of current changes.	1	10	3			
63. At the end of the course I feel more motivated to improve my knowledge etc.	3	11				
64. I think a refresher course should be compulsory every 2 years.	8	5	1			
65. Peer assessment proved more useful to me that I had anticipated.	3	9		1		1
66. I found criticism from colleagues is more difficult to take than from tutors.	4	4	6			
67. I found the course difficult initially.	4	4	3	3		
68. I found the first assignment difficult.	2	6	4	2		
69. The assertiveness session was very helpful.	7	7				
70. I found essay writing difficult to grasp.	3	4	3	4		
71. I found the second block assignments hard work.	3	9				
72. The seminar work restored my confidence.	1	1	8			
73. I found that teaching plans required a great deal of thought.	6	6	1	1		
74. The session on Criticism was very helpful.	1	10	3			

34. Structural communication enhancements to an interactive-video simulation game: in search of reflective learning

Alexander Romiszowski, *Syracuse University, Syracuse, USA*

Summary: This paper touches on several interrelated topics. The main theme is the instructional design of interactive-video simulation games intended to teach experientially. The need for reflective debriefing for effective learning in these situations is discussed. Structural communication is presented as a CAL technique capable of implementing such reflective learning. An evaluation study of a commercially available interactive-video management simulation, Decision Point, is presented, and the use of structural communication to improve both learning effectiveness and efficiency is demonstrated.

BACKGROUND TO THE STUDY

Is interactive-video simulation effective/efficient?

Decision Point is an interactive-video (IV) simulation-game, which puts the learner in the position of 'Vice President of Sales' of a hi-tech manufacturer. As the producers, Digital Equipment Corporation, describe it, it is a 'living case study': a situational simulation in which the student interacts with dramatized scenarios representing occurrences in the company, interviews key personnel and takes decisions on a total of ten issues that reflect on the success of the sales effort (Digital Educational Services, 1985).

All in all, Decision Point is a typical IV simulation game where all effort has been made to reproduce reality in as realistic a manner as possible. As it is sold, however, there is little guidance on how to introduce or follow up the experience, or indeed whether briefing or debriefing of any sort is desirable. The manual suggests that:

> '... from this kind of experience – from living through the case several times – you will learn about the complex interrelationships of causes and effects in managerial decision making ... by taking the course again and again you will be able to develop the feel for business that often characterizes top executives.'

Is this in fact so? And at two hours or so a time, is this an effective learning strategy?

Initial observations

When Decision Point began to be used by students and staff at Syracuse University, records were kept of the results achieved on successive repeat attempts. It was found that typically, students would register a marked improvement from the first to the second attempt, but then the learning curve would flatten out with little further improvement on the third and fourth attempts. The level at which this plateau would occur varied. A few students achieved close to maximum possible sales on the second play, leaving little room for further improvement, but many would flatten out well below the goals set for them by the game.

Discussions showed that one difference between the high and low achievers was the extent to which they reflected on the general principals which were involved in the scenarios that were presented to them by the interactive-video simulation. It would seem that some form of tutorial designed to encourage 'deep processing' of the general theoretical principals of management behind the practical decisions, would enhance the instructional effectiveness of the package. (For a general discussion of 'reflective learning' in many contexts, see Boud et al, 1985.)

These observations led to the design of a 'debriefing tutorial' which would allow students to reflect on the cognitive structure that they had applied to a given problem and compare it with the cognitive structure of expert managers. The methodology for the design, development and delivery of this tutorial is based on a self-instructional technique first used in the late 1960s in the United Kingdom, called *structural communication* (Zeitlin and Goldberg, 1970; Hodgson, 1968, 1971, 1974). It is based on the practical application of cognitive learning principles to self-instruction (Hodgson, 1974) and has proved itself in many educational contexts (Egan, 1976; Romiszowski, 1976, 1986) including high-level management decision making (Hodgson, 1971). For a variety of reasons, it is little, if ever, used by the current generation of computer-assisted learning materials developers but holds a great untapped potential for improving current interactive instructional systems design (Romiszowski and Grabowski, 1987).

In structural communication, a student is faced with a challenging rather open-ended problem and responds by constructing a personal multi-component response. This response is analysed by means of a small 'logic program' specially developed for this problem and based on the analyses of how 'experts' tend to deal with similar problems. This logical program generates a personalized feedback message, comprising perhaps several comments and further presentations selected from a more extensive set of comments, designed to cover all commonly occurring differences between viewpoints and approaches to the problem. This approach deals equally well with errors or theoretical positions.

Space limitations preclude a discussion here of the details of the design and authoring process of such structural communication units. A general account can be found in Hodgson (1974) and Romiszowski (1986). A more detailed account of the development of the unit used in the study described here, may be found in Romiszowski, Grabowski and Damodaran (1988). In essence, however, the structural communication tutorial was developed through a process of interviewing experts both during and after the Decision Point experience (a form of knowledge engineering) in order to generate an initial version of the unit. This version was further refined by experimental use on successive cohorts of undergraduates from the School of Management over a period of two semesters.

This experimental use simulated a future fully automated CAI tutorial mode, all problems, responses and comments being presented in a standardized format, one 'screen' at a time, but on paper. The 'logic programs' analysing a student's conceptual structure were 'executed' by the experimenters, using a printed job-aid. However, extra non-programmed student responses or queries, together with resultant experimenter comments, were allowed (indeed encouraged) and recorded as potential input to the refinement of the tutorial.

The results of the study which follow are the results of the developmental process outlined above. They should not be treated as hard research results.

RESULTS OF INITIAL STUDY

Group 1 (N=17) took Decision Point twice, with an interval of less than a week between sessions. Some took it a third and fourth time (only a small sub-group). This group used the originally supplied manual as a guide to the exercise.

Group 2 (N=14) took Decision Point twice but received a debriefing tutorial on the general principals involved between the first and second session.

Using as a measure the number of decisions taken 'correctly' (as evaluated by the authors of Decision Point), the results are as shown in Table 1.

Using the ratio of actual gain/maximum possible gain, we have a value of 23 per cent of

	FIRST SESSION	SECOND SESSION	SUBSEQUENTLY
GROUP 1	43% correct	56% correct	no apparent improvement
GROUP 2	45% correct	74% correct	no data available

Table 1. *Percentage of correct decisions*

possible gain for Group 1 and 53 per cent for Group 2. However, the analysis of the results of different decisions reveals that learning was markedly different on questions that required the application of interrelated principles and on questions that merely required the competent procedural use of the decision-support simulation software. The results were rather surprising in that the intellectually less demanding decisions were tackled less successfully initially and learning on these was less effective. The effect of the tutorial was most marked in relation to the principle-application decisions as shown in Table 2.

	GROUP 1	GROUP 2
PERCENTAGE OF POSSIBLE IMPROVEMENT ON *PROCEDURE-BASED* DECISION POINTS	31%	60%
PERCENTAGE OF POSSIBLE IMPROVEMENT ON *PRINCIPLE-APPLICATION* DECISIONS	33%	100%

Table 2. *Effect of tutorials*

The first and second attempt results for each of the ten decision points are shown in Figure 1. The top four are the procedure-based decision points that can be successfully resolved without the application of any skills or knowledge of management, provided one pays attention to the interactive-support models built into the simulation. The bottom four are the decision points that require the use of management principles and some 'trade-off' judgements. The two in the middle (report distribution and sales quotas) require the planning of a detailed strategy in a context where many similar strategies are possible.

CONCLUSIONS, IMPLICATIONS AND PROSPECTS

Interactive-video simulations and experiential learning

Interactive-video simulations are:

- an exceptionally attractive and captivating experience for the learner when they are well scripted and reflect reality 'as it is' (we have had no-one walk away from their first encounter with the Decision Point simulation and most students were willing to play two, three or more times, at an investment of two hours each time);
- potentially deceptive in terms of the real learning that is taking place. In the case discussed, some general learning that 'things in business are not as simple as they might at first appear' was all that most students learned in terms of general principles. Specific relevant principles of management were rarely learned if not known by the student before the experience;
- only a part of a full instructional design for specific objectives. They must either be preceded by careful instruction in the concepts and principles involved (as suggested by Reigeluth and Schwartz, 1987) or they must be followed by carefully designed debriefing tutorials that cause the learner to reflect on the generalizable principles

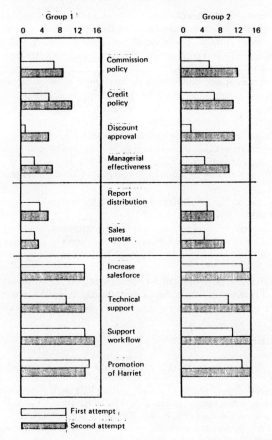

Figure 1. *The first and second attempt results, for each decision point*

that are involved and are at play in the specific cases encountered;
- just as prone to serious instructional design errors in their detailed design as any other form of instruction. In the example discussed, of ten decisions points presented to students, only four are of a reasonably adequate design if the learning of general principles is among the prime objectives of the exercise. Two questions are too difficult, or rather are evaluated in an unclear and too rigid manner to be useful as examples for successful reflection, deep processing of the data presented and the 'discovery' of new generalities. The remaining four decision points use highly sophisticated computer presentations that allow correct responses without any consideration of general principles. Any useful learning resulting from this experience would be despite, rather than because of, the design. The fact that students did not do so well on these four points is difficult to explain, but one hypothesis is that they were too bright: they refused to believe the childish simplicity of the task!

STRUCTURAL COMMUNICATION AS A DEBRIEFING METHODOLOGY

Structural communication is:

- a self-study method which seeks to simulate an in-depth discussion on a given topic;
- based on cognitive psychology and schema theory;
- an opportunity to compare the student's and author's conceptual structure on the topic and to identify and comment on any significant differences, without implying 'right/wrong';
- applicable to almost any discussion topic that involves the structuring of an explanation, or an argument, for a given problem phenomenon, viewpoint, trend, theory, etc;
- effective (eg the Decision Point study);
- little used (even known) since its development in 1968-73;
- easy to implement in CAL by means of most programming languages (though somewhat time-consuming);
- not available as a facility in any widely used courseware authoring language or system;
- as powerful, pedagogically, as many ICAI systems, yet much simpler and cheaper to implement; and
- capable of implementation by means of logic programming and existing expert-system shells and, in this form of implementation, is an excellent laboratory for further development of the technique beyond its 1970s level of sophistication and power.

Ongoing research and development is concentrating on the automation of the design, development and delivery of Structural Communication tutorials as computer-based adjuncts to other learning experiences, expositive or experiential, computer-based or not.

REFERENCES

Boud, D., Keogh, R. and Walker, D. (eds) (1985) *Reflection: Turning Experience into Learning.* Kogan Page, London.

Digital Educational Services (1985) *Decision Point: A Living Case Study.* (Interactive computer-based videodisc program and accompanying manual) Digital Equipment Corporation, USA.

Egan, K. (1976) *Structural Communication.* Fearon Publishers, Belmont, USA.

Hodgson, A.M. (1968) A communication technique for the future. *Ideas,* **7,** Curriculum Laboratory, Goldsmith College, University of London, UK.

Hodgson, A.M. (1971) An experiment in computer-guided correspondence seminars for management. *Aspects of Educational Technology, V.* Pitman, London.

Hodgson, A.M. (1974) Structural communication in practice. In Romiszowski, A.J. (ed) *APLET Yearbook of Educational and Instructional Technology, 1974/75.* Kogan Page, London.

Reigeluth, C.M. and Schwartz, E. (1987) An instructional theory for the design of computer-based simulations. Paper presented at the 1987 ADCIS conference, San Francisco, November. Published also as IDDE Working Paper (Schwartz and Reigeluth, 1987) No 23, School of Education, Syracuse University, NY, USA.

Romiszowski, A.J. (1976) A study of individualized systems of mathematics instruction at the post secondary levels. (Doctoral Thesis) University of Loughborough, Loughborough, UK.

Romiszowski, A.J. (1986) *Developing Auto-instructional Materials: From Programmed Texts to CAL and Interactive Video.* (Chapter 7 is devoted entirely to Structural Communication). Kogan Page, London.

Romiszowski, A.J. and Grabowski, B. (1987) Some neglected CAL methodologies and their potential for new interactive systems of instruction. Paper presented at the 1987 SALT Conference on Developments in the Design of Interactive Instruction Systems. Published in the proceedings. Stamford, CT.

Romiszowski, A.J., Grabowski, B. and Damodaran, B. (1988)

Structural communication, expert systems and interactive video: a powerful combination for a non-traditional CAI approach. Paper presented at the 1988 convention of AECT, New Orleans.

Zeitlin, N. and Goldberg, A.L. (1970) *Structural Communication: An Interactive System for Teaching Understanding.* Educational Technology Publications, Englewood Cliffs.

35. Using computers in the diagnosis and remediation of developmental dyslexia

Bruno Morchio and Michela Ott, *Instituto Technologie Didattiche (CNR), Genova, Italy*

Summary: The paper tries to answer the following questions:

- Is it possible to use the computer both in dyslexia diagnosis and remediation?
- What are the potentialities and peculiarities of computers in this field when compared with other tools?
- Which are presently the best strategies and methods for computer-aided diagnosis and remediation of dyslexia?

The paper also illustrates a joint research project of the Institute for Educational Technology (ITD-CNR) and the Public Health Service Unit no.12 of Genoa (USL 12) focusing the attention on the computer programs produced by the research team.

THE RESEARCH PROJECT: AN OVERVIEW

The Institute for Educational Technology (ITD) of the Italian National Research Council (CNR) is presently involved in a research project concerning the computer-aided diagnosis and treatment of developmental dyslexia. It is a joint project of CNR and USL (Public Health Service Unit) no.12 of Genova.

Aims

The main aims of the project are as follows:

- to verify whether and how the computer can be used both in dyslexia diagnosis and remediation;
- to study and evaluate the potentialities and peculiarities of computers in this field when compared with other tools;
- to develop strategies and methods for computer-aided diagnosis and remediation and to set up dedicated computer tools; and
- to create a database of all the available information on software products concerning developmental dyslexia.

Theoretical models

The reading process is characterized by two main aspects: encoding and comprehension; the research focuses on encoding problems and impairments.

The research team adopted the theoretical model that Sartori defined as standard (1984). This model (shown in Figure 1) is based on the distinction between the visual-

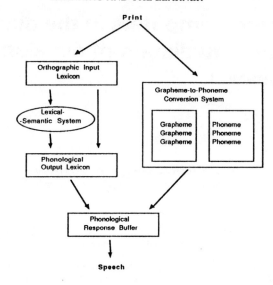

Figure 1. *The standard model of reading*

lexical route and the phonological route of reading words.

According to this model there are two different approaches to word reading: the visual-lexical decoding and the phonological recoding.

Using the lexical modality based on the recognition of the words as a whole orthographic structure, it is possible to process correctly known words only (ie both regular and irregular words whose visual logogen is stored in the input orthographic lexicon). This route, instead, prevents the correct reading of unknown words.

The phonological route is based on the phoneme-to-grapheme conversion; the reader can process both unknown words and non-words but they cannot read successfully irregular words whose incorrect pronunciation is based on a whole lexical access to the stimulus.

As the specific objective of the research is the treatment of developmental dyslexia, the mentioned theoretical model was integrated with the three-staged model of spelling proposed by Frith (1985) in order to interpret the acquisition of reading and writing abilities in the developmental stage. The model is based on the functional distinction between three stages in the spelling process: logographic, alphabetic and orthographic. Logographic skills refer to knowledge and the use of individual phonemes and graphemes and their correspondences, orthographic skills refer to the instant analysis of words as orthographic units without phonological conversion.

On the basis of these models the group designed the diagnostic tests and the remedial exercises; for the latter ones the aim was to improve the deficient function.

Population and work phases

The research involved a group of about 300 primary and secondary pupils (8-13 years old). The research work consisted of two phases:

- a diagnostic phase concerning the building and administration of diagnostic tests consistent with the theoretical interpretive models, their correction and evaluation; and

- a remedial phase concerning the building of exercises (directed to each deficient function), the definition and the organization of remedial activities and the analysis and evaluation of results.

The role of computers

To date, computers have not been used in the diagnostic phase. They have been mainly a tool for the analysis and evaluation of test results; diagnosis has been made with paper and pencil tests. A test is now being designed which will take advantage of the potentialities of computers regarding the organizational pattern, presentation form, statistical analysis and processing of data.

On the other hand, the remedial phase was completely computer-aided. After making a diagnosis for each subject and for each functional impairment, remedial training was completely put over to the computers; the computers managed the repetitive training phases which are of major importance in the treatment of this kind of handicap. As to recovery, both special purpose interactive educational software and common editing or graphic programs have been used.

In short, we can assert that in our experience the use of computers for diagnostic purposes needs further study while their use in remediation has proved successful.

HOW SHOULD COMPUTERS BE USED?

Computer programs cannot be considered as a magic tool either for diagnostic purposes or for remedial purposes, but they can play an important role in such fields when they are well structured and properly used.

Appropriate tools for specific impairments

In order to make the use of computers really fruitful, suitable computer tools should be selected in order to identify and treat specific impairments. Reading and writing problems often have different symptoms and causes, therefore both diagnostic and remedial tools must be oriented towards identifying the specificity of phenomena.

Diagnostic tools should not generically enhance reading and writing problems; on the contrary, they should point out the particular kind of impairment involved (for instance impairment in the use of the visual route or of the phonological route, or unexpected stops at one of the stages of acquisition of spelling abilities, etc).

Remedial tools too should not be oriented to generalized impairments in spelling but should aim at treating specific deficiencies and impairments.

A complete panorama of the available material is useful:

- to make a good choice among existing products; and
- to create new suitable tools, when they are not available, on the basis of the theoretical interpretative models and of the hardware potentialities.

The Software Library (BSD) at the ITD is presently collecting, storing and evaluating the best Italian and foreign software devoted to reading and writing disabilities that is available on the market.

As to the differential diagnosis of reading and writing problems, very few computer tools so far exist; however, a lot of specific material is available for their treatment.

A few computer-tools as a proposal

In the early phases of our research, ready-to-use Italian and foreign interactive programs, adapted to our scopes and theoretical assumptions, were used. Later on, a few remedial programs were designed and produced to meet particular needs.

First of all, exercises using common graphic and word-processing programs were designed. Such exercises are divided into different series according to the specificity of the impairment to be treated. In the case of special purpose interactive programs, the computer is fully used and its potentialities are fully enlightened: it can administer exercises, accept and evaluate the answers and supply immediate feedback as well as a global statistical analysis of results.

In the case of text editing and graphic programs, computer potentialities are not fully used; these programs do not allow any qualitative or quantitative data analysis and besides they provide no immediate feedback on the correctness of answers. Nevertheless, these programs can be profitably used since they require the student's involvement both in autonomous writing and in symbol decoding; moreover they are easy to use and run on most types of computers.

Within our research, two remedial programs have been designed and produced to meet particular needs. The first program is related to the visual word-recognizing ability (TACHISTOSCOPIO) and the second one to letter recognition (LETTERE). The two programs run on an IBM PC or compatibles and can be used for both diagnosis and remediation purposes.

LETTERE is a program for letter recognition. It can be used to verify and drill the visual and phonological competence in word recognition; it can also be used for 'shape recognition' exercises.

The base exercise consists of the identification of one target-letter (either lower case or upper case) among a list of options shown simultaneously. See Figure 2.

The program contains a few ready-to-use exercises but can allow one's own exercises to be created within guidelines. Not only does the program take into account all the results but it also supplies a quantitative analysis, distinguishing between different kinds of errors (substitutions and omissions).

TACHISTOSCOPIO is a program for the diagnosis and training of reading problems. As to the diagnosis, the program allows one to establish which of the two routes is being used, the visual-lexical route or the phonological one, and performs a qualitative and quantitative analysis of results (number and kind of errors).

The remediation can be defined as a tool for the methodical training of the visual route of reading and of short-term memory. The basic exercise consists of a timed presentation of a word-stimulus (a single word or a short sentence) which the student must read correctly. The program itself contains a few basic lists of Italian words chosen on the basis of their frequency, their image impact and their grammatical category, but it is also possible to input any self-made list of words.

During the execution of the exercises changes are possible. They can concern:

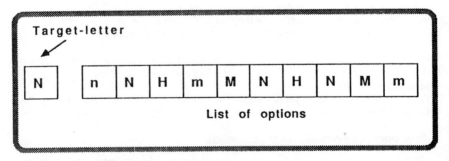

Figure 2. *The basic exercise of the programe LETTERE*

- the time of the stimulus presentation (from 100 ms to one second);
- the position of stimulus presentation (right, left, centre);
- the character dimension (small, medium, large);
- the way of presignalling the stimulus (window, pointer on the first letter, unpresignalled stimulus); and
- the response modality (oral or written).

Lastly, the results analysis is automatically undertaken and displayed.

CONCLUSIONS: WHY SHOULD COMPUTERS BE USED?

Our work is still in progress but, on the basis of preliminary results, we can draw a few conclusions on the use of computers in this particular field. On the whole the computer proved extremely reliable for remediation. Of course we do not mean that we should replace the recovery operator, but we think it is a useful tool to help, improve and vary the various remedial activities.

Advantages in comparison with traditional tools

When compared with traditional remedial tools (generally based on the constant presence of the operator close to the impaired child) the use of computers offers many advantages:

- *resource saving:* the whole recovery process can be completely computer-managed and one operator can look after many children at the same time;
- *flexibility:* it is possible for a person other than the recovery operator (eg a parent) to assist the child while they perform the exercises;
- *homogeneity:* a fixed series of exercises are administered for the same type of impairment, following constant patterns;
- *motivation:* a higher level of subjects' motivation was almost always registered, often leading to an increase in the benefit gained. 'Playing' with a computer is amusing and thus learning is easier; exercises, though repetitive, can present varied graphical patterns as well as suitable feedback that can attract and involve the student; and
- *concrete and plastic experience with language:* computers let the pupils deal with lexical stimuli in a totally new and particular way that enables them to experiment with the 'physical features' of languages.

Moreover the use of computers also provides a higher degree of individualization of the remedial routes (ie during the remedial activities individualized routes can be selected) and also makes possible a complete evaluation of performance and results through various statistical analyses of data.

The computer is an indispensable tool

As regards a few particular aspects of reading and writing impairments, the computer should be considered an indispensable tool and not a complementary one. For instance, from a diagnostic point of view it is difficult to verify the integrity of the lexical decoding strategy with pencil-and-paper tests, while where a computer is used, flash exposition to different stimuli can provide reliable data in a short time. In the same way, a lot of specific remediation activities can be profitably designed and carried out only via computer (eg computer-managed presentation of stimuli to promote the use of the visual-lexical decoding route).

In the future, computers based on new, sound technologies will become even more reliable for the diagnosis and treatment of reading and writing problems. At present most computers used in schools are 'dumb' while dyslexics could gain a lot of help from interacting with a 'speaking' machine capable of harmonizing graphical and acoustic outputs and supporting the mutual integration of the two different codes in children's minds.

REFERENCES

Frith, U. (1985) Beneath the surface of developmental dyslexia. In Patterson, K.E., Marshall, J.C. and Coltheart, M. (eds) *Surface Dyslexia*. Lawrence Erlbaum Associates Publishers, London.

Sartori, G. (1984) *La lettura. Processi normalie dislessia*. Mulino, Bologna.

FURTHER READING

Aaron, P.G. (1982) The neuropsychology of developmental dyslexia. In Malatesha, R.N. and Aaron, P.G. (eds) *Reading disorders*. Academic Press, New York.

Calfee, R. (1982) Cognitive models of reading: implications for assessment and treatment of reading disability. In Malatesha, R.N. and Aaron, P.G. (eds) *Reading Disorders*. Academic Press, New York.

Coltheart, H. (1978) Lexical access in simple reading task. In Underwood, G. (ed) *Strategies of Information Processing*. Academic Press, London.

Feenstra, H. (1987) Computer-assisted instruction of component reading skills. In Moonen, J. and Plomp, T. (eds) *Eurit 86, Developments in Educational Software and Courseware*. Pergamon Books Ltd, Oxford.

Fisher, C., Van Den Born, J.J. and Pennings, A. (1987) A prototype of a computer-based educational system for children with initial reading problems. In Moonen, J. and Plomp, T. (eds) *Eurit 86, Developments in Educational Software and Courseware*. Pergamon Books Ltd. Oxford.

Manis, F.R. (1985) Acquisition of word identification skills in normal and disabled readers. *Journal of Educational Psychology*, **77,** 1, 78-90.

Manis, F.R., Savage, L., Morrison, F.J. and Horn, C.C. (1987) Paired associate learning in reading-disabled children: evidence for a rule-learning deficiency. *Journal of Experimental Child Psychology*, **43,** 25-43.

Marshall, J.C. (1984) Toward a rational taxonomy of the developmental dyslexias. In Malatesha, R.N. and Whitaker, H.A. (eds) *Dyslexia: a global issue*. Martinus Nijhoff Publishers, The Hague.

Morton, J. and Patterson, K.E. (1980) A new attempt at an interpretation, or, an attempt at a new interpretation. In Coltheart, M., Patterson, K.E. and Marshall, J.C. (eds) *Deep Dyslexia*. Routledge & Kegan Paul, London.

Patterson, K.E. and Marshall, J.C. (eds) (1985) *Surface Dyslexia*. Lawrence Erlbaum Associates Publishers, London.

Patterson, K.E. and Morton, J. (1985) From orthography to phonology: an attempt at an old interpretation. In Patterson, K.E., Marshal, J.C. and Coltheart, M. (eds) *Surface Dyslexia*. Lawrence Erlbaum Associates Publishers, London.

Pennings, A.H. (ed) (1987) *Letterwerk*. Vakgroep Orthoppedagogiek en Klinische Pedagogiek, VOU-rapportnummer 86. 13 a, b, Utrecht.

Rayner, K. (1986) Eye movements and the perceptual span in beginning and skilled readers. *Journal of Experimental Child Psychology*, **41,** 211-236.

Reitsma, P., Ellermann, H.H. and Spaai, G.W.G. (1987) An electronic aid for practising letter-sound relations. In Moonen, J. and Plomp, T. (eds) *Eurit 86, Developments in Educational Software and Courseware*. Pergamon Books, Oxford.

Van Daal, V.H.P., Bakker, N., Der Leij, A. and Reitsma, P. (1987) Word frequency in practice programs of poor readers. In Moonen, J. and Plomp, T. (eds) *Eurit 86, Developments in Educational Software and Courseware*. Pergamon Books, Oxford.

Van Den Bros, K.P. (1984) Letter Processing in dyslexic subgroups. *Annals of Dyslexia*, **34,** 179-193.

Vellutino, F.R. and Scanlon, D.M. (1985) Free recall of concrete and abstract words in poor and normal readers. *Journal of Experimental Child Psychology*, **39,** 363-380.

36. Improving education in Bulgarian schools

Mikhail Draganov, *Bulgarian Ministry of Education, Bulgaria*
Raïna Pavlova, *Higher Institute of Mechanical and Electrical Engineering, Sofia, Bulgaria*

Summary: The organizational structures, forms and tools of education may be conducive to, or may hamper, the implementation of even the best educational and training technologies. This paper discusses the organizational structures and tools at school and national levels which could be conducive to improving learning, and their relationship to its content.

INTRODUCTION

The prime aim of Bulgaria's educational system is to prepare young people for life, in particular to:

- provide them with a general education, manners and culture to an adequate standard;
- give them an essential general knowledge in natural science and the humanities;
- bring them up as industrious and loyal citizens; and
- provide them with a vocational training in diverse subjects.

Thus formulated, the major aim of the educational system is considered in terms of the needs of the individual learners. In terms of the needs of society in general, the system has to produce highly skilled specialists for all fields of culture and material production.

The problem of vocational training is a paramount issue in Bulgaria's educational policy. The aim is for each secondary school leaver to have mastered, upon graduation, some profession.

The quality of the students' training depends both on the constant improvement of learning and on the improvement of the educational system. Naturally the improvement of learning is highly dependent on the technologies of learning and on the learning environment. It is now clear that the organizational structures, forms and tools in education could either facilitate or hamper the introduction of the best learning technologies.

THE EDUCATIONAL SYSTEM

Bulgaria's educational system is structured and functions according to a number of principals set out by the Government (People's Republic of Bulgaria, 1986). These include:

- state ownership of schools, universities and other institutes of learning;
- free education;
- providing each man and woman with the opportunity of education depending on his or her wishes, capabilities and the country's needs;

- centralized and planned management of the educational system;
- national unified curricula, syllabi and textbooks;
- equal opportunities and quality of instruction across institutions;
- providing young people with education that is relevant to their needs for life and which reflects the latest achievements in science and technology;
- education which is closely bound-up with the country's economic needs;
- state-funded maintenance and promotion of the educational system;
- involvement of industry in financing and maintenance of the system of vocational training and in the planning of educational needs; and
- conducting part of the vocational training in industrial conditions.

IMPROVING LEARNING

The general principles underlying the Bulgarian educational system imply specific organizational prerequisites for the improvement of learning.

The state-owned free secondary and higher schools make education generally accessible. Regardless of their means, young people can receive education depending on their wishes and capabilities. The centralized management of the system gives extremely wide opportunities for improving learning. The nationally unified syllabi and curricula simplify their optimization and help ensure that a well-structured content is taught throughout.

The optimized syllabi and curricula are an excellent basis for improving learning. Because they are unified, the textbooks can also be unified. Textbooks are approved on a competitive basis determined by the professional estimation they receive. Unified textbooks ensure similar, equally good conditions for improving education in different schools.

The centralized and planned management of the educational system is most conducive to improving learning through the timely and large-scale introduction of the latest and equally unified learning technologies. The planned nature and centralized management of the process of providing materials and facilities make it possible to:

- determine and follow priorities in distributing teaching aids and facilities to meet the most urgent needs and to achieve the highest economic efficiency;
- introduce unified teaching resources, thus allowing for an easy exchange and distribution of teaching aids; and
- select the most promising new technologies and to introduce them on a large scale.

The centralized management and state-funded character of education make it possible to develop courseware in a centralized manner and to distribute it free of charge to schools irrespective of their funds.

The education/industry relationship is effected through personnel training agreements between schools and industrial enterprises. These agreements are conducive to improving learning in two respects:

- finding resources and facilities for improving vocational education; and
- providing opportunities for vocational training in real industrial environments.

VOCATIONAL SUBJECTS

Bulgaria's educational system comprises three levels: primary (to the eighth grade), secondary (grades nine to eleven), and higher.

In addition to teaching various subjects, the primary school aims to find out the students' talents so that these can be encouraged later. The subject of 'crafts and creativity' is studied in the first three years and then for the next five years is continued as 'crafts'.

The goal of these subjects is to teach students to work, and thus to educate them. Simultaneously, children are taught certain skills and work habits, and their innate talents and flairs are discovered and encouraged.

Given the wide variety of secondary schools, technical colleges and vocational schools, the choice of a school suiting the wishes and capabilities of the student is a major pre-requisite for successful learning.

The choice should be regarded as an integral part of the system of improving learning, and involves a correct vocational orientation as well as an entrance examination. A system for the students' vocational orientation has been developed and is now operating. The objective for each man and woman is to make an independent and realistic choice of profession in accordance with his or her capabilities and the need for trained personnel within the economy.

There are vocational orientation centres in different regions of the country to aid children in their choice of a secondary school and a profession. In smaller towns and villages the network of schools and vocational training establishments is kept in step with the structure of the economy and the regional needs of cadres.

IMPROVING LEARNING THROUGH INDIVIDUALIZATION

In the context of a class lesson system of instruction and unified syllabi and curricula, it is possible to improve learning by making it more individualized and by applying flexible organizational forms of instruction at school and, in part, at a regional level.

General compulsory education
This is the basic form of instruction in schools and comprises 85-95 per cent of academic time. It is similar and compulsory for all students in the school.

Optional compulsory subject
This comprises two hours per week. It is compulsory for all students to choose from several subjects. These are normal school subjects that are extended in depth.

Optional non-compulsory subject
The school gives students the non-compulsory opportunity to attend a subject of their own choice for two hours a week.

Extra-class and extra-mural instruction
Depending on his or her interests, each student has the opportunity to attend various other forms of learning, such as circles in different subjects, computer clubs, craft and design courses and so on. Most of these take place in schools or in municipal centres for young engineers, Pioneer's Palaces, etc. These courses follow recommended but not obligatory unified curricula.

SUBJECT MATTER APPROACHES

Instruction in schools follows the traditional class-lesson system. Obviously, since the students in a class have different performances and abilities, we are now looking for ways to make learning more individual within the context of one teacher to many students. Computer-assisted learning is a major instrument (Pisarev and Pavlova, 1987). Classical instructional technologies also have potential for making learning more individualized, and this usually depends on the way in which the teacher approaches the students. Students of above-average performance are given additional, individual and more difficult tasks. Students with poorer achievements are also assigned additional tasks to acquire and to master certain habits and skills. Here, the flexibility in organizing the process of instruction rests entirely on the teacher. The school management encourages the teachers in their efforts to achieve better results in learning.

REGIONAL ORGANIZATIONAL STRUCTURES

The regional extra-school institutions of the educational system noted above are designed to promote the capabilities and talents of bright and gifted children, both in the field of engineering and the arts.

To aid the teaching in crafts and design classes, special intra-school centres have been established and fitted with expensive equipment to provide a real production context. The secondary school students both study and work there. This type of work experience improves education for industrial production and technology.

Special vocational qualification centres have been established to help the training of secondary and higher school students. This is a kind of integration between the secondary and higher schools on the one hand, and research institutes and industrial enterprises on the other. Each school may be a member of several of these associations.

NEW LEARNING TECHNOLOGIES AND INTERNATIONAL COOPERATION

The task of developing educational software in Bulgaria is highly organized. Research teams have been set up, funds provided and the evaluation of materials has been commissioned. The research teams collaborate with colleagues in other countries. The European socialist countries have designed a joint comprehensive research programme to improve the educational system through the introduction of computer technology. This programme falls into three parts:

- general and secondary education;
- secondary vocational education; and
- higher education.

The object is to design and introduce compatible hardware to facilitate the exchange of software tools, and educational software and hardware.

This international cooperation and the collaboration work are still in their early stages so it is not yet possible to comment on the results.

CONTENT-ORIENTATED APPROACHES

It is a legal requirement that schools must keep closely in touch with life and with the continuous advancement of the educational system. The educational system is not a *fait accompli* but is in a state of continuous reconstruction and improvement to meet the demands of the vast changes that are being effected, both in the structure and content of the economy and in societal development. The improvement of the educational system is highly dependent on optimizing the rates and content of the changes, and on improving the methods and system of its organization and management.

One approach to these objectives is to improve the subject matter in accordance with the educational goals. Instruction in Bulgarian schools is orientated towards acquiring methods of cognition and of efficient organization of learning and practice, so as to generate thinking and capable students who have a critical eye for their environment. The objective is to build habits and capacities for self-learning, improvement and creative thinking in students.

Together with providing the fundamentals of natural science and the humanities, the objective of the educational system is to set learning on a wide polytechnical basis by expanding the students' knowledge of modern technology and the regularities of socialized production. They are also taught practical skills and habits that involve them directly in production, and create in them the desire to work, to be enterprising and to be creative.

CONCLUSIONS

The new learning technologies have proved to be the principal means of improving learning. Their introduction and efficient utilization can be facilitated by employing flexible organizational forms, structures and tools. The centralized system of planning, financing and managing the educational system is a crucial factor in this process.

REFERENCES

People's Republic of Bulgaria (1986) *Education – Development for 1984-1986. National Report of the People's Republic of Bulgaria.* International Conference on Education, 40th Session, Geneva 1986.
Pisarev. A. and Pavlova, R. (1987) Some problems of computers and the individualization of learning in Bulgarian schools. In Percival, F. (ed) *Aspects of Educational Technology XX: Flexible Learning Systems.* Kogan Page, London.

37. Message Robot: A Support System for the Pace-Making of Classroom Work

Keizo Nagaoka, *Kobe University, Japan*
Issei Shiohara, *Shiohara Girls Senior High School, Kobe, Japan*

Summary: This paper discusses a new type of application of computers in education. Computer-assisted learning (CAL) generally aims at individualized education. However, in many countries, the most popular teaching format in schools is collective instruction or lecturing. The system which is described is called 'Message Robot' and is intended for use in collective instruction as an aid to pacing classroom work.

SYSTEM OUTLINE

We developed a system which has the following attributes:

Name:	Message Robot
Purpose:	Pace-setting of classroom work
Function:	Supporting the decision making of the teacher
Situation:	Collective instruction exercises
Hardware:	Response analyser and microcomputer (in the classroom)
	Mainframe (in the university)
	Interfaces/public telephone lines
	Wireless equipment for man-machine interface

The pace-setting functions of Message Robot are restricted to ending an exercise, giving a hint, making a comment, advising and so on.

Figure 1a shows the outline of the system.

TECHNOLOGIES

Numerical calculation

The time required by learners for completing an exercise or a task is described by the microcomputer as a response curve. The microcomputer calculates the data by means of the Weibull distribution. The resulting data and Weibull parameters of the response curve are used for input to an expert system.

Expert system techniques

An expert system running on a mainframe computer at Kobe University has been constructed with 250 production rules derived from experienced teachers' expertise. This expert system deals with input information as shown in Figure 1a.

The messages for supporting the teacher's decision are produced by the inference process using the input data and expertise shown in Figure 1b.

Obtained by analysis of student responses

- Response curve (ie response rate)
- Give-up rate
- Four *typical* students' responses

Classroom work conditions (input in advance)

Purpose of exercise:

1 Let students finish as many problems as possible
2 Review lightly
3 Other

Difficulty of task:

1 Difficult
2 Easy
3 Other

Class ability:

1 High
2 Low
3 Ordinary

Class motivation:

1 Positive
2 Negative

Time for exercise:

1 Sufficient
2 Not sufficient

Hints

Input at the time of use

Figure 1a. *Expert system: input data*

Knowledge-base 1 (expertise; 250 if-then rules):

- knowledge for data transformation
- knowledge for instructional strategy
- knowledge for response curve
- knowledge for students' condition
- knowledge for action timing
- knowledge for decision making

Knowledge-base 2 (temporary knowledge):

- knowledge arising from classroom working (eg time, response rate)

Figure 1b. *Expert system: teachers' expertise*

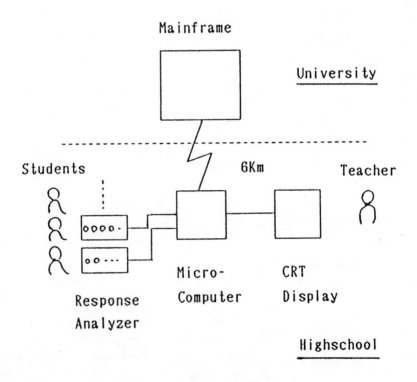

Figure 2. *Message robot system*

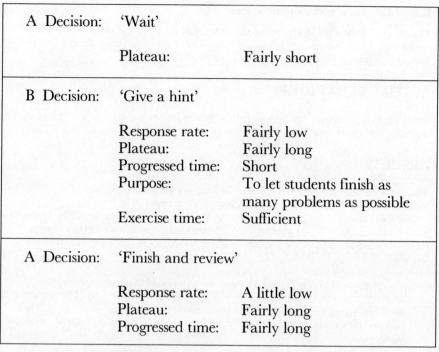

A Decision:	'Wait'	
	Plateau:	Fairly short
B Decision:	'Give a hint'	
	Response rate:	Fairly low
	Plateau:	Fairly long
	Progressed time:	Short
	Purpose:	To let students finish as many problems as possible
	Exercise time:	Sufficient
A Decision:	'Finish and review'	
	Response rate:	A little low
	Plateau:	Fairly long
	Progressed time:	Fairly long

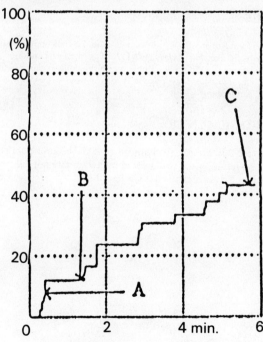

Figure 3. *Actual behaviour*

Long-distance communication

The microcomputer in the classroom and the expert system in the university are connected via interfaces and the public telephone system. This means that computer resources become available for use within education, as shown in Figure 2.

ACTUAL BEHAVIOUR

An example of the actual behaviour of the system is shown in Figure 3. Three messages-reasonings sets, corresponding to three time points, were displayed on a CRT.

RESULTS

The system is both effective and efficient for learning and the motivation of students. It is useful for the training of unskilled teachers or student teachers.

Our first version of such a system was named 'Face Robot' (Nagaoka, 1984; Nagaoka and Shiohara, 1985), which indicated the learning condition as a face graph display. Two major improvements have been implemented in the Message Robot system; they are as follows:

- though the face graph is good for rapid assimilation of the learning conditions of students, it is difficult for those with little experience to understand. The messages produced by message robot are more obvious and exact; and
- as noted previously, it is important to let the teacher be free in a classroom to make more communication with students.

REFERENCES

Nagaoka, K. (1984) Face Robot with response analyser in the classroom. In Alloway,B.S. and Mills, G.M. (eds) *Aspects of Educational Technology, XVIII*. Kogan Page, London.
Nagaoka, K. and Shiohara, I. (1985) Face Robot for pacemaking in classroom work. In Duncan, K. and Harris, D. (eds) *The Proceedings of the 4th World Conference on Computers in Education (WCCE 85)*, North Holland, Amsterdam.

ACKNOWLEDGEMENTS

The authors thank T Nishimura, T Okumura and M Nakamura for their helpful assistance. The research reported was assisted by a foundational aid from the Telecommunications Advancement Foundation (TAF).

Workshop report
38. Workshops that work!: some pre-workshop thoughts

Phil Race, *Polytechnic of Wales, UK*

Summary: The purpose of the workshop is to share experiences and develop criteria. This short paper was prepared in advance of the workshop, based on the author's own experiences of designing and conducting workshops.

WORKSHOPS: SOME 'DEFINITIONS'

'A workshop is a group event where each participant emerges able to do things better than they could at the start of the workshop.'

'A workshop is an event where each participant actively contributes for most of the time.'

'A workshop is an event where participants learn a lot from each other.'

'The outcomes of a workshop are dependent on the contributions of participants, rather than on input from the leader.'

'A workshop is not a lecture or a seminar, though it may include short episodes in such modes.'

The aim of this workshop is to identify criteria which may help ensure that workshop programmes and processes achieve their objectives. I have listed below various criteria under a range of headings relating to principal features of workshop programmes. First, I consider general issues common to most workshops. At the end I will include some general recommendations based on experience.

USES OF WORKSHOP OBJECTIVES

- To help ensure that the right people come to the workshop. When workshop objectives are known in advance, participants who can already achieve them are able to see that they may have little reason to attend.
- To help focus participants' attention on the main purposes of the workshop.
- To assist in the planning of the timing of workshop components.

Participants' modification of workshop objectives

It may be best (when possible) to allow participants-to-be to plan workshop objectives from the start (eg if a pre-workshop event is possible to arrange, or at the end of the first workshop, plan for the next one and so on).

Collecting participants' expectations provides a means for fine-tuning workshop objectives to meet the needs of a group.

If objectives are visibly modified to take into account participants' expectations, the group will feel more 'ownership' of the event. Participants are then more likely to follow-up the workshop in terms of trying out ideas and practices.

DRAFT CHECKLIST FOR WORKSHOP PROCESSES

- Can the workshop be accelerated (and participants' experience brought to a common starting point) by issuing a pre-workshop task? The completed task can be supplied to the workshop leader before the event, and the workshop tailored to take into consideration matters arising from the ways participants approached the task.
- Especially with participants who do not already know each other, it is useful to have a relevant, non-threatening 'ice-breaker' to get them talking to each other.
- A U-shape works better than rows. Participants need to be able to see each others' faces.
- Are workshop processes participant-centred, rather than 'leader-led'?
- Is there a good mixture of activities, including appropriate use of individual work, work in pairs and small groups, individual/group report-back, brainstorming (oral, acetate, paper and so on)?
- Does 'input' from the workshop leader take a minimum proportion of the time available? (eg is handout material used to avoid lengthy expositions?)
- Where participants have generated material/ideas, are these then 'crystallized and circulated to participants? (eg by 'workshop products' being produced from participants' acetates and flipcharts). Are workshop products produced and circulated quickly?
- Is it possible to ask what participants think of the workshop without waiting till the end of the event? A quick round-the-table response to 'How are you feeling about things so far?' can be most valuable (if sometimes terrifying!).
- When dividing participants into syndicates of two, three or four, it is useful deliberately to 'mix' them. Syndicates formed spontaneously from participants who happened to be sitting together (and probably already know each other) are in general less interesting than ones where participants are 'strangers'.
- If there are one or two 'negative' participants, it is worth rearranging syndicates for each task so that the negative influence is spread out rather than being concentrated on a few unfortunate (positive) participants.

SOME TIMETABLING CONSIDERATIONS

- Participants like to see timings and content details for various sections of the workshop. However, participants become restless if the workshop is seen to be running 'behind schedule'. Therefore plan timings carefully so that the probability of being able to adhere to them is maximized (eg include two or three parts in a 'slot' so that if one part over runs, the remaining parts can be 'squeezed' slightly).
- Always finish on time (coffee, lunch, close of workshop). Participants may become quite negative if workshops over run!
- If near the scheduled close of an event much remains to be done, use the time left to arrange a follow-up (including its draft objectives). Alternatively, allow an optional continuation after a break (letting those with trains to catch or children to collect slip out informally rather than walk out disruptively!).
- Start on time. This is necessary to avoid alienating those who have arrived promptly. But, do not start with anything on which everything else will depend: those who arrive late would be permanently disadvantaged (and may become hostile/unproductive). Therefore plan something useful, but not essential, for the first part of the workshop.
- A 30-minute coffee-break with a punctual return is better than a 15-minute coffee-break from which participants straggle back for several minutes.
- A 60-minute break for lunch may be insufficient in some restaurants!
- If an issue comes up which may mean major departures from the timetable, negotiate

a programme change/substitution with participants (rather than squeeze it in and run late).

EVALUATION OF WORKSHOPS

Real evaluation of workshops is likely to be achievable only months or years after the event, when it may be possible to analyse what participants did as a result of things they got out of a workshop. However, it is possible to obtain more instant feedback in a number of ways:

- *Oral feedback:* this can be gathered during or after a workshop. One problem is that the findings can be coloured by 'politeness' and wishes not to disagree with the consensus of views among others attending.
- *Feedback from workshop leaders:* it is often useful to address the question: 'What would you do differently if conducting the same workshop tomorrow with a new group of participants?'.
- *Feedback from participants' bosses:* when it is possible to gather feedback from people such as supervisors, heads of department, and so on, such feedback often has the advantage that things may be included which the participants would have been reluctant to give directly to the workshop leader.
- *Post-workshop feedback:* it is sometimes possible to gather participants' considered reactions to a workshop, for example some weeks after the event.

ADVANTAGES OF WORKSHOPS OVER OTHER TRAINING STRATEGIES

The advantages may include the following:

- Workshops should be more open-ended than other kinds of training event, so can be altered to meet new needs arising, or participants' expectations and wishes.
- Participants emerge from a good workshop with the feeling they have contributed actively, sharing 'ownership' of the outcomes of the workshop. They are more likely to build on what they have done.
- Workshop situations can be used for role-play and simulation in a non-threatening environment. Participants can (for example) rehearse how they may best respond to difficult situations, or try out controversial approaches and gain feedback from fellow participants.
- If participants are kept active it is usual for them to gain at least as much from each other as from the workshop leader or workshop resource materials.
- When a workshop is repeated with new groups, the workshop leader can cross-fertilize findings from previous workshops. This helps ensure that all possible dimensions are included in analyses and discussions.
- To some extent, workshops can be 'open learning experiences' for participants who can learn at their own pace and in their own way, within reason.

GENERAL RECOMMENDATIONS

Number of participants

Six to sixteen participants work well. If there are more than 20 it is likely that participants will not feel that they are involved sufficiently actively (report-backs can become boring, and so on). If there are less than six participants the experience-base is usually rather too limited.

For 16 or more participants it is desirable to have more than one 'leader' so that participants can be split into smaller groups for most activities.

Co-leaders

Never work at short notice with someone you have not worked with before!

If you want to have an 'equal' co-leader, it is best that they are someone you have worked with several times already.

Co-leaders are best trained by 'assisting' you on two or three workshops.

New workshop repertoire is best gained by assisting an expert in the field concerned on several occasions before launching out on your own.

Things to arrange in advance

If working away from your 'home-base', when dealing with the person on-site who is responsible for organizing your workshop, it's always worth mentioning in writing things like overhead projector, flipchart, room with moveable seating, extra rooms for syndicate work, timings of coffee/lunch, and so on.

Things to have with you

It is useful to have the following general items:

- acetate sheets and OHP;
- place cards;
- five or so extra copies of any handouts to be used;
- 'Blue-Tack'; and
- Spare copies of the workshop programme.

Section 5:
Supporting staff

39. Improving learning: the impact of learning on professional training and staff development programmes

Derek Gardiner and Peter Mathias, *CCETSW, London, UK*

Summary: This paper draws on two recent studies and considers their findings in the context of research into student learning in higher education, and of work in organizational psychology. Despite the differences in the focus and purpose of the studies, a large number of similarities were found. These similarities and common elements could be developed into a more general model which can be used to plan and understand a wide range of change-promoting and learning activities. In essence, the model proposes that conceptions of learning and change held by those involved influence the design, implementation and outcome of educational and organizational change enterprises. Three levels of conception are identified and their influence/impact demonstrated in case studies. The first level is characterized by surface-reproductive conceptions of the content of learning and change. The second level is concerned with deep-constructive conceptions with a focus on the processes of learning and change. The third level concerns conceptions of learning and change which also encompass learning-to-learn and the transfer of learning (ie meta-learning). The model allows descriptions and interpretations of interactions, and of change through time. It is thus potentially a powerful tool in explaining and giving meaning to educational and organizational change processes.

RECENT RESEARCH INTO STUDENT LEARNING IN HIGHER EDUCATION AND ORGANIZATIONAL DEVELOPMENT

Adult learning in higher education

The main thrust of recent research into adult learning comes from studies carried out in Goteborg, Sweden, since the middle of the 1970s. They represent a major refocusing of educational research by looking at learning from the learner's perspective. This means that attention is given to *what* is learned and *how* that learning occurred, it does not try simply to measure *how much* is learned. This perspective is about how people see and construe their world and the way this influences learning.

The early studies concerned how students studied books and articles. Two main approaches used by students were identified which the researchers called *surface approach* and *deep approach* (Marton and Saljo, 1976). The surface approach involves trying to memorize facts from the text of the article or book. It is essentially a passive, reproductive approach to learning. The deep approach is characterized by a search for meaning. It is active and constructive (ie the learners actively try to construe meaning for themselves).

These different approaches to studying were found to be directly associated with qualitatively different outcomes of learning; thus using a surface approach never produced a deep outcome. Clearly, if students are versatile and able to use both approaches, then they could respond appropriately to either reproductive or constructive learning tasks.

These findings were also demonstrated in research into students' everyday approaches to their coursework.

Underlying these different approaches to learning, and the consequent differences in outcomes of learning, were distinctly different conceptions held by the students of what learning actually involves. Saljo (1976) found five levels of understanding of the concept of learning. The first three are relatively simple, reproductive conceptions. The last two are more complex, constructive conceptions.

Of particular interest to us is the further work undertaken by Saljo (1979) in relation to the impact on learning of the perceptions students had of the context in which their learning was to take place. The approaches reported above were the approaches chosen by students to meet the learning task *as they perceived it* and *in that particular context*. While further work elsewhere has considered the influence of the institutional and departmental milieux on learning (eg Entwistle and Ramsden, 1983), Saljo looked especially at the influence of students' perceptions and expectations of the nature and focus of assessment on their approaches to learning, and the outcomes of that learning.

Other work in Sweden showed that when students felt over-burdened with the amount they had to learn, they tended to revert to surface approaches, and that those using surface-level approaches were unable to sustain high levels of study time as the academic year went on. Students who characteristically use surface approaches seem likely to be disadvantaged in higher education generally and particularly so in professional education where they must demonstrate knowledge-in-use and construe meanings from their own experience and those of colleagues with whom they work.

Even when teachers in higher education intend that students should have deep outcomes to their learning, these kinds of outcomes can be constrained by surface-level teaching, by forms of assessment which require (or value) only reproductive learning, or by giving students too much to learn.

At the heart of all of this work are the conceptions which teachers and learners have of learning itself. Unless they can understand that learning means more than simply remembering and reproducing information, and involves the students in actively construing meanings for themselves, then students' learning will simply result in surface level approaches and outcomes.

The Swedish work has been replicated and extended in England, Australia and Holland. Some of the further work has been concentrated upon the impact of differing contexts of learning (Svensson, 1976). Some work has considered the perceptions students have of what they are required to learn (Biggs, 1985), while other studies have looked at the relationship between conceptions of learning and the conceptions students have of teaching, understanding and insight, and the relation of theory to practice (Van Rossum et al, 1985).

A central finding from this body of work is the recognition that deep outcomes of learning, however much they may be intended, will be constrained by a large number of factors, including on the one hand the conceptions which learners have of learning itself, and on the other hand, the approaches of teachers, the nature and forms of assessment, and the departmental and institutional contexts (which increasingly have, in turn, been influenced by broader societal and political factors). This links with developments in the training and organizational change literature.

Recent literature on training and organizational change

The 1980s have seen the elaboration of an interventionist approach which sets training and trainers more firmly within an organizational context than the traditional educational approach concerned with individual learning irrespective of the organizational context within which it takes place.

Bramley (1986) argues that the interventionist approach is designed to overcome the shortcomings of the educational one which consist of:

- difficulties in transferring, maintaining or applying skills acquired in training sessions to everyday work;
- the learning development of, at best, tenuous links between individual learning and organizational effectiveness; and
- the lack of recognition that the context in which individuals work affects performance as well as does the possession of skills, abilities and competence.

Within interventionist training, learning is seen as instrumental to organizational effectiveness. It is as necessary for trainers to think about organizational and group learning as it is for them to offer opportunities for individual learning and development. Improved learning means improved organizational effectiveness, and training interventions are judged and valued accordingly.

The importance of such developments to the present paper is the finding that the extent to which trainers are able to develop an interventionist approach to their work depends on the structure and climate within the organization.

For example, Pettigrew, Jones and Reason (1982) found five perspectives on the training role in a study of trainers in the chemical industry. The five perspectives were distinguished on the basis of perceptions of the purpose of training. Of these, the first key to trainer effectiveness was held to be the capacity to modify and adapt the role and purpose of training according to the organizational context. The second key was the way in which the trainer manages the boundary between their activity and the rest of the organization.

Thus it appears that training and learning within organizations, and particularly their outcomes in terms of individual and organizational effectiveness, are subject to the multiple influences of the organizational process. Our argument is that the varied perceptions of the role of training, and the differing conceptions of learning which may be held by various actors, are central to the process and directly related to outcomes. This influence is exerted throughout the negotiations and interactions essential to the design and implementation of training activities within organizations. The staff development programme described later contributed to our thinking in this area.

The interface between the adult learning and the training literature

From our reviews of the literature, we are particularly interested in the following features:

- For some people there are apparently single, right ways to do things in their world; thus for them, learning, training and understanding how organizations work or change, involves finding out the right way things happen and trying to do it. They also have a belief that there are single right outcomes to these activities. We characterize these absolutist conceptions as 'level one', which underlie surface-reproductive approaches and outcomes.
- For other people, there is a recognition of diversity in each of these conceptions (of learning, training, organization, and so on) and, consequently, there are opportunities to choose courses of action. These courses encompass surface-level activities, but also include deep-level ones. The latter allow the possibility of deep outcomes to these activities derived from 'level two' conceptions.
- In choosing courses of action, some people are able to give attention to congruence and the match/mismatch of the task and learning approach necessary to accomplish it. Those who are able to make appropriate choices of approach to lead to the required outcome, will need to have developed a repertoire from which they can make these choices. This meta-learning ability, the capacity to learn to learn, and to transfer learning (Gardiner, 1984), we characterize as 'level three' conceptions of

training, which allow this range of approaches and outcomes which may be both content and context dependent.

We also found, in addition to being able to define the above three levels of approach and outcome, that:

- the levels of outcome actually achieved, will be dependent upon the interactions between those involved in planning, design, implementation, evaluation and the approaches they use. These, in turn, will be constrained by the levels of conception of learning, training and organization, which they hold; and
- the roles which those responsible for the development of training or educational programmes can adopt are influenced by the culture and climate of the organization in which they find themselves. This applies equally to the public and private sectors and to higher education and commerce. Attempts to change role or alter educational practice can therefore be enhanced by, and contribute to, an understanding of organizational change and development.

Underlying each of these features, are the conceptions held by individuals and groups, of 'learning', 'training' and 'organization'.

We can now turn to describing two case examples of learning and change where data can be gained by looking at these kinds of features. We later synthesize the findings into a preliminary model of learning and change in a wide variety of educational, training and organizational development enterprises.

CASE STUDY 1: STAFF DEVELOPMENT PROGRAMME

Between 1984 and 1986 one of the authors took part in the design and implementation of a staff development programme for a group of voluntary organizations operating in the social services area.

The programme was designed, run and evaluated under contract to a committee set up to represent the interests of the commissioning organizations and to manage the development. Full details of the evaluation can be found elsewhere (Mathias, 1986). It showed that over half the participants changed their approach to the training material as the course progressed. The problem was that the course designers had hoped to encourage holistic approaches but the direction of change was from holist to serialist (Pask, 1976).

The training material consisted of audio, text and some video. At the insistence of the course designers, two one-day workshops and a residential period of three days were included in the programme. In addition, each participant was provided with a study supervisor whose purpose was to provide expertise and feedback.

The programme extended over four months and the range of time spent by participants on the programme was from approximately 40 to 130 hours. The material was designed in four units and the finding, that at the end of the fourth unit half the participants had changed their approach from holistic to serialistic, was unexpected.

In retrospect, it seems that the terms of the enterprise and the detail of the contract between those who were to produce the programme and those who commissioned it were not established sufficiently clearly at the beginning.

In particular, the course writers assumed an interventionist strategy to training, seeking to influence the effectiveness of the organization as well as the individual competencies of programme participants. This conception of purpose was not shared by the commissioning committee. Additionally, the course writers failed to realize early on that the commissioning organizations needed to develop the capacity to keep the programme running once the pilots were over. The training committee was under pressure to deliver 'no-nonsense, relevant training' more effectively than in the past. The culture and climate of the enterprise became a high-pressured, competitive one in which everyone seemed to feel they had much to prove.

The climate influenced the course designers to evaluate the course and control the resulting information, partly in defence of their own position: to prove that a good job had been done. This led to the over-use of questionnaires in which participants were asked to identify and reflect on their own performance.

The repetitive, frequent use of the same evaluation sheet may have pushed the participants towards serialist approaches to the material. Marton and Saljo (1976) reflect on a similar finding where students 'technified' their training to meet the assessment task. The implications for systems of assessment are clear: students can be driven towards serialist approaches by the form which assessment takes.

Other data from the evaluation suggest that participants were constantly scanning the world of the programme in search of salient cues and clues about the significance of the material, their own performance and the expectation of key figures (Mathias, 1986). Such cue-seeking or strategic behaviour has been found elsewhere in the literature (Miller and Parlett, 1973; Entwistle, 1987).

In summary, the quality of the participants' experience, the strategies they adopted and the outcomes they achieved seem to have been influenced by the following factors:

- negotiations about the terms of the programme between course writers and training committee in which differing conceptions of training were significant, but not fully dealt with;
- the design of the course which included study supervisors whose own conceptions of training and learning influenced behaviour in their interaction with participants; and
- conceptions about the exercise held by participants: in the early stages, as they related to career prospects, and in the intermediate stages, as they were influenced by the structure of the material and the behaviour of supervisors, managers and course organizers.

CASE STUDY 2: TEACHING AND LEARNING IN SOCIAL WORK EDUCATION

One of us recently undertook some research to study teaching and learning interactions in professional education (Gardiner, 1987) which focuses particularly on teaching and learning in supervision in social work qualifying training. Approximately half of the time on social work training courses is devoted to practice placements in agencies, where students practice under the supervision of a qualified worker. The supervisory relationship is a key component in the development of six practice skills, but it is under-researched.

This study was essentially illuminative in nature, methodology and purpose, from the perspectives of supervisors and students. It began by presenting some illustrative experiences which were not adequately explained using the traditional model of supervision. A literature review showed the roots of that model in American casework supervision literature of the immediate post-war period. The research task was to generate descriptions and interpretations of teaching and learning in supervision which were meaningful to the participants themselves, and which could contribute to the development of a new, grounded model of learning in professional education for the 1980s.

Data were gathered by a range of methods including questionnaires, interviews and tape recordings of supervision sessions, and were presented as illustrative case examples. These accounts of the content and process of supervisory sessions pointed to the importance of the conceptions which the supervisors and students had of the learning process as a factor in explaining the patterns of interaction seen in the supervisory relationship.

Three qualitatively different levels of teaching-learning interaction in supervision were identified, derived from and constrained by students' and supervisors' conceptions of learning. The three levels reflect, respectively, a focus on the content of learning, a focus on the process of learning, and a focus on meta-learning (ie learning to learn, and the transfer of learning). Feedback to participants and other supervisors, tutors and policy-makers was included in the study to validate the findings and to develop the model.

The findings which are relevant to social work education have been reported elsewhere (Gardiner, 1984; 1987) so less attention is given here to the specific details of the teaching-learning interactions which were described, although it should be noted that they represent the building blocks of the model we shall describe.

TOWARDS A MODEL OF LEARNING CONCEPTIONS IN CHANGE ENTERPRISES

Earlier in the paper some common features in the literature, which are exemplified and developed by the case examples, were described. These are summarized below:

- for some people there are single right approaches to learning, training, organizational change and understanding organizations;
- for others there is a recognition of diversity in each of these, therefore there is opportunity for choice of actions and outcomes;
- in making choices, attention needs to be given to congruence and match/mismatch of the actors' levels of conception;
- outcomes will be dependent upon the interactions between those involved in planning, design, implementation and evaluation derived from their levels of conception; and
- the climate and culture of the educational enterprise or organization within which learning takes place should be taken into account when planning change activities.

The constraining effect of conceptions of learning and training have been illustrated in the case studies. Thus, in the process of commissioning, designing, implementing and evaluating learning and training programmes, the impact of the levels of conceptions should be identified.

The model which we use to explain these events and experiences is an interactive one which describes and explains the patterns of interaction between those involved. Thus interaction one will be the pattern resulting from actor(s) A and actor(s) B having level-one conceptions of the purpose of their meeting. Similarly, interactions two and three result from congruency of conception between those involved.

If there is match, or congruence in any level (eg between a teacher (actor A) and a student (actor B)), or a commissioning committee (actors A) and course writers (actors B), outcomes may be satisfactory up to the level of the match of their conceptions. However, a mismatch may well produce persistent conflict, clashes and confusion. It is likely that major problems will occur if either actor(s) A or actor(s) B are operating at level one, with the other(s) at levels two or three. Clearly if outcomes at levels two or three are intended, the interactions of those involved must at least reach such a level.

Thus, recurrent problems like lack of application, poor take-up, overt hostility from

	LEVELS OF CONCEPTION		
	1	2	3
actor(s) A	conception A_1	conception A_2	conception A_3
interaction pattern	interaction 1	interaction 2	interaction 3
actor(s) B	conception B_1	conception B_2	conception B_3

Figure 1. *Patterns of interaction*

other parts of the organization, or the unexpected or unintended use of learning strategies inappropriate to the task, can be explained or avoided by doing work on the levels of conception in the initial stages of planning with those who require the change, and in the implementation and evaluation phases with those who are the subjects of the programme.

Because there is a direct relationship between approaches and outcomes at individual and organizational levels of change enterprises, improved performance comes from:

- identifying organizational factors which may influence course design, learning strategy and learning outcome;
- looking for congruence in overall design between intended outcomes and approaches required by the learning programme; and
- deciding whether attention needs to be given to the introduction of a programme which will promote shifts in levels of conception in participants, thus extending the range of possible outcomes.

We have found this model useful in describing and explaining experiences in the two evaluative studies reported above. We have also offered the model to a number of colleagues in higher, further and professional education. They have also found it useful in helping them to make sense of a wide range of learning, teaching assessment, evaluation and research activities.

At this point, the model is tentative and incomplete. It is offered here only in outline. We are encouraged by initial responses to it, will continue to develop and refine it, and will report its further usage in the relevant literature.

REFERENCES

Biggs, J. (1985) The role of meta-learning in study processes, *British Journal of Educational Psychology*, **55**, 185-212.

Bramley, P. (1986) Evaluation. In *Gower Handbook of Management Development*. Gower, London.

Entwistle, N. (1987) A model of the teaching-learning process. In Richardson, Eysenck and Warren-Piper (eds) *Student Learning*. SRHE/OU, Milton Keynes.

Entwistle, N. and Ramsden, P. (1983) *Understanding Student Learning*. Croom Helm, London.

Gardiner, D.W.G. (1984) Learning for transfer, *Issues in Social Work Education*, **4,** 2, 95-105.

Gardiner, D.W.G. (1987) *Teaching and learning in social work practice placements: a study of process in professional training*. PhD Thesis, Institute of Education, University of London.

Marton, F. and Saljo, R. (1976) On qualitative differences in learning: 1 outcome and process, *British Journal of Educational Psychology*, **46,** 4-11.

Mathias, P. (1986) Distance learning: an evaluation of a course, an exploration of the strategies used by students and a description of the experience of studentship. Unpublished report: Dept of Occupational Psychology, Birkbeck College, London.

Miller, C. and Parlett, M. (1973) *Up to the Mark*. Occasional paper 13. Centre for Research in Educational Sciences, University of Edinburgh, Edinburgh.

Pask, G. (1976) Styles and strategies of learning, *British Journal of Educational Psychology*, **46,** 128-148.

Pettigrew, A.M., Jones, G.R. and Reason, P.W. (1982) *Training and Development Roles in Their Organizational Setting*. Training Division, MSC, Sheffield.

Saljo, R. (1976) Qualitative differences in learning as a function of the learner's conception of the task, *Studies in Educational Science*, 14, University of Goteborg.

Saljo, R. (1979) Learning in the learner's perspective 1: some commonsense conceptions. *Reports from Institute of Education*, 77, University of Goteborg.

Svensson, L. (1976) *Study Skills and Learning*. Acta Universitatis, Gothoburgensis.

Van Rossum, E., Deijkers, R. and Hamer, R. (1985) Students' learning conceptions and their interpretation of significant learning concepts, *Higher Education*, **14,** 617-641.

40. Initial teacher training at a distance

David Wright and Duncan Harris, *Faculty of Education and Design, Brunel University, UK*

Summary: This paper discusses an important new development in initial teacher training exemplified by the physics with technology two-year part-time distance learning PGCE course offered by Brunel University.

INTRODUCTION

The course was developed in response to a need discovered by the Institution of Electrical Engineers (IEE). The IEE found that an appreciable number of their women members were interested in the possibility of training to teach in secondary schools. These members, many of whom were on career breaks, were unable or unwilling to make use of conventional full-time teacher training courses because of family and other commitments.

Discussions between the IEE, the University Faculty of Education and Design, and Local Education Officers followed and led to the proposal for a PGCE course in Physics with Technology. Following their initial enquiries of their members, the IEE discovered that the interest also extended to a significant number of male members.

It soon became apparent that the demand for the course was not confined to members of the IEE. The majority of enquiries came from London and South East England. The course team decided at an early stage that, provided proper support could be arranged, students would be accepted from a much wider catchment than the Home Counties. The course is not a conversion course, as normally understood: students are graduate engineers, physical scientists or technologists.

THE COURSE

The basis of the course was to be:

- student lives at home, carries out school experience near home in collaboration with their LEA;
- all course materials provided on a distance learning basis;
- weekend and one-day meetings arranged at roughly bi-monthly intervals; and
- tutorial support available by telephone and occasional visits to local groups.

Most of the course makes use of written material from the Faculty. The design of the materials assumes that the students have met most, if not all, of the authors. The materials have followed five decisions identified by Fyfe (1981):

- attractively presented;
- involve active learning;
- teaching as personal as possible;
- functions of materials clear; and
- media input simple (none currently in this aspect of the course).

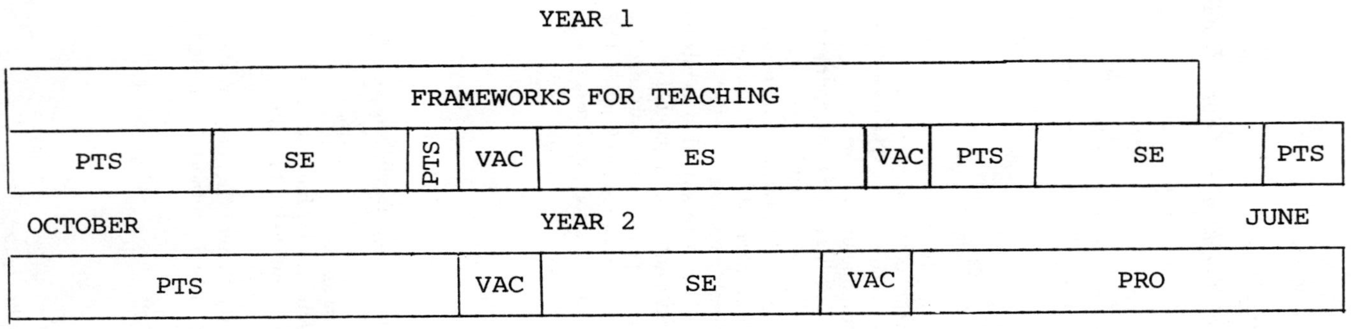

YEAR 1

FRAMEWORKS FOR TEACHING

PTS	SE	PTS	VAC	ES	VAC	PTS	SE	PTS

OCTOBER   JUNE

YEAR 2

PTS	VAC	SE	VAC	PRO

PTS Physics and Technology Teachings Studies

ES Educational Studies

SE School Experience

PRO Project

VAC Vacation

Figure 1. *Overall structure of the scheme*

However, for these students a unit was much longer than Fyfe's suggested 3.5 hours work. Subsequent feedback suggests that the decision was correct.

One section of the material consists of physics and technology teaching studies which includes broad-balanced science. Each unit of the material focuses on a topic (eg electricity, waves etc) and looks at the way in which this topic may be taught and the concepts and ideas learned in school.

The Open University approach using mainstream texts and tributary texts doesn't seem appropriate since for teacher training applications all of the material has to be understood and grasped. The course, if it is to be successful, must give the students confidence and to that end each topic indicates most of the material likely to be met in 11 to 18 schools with many questions, most of which are based on current popular school texts being used. Although many of these questions are apparently simple, the students accept them as an essential part of their armoury for helping learners in school.

The physics technology link is particularly important for this group of students since many of them have important skills, knowledge and understanding from their experience as engineers. The importance of broad-balanced science developments in the 11-16 curriculum, AS levels and the changing nature of technology are emphasized. Practical work also occurs, some of which is carried out during visits to the university and some of which takes place in a local school. The overall structure of the scheme is shown in Figure 1.

The education part of the course is in collaboration with the Open University (Holmberg, 1981) and begins with the Open University Course EP228 'Frameworks for Teaching' which initially runs in parallel with the physics and technology contributions.

The second major part of the education studies course is made up of five units prepared specially for the course and in the main written in-house. The five topics covered under educational studies consider both fundamental and recent developments in teaching. Where appropriate, these have been related to the teaching of physics and technology.

The first topic investigates the value judgements inherent in teaching and the nature of the knowledge we profess as teachers. The second topic adopts a psychological perspective in order to consider motivation, attention and perception, learning and memory, concept formation and intellectual development. The third topic examines assessment and its relationship to learning. The fourth examines one aspect of that whole process designed to ensure a closer fit between schools and the world of work: the extent and impact of TVEI on schools. The final topic focuses upon the fundamental classroom process of language, its nature, uses, development and the relationship between language and learning. Writing and reading are considered in the same way.

Students need to meet tutors who write materials, prepare themselves for independence in learning (Boud, 1981) and have some hands-on experience with school apparatus. There are two residential weekends and an additional three to six days (according to the needs of the group) with these foci.

ASSESSMENT

Written assignments are used for the education studies and physics and technology teaching studies part of the course. The performance of the student teacher on school experience is assessed by the local tutor in consultation with a university tutor.

It is already clear that some students, when under pressure, revert to teaching strategies that were used on them. Current teaching/learning environments emphasize teaching strategies to enable learning with the teacher or by the learner. Mature students as teachers in training need to reflect on their approaches, there needs to be 'rebuilding and review' (Candy et al, 1985)

Students are expected to devote some 20 hours per week to the whole course. Initial feedback indicated that most students were spending longer than this on the written material and assignments.

STUDENT SELECTION

Interviews are arranged for each place on the course, provided the prospective student is likely to be successful on the course and meets the usual entry requirements. The interviewing procedure is more complicated than for a normal PGCE course: each candidate being interviewed by the local authority science advisor/inspector in conjunction with a university course tutor. This method is used to introduce the local authority to the course and to enable discussions to take place, as well as ensuring that the student is acceptable to the authority. It is clear that students, although not given any expectation of employment at the end of the course, would probably be employed by the same local authority represented by the science advisor/inspector.

As well as assessing, within the limitations of the interview, the qualities expected in a teacher, a definite attempt is made to determine the likely response of the candidate to returning to apparently simple\ideas and equipment. It will be appreciated that the students are mature candidates, many of whom have been in positions of responsibility in industry.

SCHOOL EXPERIENCE

School experience is an essential part of any teacher training course, an equivalent of 16 weeks is required. In the course there are four components:

- The initial observation concerned with the students observing classroom activities (eg styles of teaching). The students are prepared for this by means of discussions during visits to the university as well as by distance learning material. Each student is given a set of suggested foci so that the visit to school will fit into a well-structured framework.
- The second block of school experience is a gradual introduction to teaching, beginning with small groups and progressing to full classes. Students can expect to have their difficulties during this block so strong guidance and support are necessary.
- The third block lasts for some ten weeks and is assessed. A student who is unsuccessful will not be awarded a PGCE. However, problems should be apparent before the end of the previous block so remedial action can be taken.
- There is, in addition, a project in the final (fourth) school experience. This project links the learning process in school with physics and technology.

Each phase of the experience has a preparatory introduction (eg observation for phase 1) and an evaluatory phase, the latter being a crucial part of debriefing (Pearson and Smith, 1985).

EXPECTATION AND STUDENT SUPPORT

It is clear that a great emphasis is placed on the support of students on school experience and this is particularly important during the second and third blocks. In order to prepare students, they are counselled in advance and guided by means of written material. Inevitably, the day-to-day support is especially important and must come from the school, usually the appropriate head of department deputizing for the LEA science adviser. In the event of problems requiring special support, the course tutors have to attend or communicate with the students by means of the telephone. Local group meetings are a necessary part of this support system.

We have already emphasized the link between the subject material and the preparation for the blocks of school experience; there is an additional link for practical work.

There are several specific problems in connection with the needs of the students and the nature of the course. The following points are apparent:

- as has already been noted, students frequently revert to their own experiences as pupils when faced with new material and stress;
- a student may have a false impression of the degree of difficulty of a topic and may not appreciate their own lack of understanding; and
- students may feel isolated and insecure, particularly before their school experience blocks.

Although this course is not intended as a conversion course, we place great emphasis on the need to challenge the ideas already accepted by the student from their own experience.

THE FUTURE

Audio conferencing and normal videotapes are planned as part of the course, interactive video is being considered as a possible development. An interactive video system would allow students to appear to visit the classroom, perhaps during a practical session. Classroom problems could be incorporated so that the response of the student would affect the next stage of the programme. The main difficulties are those of initial cost in the development of the interactive video programme and the cost of the equipment required by the student. Inevitably programmes would have to be of short duration, so it would be uneconomical unless funding could be obtained on, perhaps, a national basis and local centres were available for the students to visit to view the programmes.

It is too early to evaluate the long-term success of the course; this will only be possible when students are successfully teaching in schools on a long-term basis. We are aware of the particular needs of mature students in this area and first indications are that these mature students with industrial experience will indeed make an important contribution to the physics and technology teaching profession.

REFERENCES

Boud, D. (1981) Independence and interdependence in distance education: responsive course design. In Percival, F. and Ellington, H. (eds) *Distance Learning and Evaluation: Aspects of Educational Technology XV*. Kogan Page, London.

Candy, P., Harri-Augstein, S. and Thomas, L. (1985) Reflection and the self-organised Learner: a model of learning conversation. In Boud, D., Keogh, R. and Walker, D. (eds) *Reflection: Turning Experience into Learning*. Kogan Page, London.

Fyfe, W. (1981) The production and evaluation of materials for a distance learning course. In Pericval, F. and Ellington, H. (eds) *Distance Learning and Evaluation: Aspects of Educational Technology XV*. Kogan Page, London.

Holmberg, B. (1981) Approaches to distance education. In Percival, F. and Ellington, H. (eds) *Distance Learning and Evaluation: Aspects of Educational Technology XV*. Kogan Page, London.

Pearson, M. and Smith, D. (1985) Debriefing in experience-based learning. In Boud, D., Keogh, R. and Walker, D. (eds) *Reflection: Turning Experience into Learning*. Kogan Page, London.

41. Microteaching in postgraduate teacher training

G Kendall, *University of Natal, Pietermaritzburg, South Africa*

Summary: This paper provides opportunity for the author to report back to the United Kingdom, data collected for his doctoral thesis which was concerned with a comparative study between the factors affecting the use of microteaching in postgraduate teacher training in the United Kingdom and Southern Africa. The survey undertaken obtained information on the use of microteaching and was concerned particularly with organizational practices (ie size of group, number of sessions, staff involvement, use of recording equipment, timetable structures, studio facilities etc). In addition, attitudes of staff members in relation to the various aspects associated with microteaching (ie physical and technical facilities, preparation and supervision of students, immediate objectives, effects on students, relation to other education courses, economic factors etc) were obtained.

INTRODUCTION

Since its introduction in the 1960s, microteaching has attracted attention as a training technique by practitioners and as a research technique by researchers in education (as identified in Allen and Ryan, 1969). The two activities have not necessarily given each other the support originally visualized since the logistics of operating a microteaching programme and of incorporating it into an already overloaded teacher-training course were such that it appeared impossible to build such a programme on a sound research basis and, on the other hand, researchers tended to reject the ad hoc approach of those involved in teacher training. There have also been research studies in which the staff of a teacher-training institution participated before making more widespread use of microteaching, but the planning, preparation and execution of a programme for a small experimental group is a very different exercise to the one required for the total population of students. Hence there seemed to be a need for a research study with a wider base to investigate the details of microteaching programmes as they were being offered in teacher-training courses and to see how these compared to the research findings (see also McIntyre et al, 1977).

RESEARCH DESIGN

The present study has attempted to investigate the details of microteaching programmes for postgraduate teacher training by the use of:

- an organization questionnaire to obtain information about what actually was happening, according to the members of staff responsible for the microteaching programmes;
- an attitude questionnaire to provide information about what the staff members felt about microteaching with reference to particular aspects of the whole programme; and
- a search of the research literature.

Number of responses

	Univ	Poly	Coll	Total
United Kingdom	94	26	47	167

Table 1. *Number of respondents*

The study is more fully reported in Kendall 1985, 1987a, 1987b.

Responses were received from 30 university education departments, 12 polytechnics and 22 colleges; the number of respondents are shown in Table 1.

The responses were grouped in five main areas: science, social studies, language, education and miscellaneous (combining arts and mathematics), as shown in Table 2.

The additional numbers indicated by '+' are used to show where there were no detailed responses about the organization of microteaching, the percentages therefore refer only to

	— United Kingdom —			Total UK%
	Univ	Poly	Coll	
SCIENCE	28	6	6	(31%)
Biology	7 +1		1 +1	
Chemistry	8 +1		1 +1	
Physics	8 +2			
Science	2	3	4 +1	
Physical Sc.	2			
Technology	1			
Home Econ.		3		
SOC STUDIES	18	1	5	(19%)
Geography	8 +2	1	1	
History	9 +2	+1		
Rel. Educ.	1 +1			
Soc. Studies	+1	+1	1	
Economics		+1	2	
Commerce			1	
LANGUAGES	14	2	6	(17%)
English	4 +2	+2	1	
Modern Lang.	9 +3	1 +2	5	
Classics	+1			
TESL	1	1		
EDUCATION	3	5	8	(13%)
Primary	1 +2	2	3 +4	
Middle	1 +1	+1	2	
Further Educ.	1			
Secondary Educ		3 +2	2	
Slow Learners			1	
Educ/AV			+1	
MISCELLANEOUS	14	4	8	(20%)
Art/Design	1 +1	2 +2	1	
Music		1	1 +1	
Physical Educ.	3 +1		2 +1	
Mathematics	10 +2	1	4 +1	

Table 2. *Number of responses in different subject groups*

the detailed responses to the organization questionnaire.

Universities returned a comparatively large number (33.3 per cent) of science responses and a small number (6.9 per cent) of education, whereas colleges showed a higher proportion (32.6 per cent) of education responses. Polytechnics produced the most representative sample.

CONCLUSIONS FROM THE SURVEY

In 1975, Hargie and Maidment undertook out a survey directed at 220 'target' establishments, classified as local authority, voluntary, university and polytechnic, operating all types of initial training, not just postgraduate, at a time when '... the end of the first decade of microteaching in the United Kingom was approaching' (Hargie and Maidment, 1979). There were 177 responses, including 84 which gave a more detailed description of existing or planned microteaching programmes. No distinction was made between the use of microteaching in one-year postgraduate courses and four-year diploma or BEd courses for initial teacher training.

Hargie and Maidment's survey preceded '... the most far-reaching and long-term changes in the system for training teachers in its long history' and which led to the outright closures, amalgamations and redesignations of colleges that have occurred. The present survey may be able to provide answers to some of the questions posed about the possible direction of microteaching that arose from the earlier survey, but only in relation to postgraduate teacher training.

With reference to the four points that Hargie and Maidment make about microteaching in the United Kingdom, the present survey suggests a number of conclusions for postgraduate teacher training.

The degree of market penetration

It appears that the use of microteaching is more likely to be on the decline than on the ascendency. Although a few institutions indicate that they are exploring its use for the first time, there is more evidence of tutors no longer making use of the technique. A number of factors appear to have contributed to this trend. The decline in the national economy has introduced cuts in capital development and, more importantly, in the maintenance and running expenses of existing facilities. There were many reports of lack of technical assistance, of technical assistance being restored again after an interval and of equipment not being provided when requested.

Teacher-training staff appeared to be under increasing pressure, again due to the financial restrictions imposed on the institutions by central government. The move towards increasing productivity and greater efficiency in teacher-training departments has also made it more difficult for tutors to provide those aspects of the training which are expensive in time. Hargie and Maidment's estimate that '... we expect student involvement in microteaching to increase in proportion, if not in absolute terms' (Hargie and Maidment, 1979) might well have been achieved, however this is no indication of the growth of microteaching but an indication of the tremendous decline of teacher-training places.

The degree of differentiation

The evidence from the survey shows an increasing tendency towards differentiation in the use of microteaching. A few institutions continue to offer the Stanford model of microteaching but an increasing number appear to be developing more economical models by using live and audio facilities. The change in the whole climate of teacher training towards more school-based courses has also added to this differentiation, with some tutors exploring a microteaching model more suited to the school classroom situation as opposed to the special microteaching laboratory on campus.

The degree of capitalization

Electronic equipment for video recording has become more reliable, more effective and cheaper. The trend towards microteaching studios with several black and white television cameras and a video mixer in a fixed location, although still used where they have been established, appear to have given way to a portable colour camera and video recorder with the facility for end-on electronic editing. This supports the tendency for microteaching to be used in improvised rooms and school classrooms.

The degree of utilization

The survey suggest that there has been a fuller integration of microteaching into other areas of the curriculum, but this appears to have had a counter effect on the use of microteaching in teacher training as existing facilities have been put under even greater pressure. Because of the demands from other courses and the greater pressures on, sometimes diminishing, technical assistance, to avoid timetable clashes and possible disappoint many tutors have chosen not to require the sophisticated facilities and to operate microteaching in a simpler way or not at all.

The present survey certainly supports the view '... that the "dizzy decade" of microteaching development in the United Kingdom, from 1966-75, is being succeeded by a "quiet quinquennium" ...' (Hargie and Maidment, 1979) but, in postgraduate teacher training with its increased emphasis on a subject method professionally oriented approach, microteaching appears to have reached a fairly minimal use.

The overall picture of microteaching that this survey conveys is of a pattern of organization very different from the original Stanford model. The 'purer' form of microteaching appears to operate in relatively few institutions and, where it exists, is usually organized by education staff as a compulsory course for all PGCE students, independent of subject method courses.

The professional preparation of graduate student teachers is organized through the subject method tutors and the course pattern that has evolved consists of an early short teaching practice and one-day-a-week school experience during the remainder of the course. Many tutors, instead of operating a formal microteaching programme on campus, are looking for a school-based alternative. The subject method is the main focus of the course, although some attention appears to be placed on general 'teaching skills' and in addition there are subject-specific skills, such as demonstration in science, language exercises etc, as shown in Table 3.

The majority appear to use microteaching, if video recorded, for its cosmetic effect and as a preparation for the classroom experience in the early teaching practices. Although some acknowledgement is paid to a skills or behavioural modification approach, the time allowed and the opportunity available for students is generally so minimal that little, if anything, is likely to be achieved.

For greater detail see Kendall 1985, 1987a, 1987b.

FACTORS AFFECTING THE USE OF MICROTEACHING

The following factors appear to affect whether microteaching is used and, if so, the way in which it is used.

Subject method versus educational organization

Science staff made greater (41 per cent) use of technical assistance than those from other subject groups (approximately 15 per cent). Science and education tended to use longer

Skill specified	– – – UK – – –			
---	Univ	Poly	Coll	Total
Questioning, answers.	14	8	19	41
Explanation, explaining, exposition, giving information, instructing, presentation, teacher talk, use of examples.	15	8	9	32
Use of teaching (visual) aids, flash cards, OHP, blackboard.	11	2	8	21
Set, introduction, warm up, start, beginning, initiating.	8	3	9	20
Variety, variation of stimulus, stimulus skills, teacher live-liness, enthusiasm, arousing and sustaining interest.	5	3	11	19
Preparation, planning, manage-ment, organisation, timing, structure of lesson, pace.	7	2	10	19
Demonstration.	9	2	4	15
Use of language, clear speech, voice, communication, teaching oral.	7	3	5	15
Various, range of skills, teaching styles, global approach, methods.	7	2	4	13
Subject skills, use of science equipment.	5	1	5	11
Reinforcement, drilling.	1	3	6	10
Content, concepts, specific factual problems, problem posing, accuracy, right level of difficulty, effective learning.	6	–	4	10
Observation, evaluation, task analysis, objectives.	4	3	1	8
Movement, mobility, physical dexterity, non-verbal, bearing.	2	1	4	7
Closure.	–	2	1	3
Reading, from prepared text, story telling.	1	–	2	3
Interaction skills, reaction to feedback, pupil response.	–	–	1	1
Group work, discussion.	–	–	1	1
Control.	–	–	1	1

Table 3. *Subject-specific skills*

sessions for microlessons than the other groups. Education staff were more likely to be operating with mixed-subject groups, were more likely to make use of children and were more likely (50 per cent) to supervise microteaching with some assistance, whereas the majority of the other groups' lecturers supervised alone. This was particularly the case for the language group (91 per cent) and less true for the science (63 per cent 'sometimes' and 31 per cent 'always'). Those groups indicating 'never' were language (50 per cent), science (45 per cent) and miscellaneous (41 per cent).

Education staff were more likely (73 per cent) to make use of reteach lessons and science staff were the least likely (23 per cent). Education staff made the most (38 per cent) use of audio recording and the language staff made the most (41 per cent) use of 'live' microlessons, the majority of staff not using either, particularly the social studies (88 per cent) and science (74 per cent).

Education staff were less likely (44 per cent as compared with 75 per cent) to use microteaching before school teaching practice and more likely (50 per cent as compared with 29 per cent) to be using microteaching in-between teaching practices. The main difference appeared to lie between microteaching organized and supervised by education staff and microteaching as part of a subject method course. The former appeared more likely to operate a form of microteaching closer to the Stanford model, including, as well as reteach lessons, observation schedules, use of children in the longer period available between teaching practices as indicated above, but also lecture, handout and demonstration preparation, discussion after playback, more than two microlessons for each student, more sophisticated black and white television and an assessment both specific and global.

School-based versus campus-based teacher training

The most significant factor which has arisen out of the total exercise of analysing the data, is the underlying philosophical approach to teacher training. The developments of teacher training in the United Kingdom in recent years have highlighted the change in this philosophy. The traditional college-based model has been replaced by a more innovative school-based model of teacher training. The crux of the issue seems to be that, if teacher-training is seen as an activity which takes place on a college campus and consists largely of lecture, tutorial and seminar activities leading to formal written examinations, then microteaching is an exciting innovation and has a lot to offer, whether it is live or recorded, involves real children or peer groups, is a global teaching activity or concerned with specific skills.

On the other hand, if teacher training is seen to take place in a school environment with the student working alongside interested and cooperative practitioners, and involved in what are seen as real issues and problems with real classes of real children, then microteaching appears limited by its artificiality. There may still be a place for microteaching but it is likely to be restricted to the early preparation a student teacher needs before first entering the real classroom.

REFERENCES

Allen, D.W. and Ryan, K.A. (1969) *Microteaching*. Addison-Wesley, Reading, Mass.

Hargie, O.D.W. and Maidment, P. (1979) *Microteaching in Perspective*. Blackstaff Press, Ulster Polytechnic.

Kendall, G. (1985) A comparative study of the use of microteaching and an analysis of the factors which affect its use in one-year postgraduate teacher training courses. Unpublished PhD Thesis, University of Natal.

Kendall, G. (1987a) A survey of attitudes towards the use of microteaching in postgraduate teacher training institutions in the United Kingdom and South Africa. *South African Journal of Education,* **7,** 1, 20-33.

Kendall, G. (1987b) A factor analysis of staff attitudes to the use of microteaching in postgraduate teacher training courses in Southern African universities. *South African Journal of Education,* **1,** 1, 81-5.

McIntyre, D., MacLeod, G. and Griffiths, R. (eds) (1977) *Investigations of Microteaching.* Croom Helm, London.

Section 6:
Other issues

42. Self-instructional materials and students' attainment of application skills: a short intensive orientation course in the first year at the University of Bahrain

Fatima H Al-Ahmed, *Directorate of Curricula, Ministry of Education, Bahrain*

Summary: An experimental study has been undertaken in which a comparison was made between the attainment gains of two groups of Bahrain first-year university students. The use of self-instructional materials produces significant gains in learning when compared with conventional teaching. These differences are also seen when the attainment of applications skills of higher order cognitive skills (work-study skills) is compared to the attainment of basic language skills (lower order cognitive skills). The attainment of higher order cognitive skills is very poor in conventional classroom situations. The significance of these results is discussed in terms of curriculum design and students' performance in the classroom.

INTRODUCTION

The need for modification of the present English syllabus used in the first year at Gulf Polytechnic, University of Bahrain has been recognized. In this study the effects of lessons based on the application of a systems approach of curriculum design and lessons conventionally taught were compared. The experiment was conducted in English language in both basic language skills and work-study skills (application skills). The author's main purpose was to find out if students' attainment is influenced by self-instructional materials. Rowntree (1981) has distinguished between lower cognitive level objectives (knowledge, comprehension and application) and higher cognitive level ones (analysis, synthesis and evaluation) which were originally classified and arranged by Bloom (1956) with regard to difficulty: level 3 being more demanding than level 2, level 4 more demanding than level 3, and so on. A further aim of this study was to compare the performance of students in the basic language skills (lower cognitive level objectives) with that in the work-study skills (higher cognitive level objectives) in order to ascertain whether any gains achieved by students were attributable only to lower-cognitive level objectives. It might be difficult to make this comparison as Rowntree (1981) noted:

'It is generally easier to set tests at the lower rather than at the higher cognitive levels. If you are not careful you may find, for instance, that your assessment is operating chiefly at Bloom's levels 1, 2 and maybe 3.' (p 182)

The design of this experimental study involved two groups of part-time technician certificate students (N=20) and full-time technician certificate students (N=17). Those students were 18+ years old and taught by the present author while working part-time in the first semester of the first-year level at the university.

METHODOLOGY

In each skill area, this author identified two study units, designed and produced self-instructional materials and developed teaching guides and associated tests. The purpose of selected units was to bridge the gap between the secondary school-leaving stage and first-year university by means of a short intensive orientation course for one semester. The aim of this proposed orientation course was to reinforce the structures that students had already studied in the secondary school and prepare them for first-year university.

Units chosen were classified as:

- orientation course 1: Basic and related English skills (two units); and
- orientation course 2: Work-study skills (two units).

Each of these units was made available as follows:

- by a set of aims and objectives as stated in table 1;
- by self-instructional texts; and
- by pre- and post-tests relating to objectives of each unit beeing given to all the groups in the study.

The orientation course materials were taught by the author of this study in three experimental groups:

- Group A: 20 students attending the part-time technician programme were briefed

Orientation course 1 (2 units) Basic / Related English Skills	Orientation course 2 (2 units) Work-Study Skills
Aim : to increase comprehension and promote fluency in using English socially.	Aim : Use work-study skills to learn foreign language. -to develop work-study skills such as visual and reference materials.
Specific Objectives: -students will be able to: -demonstrate accuracy in basic and related language skills such as listening. speaking, reading and writing.	Specific Objectives: -students will be able to: -seek out information from maps, graphs and tables. -select study-skills such as looking up words in a dictionary alphabetising, using an index card and locating information. -comprehend the number system, terms and operation used in mathematics. (i.e., Mathematics language expressions).

Table 1. *An example of aims and objectives related to orientation units*

with the instructions of each unit and were given an hour to answer the experimental materials in class. Those who had not finished were asked to take each unit home and return it within a week.

- Group B: 17 students attending the full-time technician programme were presented with the same materials. They were briefed with instructions on each unit for about ten minutes in class and then were asked to finish the materials in their free time and return each unit within a week.
- Group C: 16 students worked as a control group who received their normal lessons. Those students were given the pre-tests related to the experimental units at the start of the experiment and after two weeks they were given the post-tests. The other two experimental groups of students had taken the same pre- and post-tests.

RESULTS

Results of the two experimental groups and the control group are show in terms of mean

GROUP	COURSE	UNIT	PRE-TEST	POST-TEST	GAIN-RATIO	NO. OF STUDENTS
A	1	1	$\bar{x}$ 17	$\bar{x}$ 82	78 %	20
			s.d. 9.53	s.d. 9.79		
		2	$\bar{x}$ 16	$\bar{x}$ 78	74 %	
			s.d. 9.16	s.d. 9.79		
	2	1	$\bar{x}$ 18	$\bar{x}$ 86	82 %	
			s.d. 9.79	s.d. 8		
		2	$\bar{x}$ 16	$\bar{x}$ 85	82 %	
			s.d. 9.16	s.d. 8.66		
B	1	1	$\bar{x}$ 28.8	$\bar{x}$ 78.2	70 %	17
			s.d. 4.52	s.d. 12		
		2	$\bar{x}$ 15.9	$\bar{x}$ 84	80 %	
			s.d. 9.06	s.d. 9.11		
	2	1	$\bar{x}$ 13.5	$\bar{x}$ 84	81 %	
			s.d. 7.6	s.d. 9.11		
		2	$\bar{x}$ 15.9	$\bar{x}$ 82.9	79 %	
			s.d. 9.06	s.d. 950		
C	1	1	$\bar{x}$ 10	$\bar{x}$ 25	16 %	16
			s.d. 0	s.d. 8.66		
		2	$\bar{x}$ 13.75	$\bar{x}$ 36.25	26 %	
			s.d. 7.80	s.d. 9.26		
	2	1	$\bar{x}$ 20	$\bar{x}$ 41	26 %	
			s.d. 10	s.d. 9.9		
		2	$\bar{x}$ 23.75	$\bar{x}$ 43.75	26 %	
			s.d. 9.26	s.d. 9.26		

Table 2. *Mean gain ratio for the treatment and control groups in Orientation Course 1 (Basic/Related English Skills) and Orientation Course 2 (Work-Study Skills)*

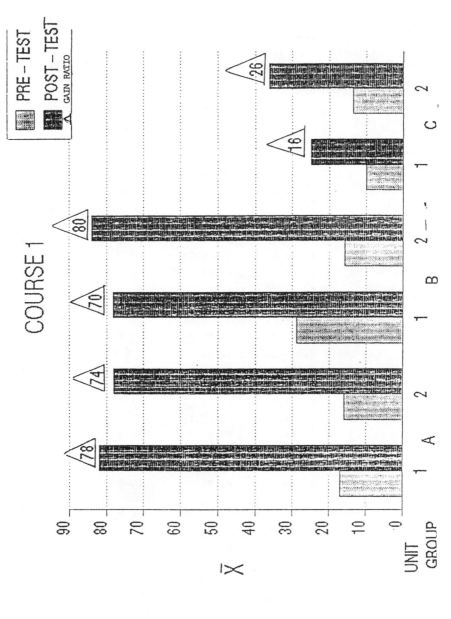

Figure 1a. *Mean gain ratio for the treatment and control group in Orientation Course 1 (Basic and Related English Skills)*

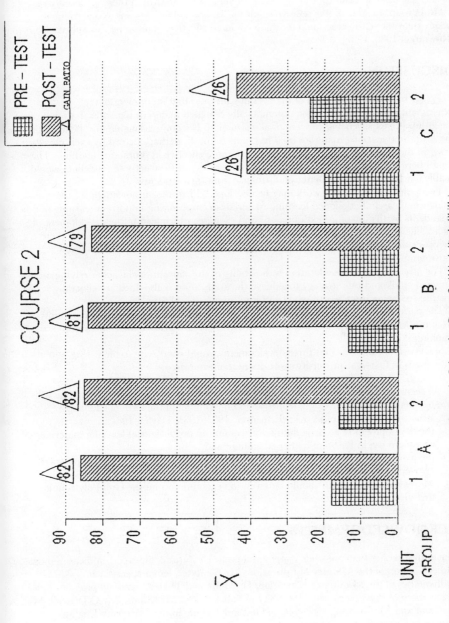

Figure 1b. *Mean gain ratio for treatment and control group in Orientation Course 2 (Work-Study Skills)*

pre- and post-test scores for each course (Oppenheim, 1966) in Table 2 and Figure 1. These results indicate much higher scores obtained by experimental groups on the post-tests. These groups of students used systematically designed learning materials as the basis for the lessons. The gains they achieved are significantly better than those achieved by the control group. In spite of this positive result the author's main aim was to determine to what extent the self-instructional teaching could be effectively taught by this approach (Rowntree, 1986; 1987).

DISCUSSION

It is clear from an examination of the overall gain ratio that attainment of the experimental groups (A, B) using systematically designed materials is greater than that of the group (C) experiencing conventional instruction. It seems reasonable to conclude that the structured learning materials used in group A and B, perhaps helped by their novelty value in the experimental situation, have been more effective in promoting learning. The results here might suggest that the provision of such detailed, structured guidelines would enable teachers to derive a better performance from their students.

Two points raised by this work may be developed. First, the author might see the influence of carefully designed learning materials in emphasizing important learning points to students by the use of in-text questions and exercises which lead to the development of such skills. It is interesting to know that such materials can be used by students at their own pace and in their own time (since they are available to students outside normal classroom times).

The other point for consideration is the ability of the conventional teacher relying on ill-designed chalk-and-talk strategy to achieve the application skills which are generally regarded as being more worth while and important.

The performance of the control group suggests also that the existing teacher training programmes leave a lot to be desired in terms of classroom performance and lesson-planning skills.

In conclusion, it seems that three developments would contribute to increasing attainment in first-year university short orientation courses:

- it seems to be desirable for those involved in curriculum planning to ensure that all teachers receive detailed guidelines to lesson planning in the form of carefully structured aims and objectives (Rowntree, 1981; 1986; Davies, 1981);
- the development of a curriculum resources unit to produce local learning materials for classroom use in Bahraini higher education; and
- the learning of self-instructional units through interactive educational computers (the University English language centre is provided with educational computers). Moreover such students should be given full exemption from the Gulf Polytechnic first-year orientation course.

ACKNOWLEDGEMENTS

The author wishes to express her grateful thanks to Dr Zahran, an expert in measurement and evaluation in the Ministry of Education; Mr Khunder, senior specialist in mathematics in the Ministry of Education; Dr Mohamed Thabet, associate professor in the Department of Psychology, the University of Bahrain; and Mr Milton, Mr O'Driscoll, Mr McGreal and Mr Greason, specialists in Gulf Polytechnic in the University English Language Centre, who gave unstintingly of their time and advice during the testing and developing of the experimental self-instructional units.

REFERENCES

Bloom, B.S. (ed) (1956) *Taxonomy of Educational Objectives, Handbook 1: The Cognitive Domain.* Mackay, New York.

Davies, I.K. (1981) *Instructional Techniques.* McGraw-Hill Book Company, New York.

Oppenheim, A. (1966) *Questionnaire Design and Attitude Measurement.* Heinemann, London.

Rowntree, D. (1981) *Developing Courses for Students.* McGraw-Hill Book Company, London.

Rowntree, D. (1986) *Teaching Through Self-Instruction.* Kogan Page, London.

Rowntree, D. (1987) *Assessing Students: How Shall we Know Them?* Kogan Page, London.

43. Aspects of analysis in the derivation of a training requirement for thermal imaging recognition training

Major Dennis Quilter, *Army School of Training Support, Beaconsfield, UK*

Summary: This paper is concerned with the derivation of a training requirement for thermal imaging (TI) recognition training using front-end analysis techniques. The use of hierarchical task analysis (HTA) and decision flowcharts is described as a means of specifying an ideal model of the job performance. This is then expanded to include the conditions under which the performance is carried out and the standard of performance anticipated in the task. The difficulty of establishing standards where the job (ie battlefield) environment does not exist is discussed.

The paper deals with the utility of the 'ideal model' to:

- apprise industry of the training requirement;
- indicate whether feasibility studies should be implemented;
- evaluate existing or proposed solutions to the training problem; and
- undertake a cost-benefit analysis of the training solutions.

INTRODUCTION

A number of different thermal imaging (TI) sights have been, or are being, introduced into the British Army. These devices are employed in surveillance, acquisition of target, and target engagement. In each of these roles there is a requirement to identify what is observed as basis for subsequent tactical decisions. Crucially the recognition of targets as 'enemy' precedes weapons engagement.

Armoured fighting vehicle (AFV) and aircraft recognition training in the normal visual mode is currently conducted in the Army. However, because thermal images are very different from visual images, particularly at medium and long ranges, there is no natural transfer of recognition ability from normal to TI images. This new need for operator training was recognized and the Director of Army Training commissioned the Army School of Training Support (ASTS) to study the problem. The aim of the study was to:

'recommend training methods which maximize the ability of operators to detect, recognize and identify thermal imaging (TI) targets within the performance capabilities of the various devices.'

This paper describes the methodology employed to derive a training requirement which enables the above aim to be met.

NEEDS ANALYSIS

It is generally accepted (Kaufman,1976; Thomas, 1982) that needs analysis is conducted to establish broad goals which should be pursued to remedy a deficiency in job performance. This concept of 'deficiency' is central to needs analysis and can be applied in three areas:

- environmental deficiencies including equipment infrastructure and operational area problems;
- manpower deficiencies either in quality or quantity; and
- training deficiencies.

Often all three are interrelated, but care must be taken that attempts to rectify problems are strictly related to manifest deficiencies. Thus it is not axiomatic that training is a solution to a defined job performance problem.

In the current study the TI devices are either in service or are shortly to come into service and have been subject to the usual human factors analysis (eg ergonomics). Earlier concept definition studies had not recommended any changes in personnel selection criteria to take account of the introduction of thermal imagery in the Army, and hence the devices have been allocated to existing unit personnel. It was the user who gave evidence for the existence of a skill/knowledge deficiency by declaring that he did not yet have the ability to identify potential TI targets on the battlefield. An equipment solution to the problem via automatic means (eg automatic target cuers) is not yet feasible, although work is being conducted in this area. Therefore a training solution seemed appropriate.

At the inception of the study some training in TI recognition was being conducted as Army training establishments responded to the problem. This training was, however, varied across different users and at an embryonic stage. Industry was also aware of a potential market for TI recognition training support materials (and therefore profit) but was hampered by the dearth of source material which mainly lay in the hands of the military. Clearly a methodology had to be applied which would permit the evaluation of existing and proposed solutions and also give encouragement to future development. It followed that the training requirement should be derived via front-end analysis (FEA) techniques as an adjunct (in some cases rather belated) to the main equipment development cycle. The overall methodology adopted for the study is shown diagrammatically in Figure 1.

FRONT END ANALYSIS

Since 1969, the British Army has had in place the 'systems approach to training' (SAT) as both a conceptual and a practitioners' tool to aid the design of training. The main elements of this system are:

- analysis;
- training objective specification;
- design; and
- implementation of training and validation.

The methodology adopted for the TI recognition training study fits into SAT's conceptual framework where the key analytical tools employed are hierarchical task analysis (HTA), decision flowcharts and job performance objectives (JPOs).

Hierarchical task analysis and decision flowcharts

HTA breaks down a major task (eg 'destroy a target with a main battle tank') into its

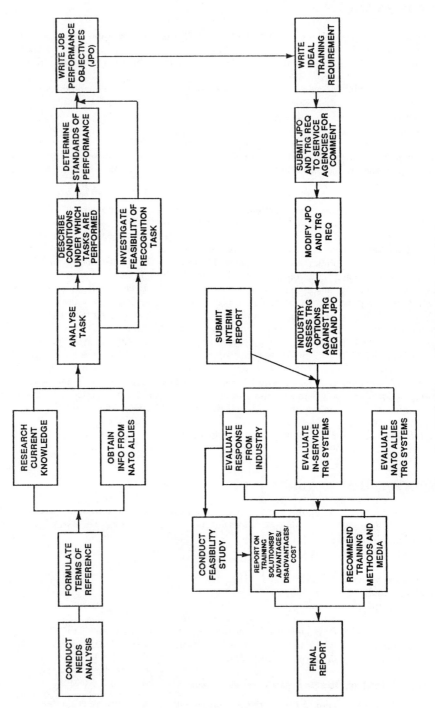

Figure 1. *ASTS TI recognition training study-methodology*

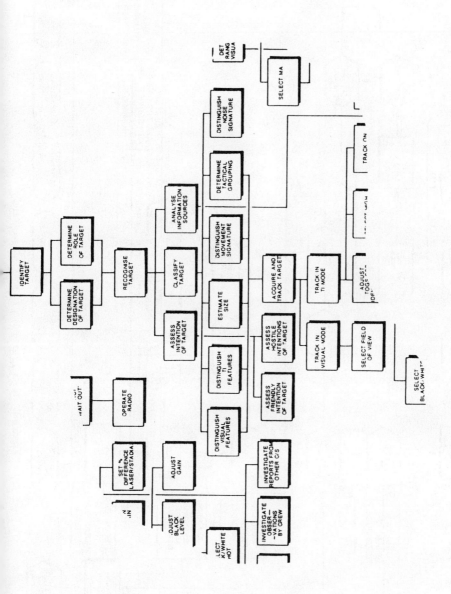

Figure 2. *Section from a hierarchical task analysis*

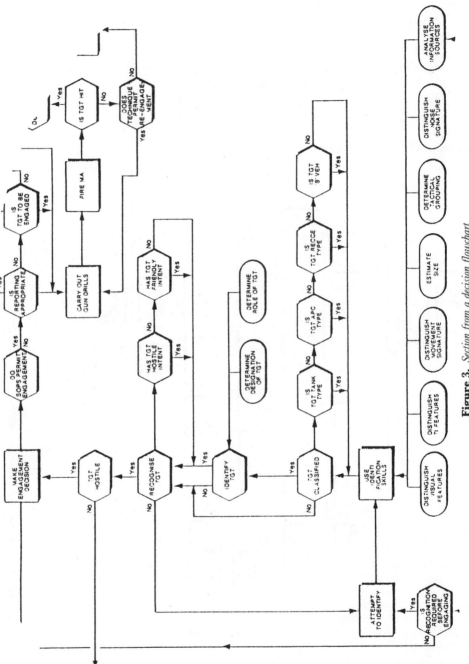

Figure 3. *Section from a decision flowchart*

constituent minor tasks. A section of a HTA from the study is shown in Figure 2. These tasks are written in behavioural terms and at a later stage permit the derivation of the enabling skills and knowledges that underpin operator performances. HTA provides a clear description of the behavioural sub-tasks that lead to a complete performance of the major task but it does not show the decision-making processes upon which the performance of the sub-tasks depends. Decision flowcharts were thus derived, emulating the algorithms a competent operator would apply in a battlefield situation.

It can be seen from Figure 3 that the decision flowchart provides a blueprint for the subsequent development of any trainer designed to practise a trainee in the application of such algorithms.

Job performance objectives

Together, HTA and decision flowcharts model the performance of a competent operator, but a description of a job cannot be complete unless it includes the conditions under which the job is performed and the standards of competence required. These aspects (performance, conditions, standards) are written into the JPO.

The military training consultant is here faced with the dilemma that although the full operational environment does not exist until battle is joined, he is nonetheless required to define that environment. The conditions are defined by reference to operational analysis data. This provides information on anticipated tactical scenarios and the command, communication and control procedures appropriate to the way in which the weapon systems are to be deployed. To this are added meteorological, geographical and psychological environmental data. Standards are derived from empirical data or from the best subjective data available.

The JPO thus represents the closest approximation to the operational task that can be achieved. In this respect it is an ideal model of the training that would lead to job competence. However, aside from the obvious difficulty of reproducing a realistic battlefield environment for training, the development of any training system is susceptible to financial and infrastructure resource constraints. Realistic training, even if affordable, may also be restricted where current technology is incapable of producing an effective solution. In some cases realistic training may also be too dangerous. The great utility of JPOs is that if they are written in the same performance, condition and standards format that is required of training objectives (TO) under the systems approach to training, then these constraints are made explicit via the differences between the two objectives. The advantages of this can be seen in the procedures now used to define the training requirement.

DEFINING THE REQUIREMENT

First the JPO and task analyses were submitted to selected commercial organizations together with a draft requirement. This included the learning design features derived from an investigation into perceptual recognition theory carried out concurrently with the front-end analysis phase. Together, these documents gave industry an opportunity to propose high-, medium- and low-cost options as training solutions.

Second, the JPO served as a tool which was used to evaluate proposed solutions to the training problem set against the needs analysis concept of 'deficiency'. For example, one possible solution to the TI recognition training requirement is instruction using slides of the equipments to be learned. This has the benefit of low cost but is deficient because of lack of dynamism; lack of a universal set of possible targets under all environmental (meteorological, organizational, psychological, physical) and range conditions; the lack of contextual cues such as intelligence, recce and battle picture information; the lack of assistance by crew members or other friendly forces; and the absence of 'hands on' use of the operational equipment (sights, target image adjustments, fields of view, etc). A comparison between the job performance objectives and training objectives which define any proposed training solution thus readily yields the deficiencies between the job performance and the output of training.

Thirdly, these comparisons have been used as a basis for a cost-benefit analysis of 'in-house' and commercial training solution options to the TI recognition training problem. This has led in turn to a feasibility study into the application of interactive video (IV) technology to the training problem.

Taking account of any feasibility studies, and following the cost/benefit stage, the training consultant is now in a position to state the training options to the user (client) in terms of the advantages and disadvantages of each, set against cost.

It is now a matter of policy as to which training option is accepted. The policy maker must weigh the priority of the task against current constraints. TOs in this context are an expression of the performance, conditions and standards accepted or achievable in training, while the deficiencies between these objectives and the JPOs are clearly recognized. If the task priority changes, or constraints are eased in the future, then resources can be directed to match more closely the respective JPOs and TOs.

CONCLUSION

The process of utilizing JPOs as an ideal model against which to evaluate solutions ultimately enables the consultant to write a specific training requirement; a necessity in today's climate of competitive tendering and fixed-price contracts.

REFERENCES

Kaufman, R. (1976) *Needs Assessment: What it is and how to do it.* University Consortium on Instructional Development and Technology, San Diego, California.
Thomas, E.A. (1982) Training needs identification: a turning point. *Performance and Instruction Journal,* **21,** 8, 6-8.

44. An evaluation method of the THE multi-media CAI system using semantic structure analysis

Makoto Takeya and Naoto Nakamura, *Takushoku University, Hachioji, Tokyo, Japan*
Tatsunori Matsui and Fumiyuki Terada, *Waseda University, Shinjyuku-ku, Tokyo, Japan*

Summary: Semantic structure analysis is a means of analysing data taken from questionnaire rating scales and is important in evaluating the effectiveness and availability of the CAI system from student viewpoints. First, a semantic structure analysis method (SS analysis) as an analysis method for a graphic representation of a questionnaire item is presented. The paper then discusses a method for constructing and utilizing a synthesized item-relational structure (semantic-structure, or SS, graph). Second, we mention briefly our multi-media CAI system, a microcomputer-controlled videodisk system called the THE system. An application of SS analysis to evaluate THE CAI system is presented. Third, the paper shows an SS graph as the SS analysis results on effectiveness and usability of hardware and courseware functions of the THE CAI system.

SEMANTIC STRUCTURE ANALYSIS

The SS analysis method is a relational structuring method among questionnaire items based on rating-scale data (Takeya, 1987). When the investigation results are shown graphically with respect to these items, we can more easily understand the structure of students' opinions. This graphic representation is called a semantic-structure (or SS) graph.

In this section, the fundamental principle of the SS graph is discussed. Table 1 shows examples of two student rating scores arranged in order of total scores. Individual data in each example are presented for five questionnaire items and ten students. Each item score consists of five categories (ie from one to five shown in the body of the tables). In Table 1, as far as sequences of items and total scores of individual items are concerned, the structures of the two examples are equivalent to each other.

First, in example 'a', response scores of items one and two are compared. Each student score for item one is larger than or equal to the corresponding student score for item two. In this case an arrow is drawn from item two to item one. After making comparisons, each pair of item scores is executed in order; we can get the results of an SS graph as shown in Figure 1a.

In example 'b', comparing item one with item two an arrow is drawn in the same manner. Next, the relationship between items two and three is investigated. There are some students whose scores for item two are less than the corresponding scores for item three: students three, seven, eight and ten. In this case an arrow is not drawn. The results are shown in Figure 1b. Thus the structure in each example is different.

Item

	①	②	③	④	⑤	Total
1	5	5	5	4	4	23
2	5	5	4	4	4	22
3	5	4	4	4	3	20
4	5	4	4	3	3	19
5	5	4	3	3	2	17
6	4	3	2	2	2	14
7	4	3	2	2	1	12
8	3	2	2	2	1	10
9	3	2	2	1	1	9
10	3	2	1	1	1	8
Total	42	34	30	26	22	

(a)

Item

	①	②	③	④	⑤	Total
1	5	5	4	5	4	23
2	5	4	5	2	5	21
3	5	3	5	2	5	20
4	5	5	2	4	2	18
5	5	5	2	3	1	16
6	4	4	2	3	1	14
7	4	2	4	2	1	13
8	3	2	3	2	1	11
9	3	3	1	2	1	10
10	3	1	2	1	1	8
Total	42	34	30	26	22	

(b)

Table 1. *Examples of rating score tables*

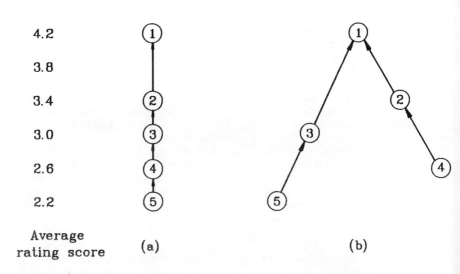

Figure 1. *Models of SS graphs corresponding to Table 1*

In the case where an arrow may be drawn from item j to item k, it means that each student's score for item j is never less than corresponding students' score for item k. However, in general we cannot obtain this 'ideal' data structure. In actual data among many students, we have to set some tolerance conditions for arrow drawing.

Theoretical aspects of SS analysis are presented in Appendix 1.

THE MULTI-MEDIA CAI SYSTEM

Next we will discuss application of the SS analysis to evaluation of our multi-media CAI system called the THE system (Terada et al, 1981). Hardware construction of THE system is a personal computer connected to a laser optical videodisk player (Figure 2).

With good software, the THE system is expected to have the following features:

- *Rich image and sound storage.* The THE system can store information incomparably richer in quantity than VTR or cassette tape.
- *Quick random access.* The image or sound needed is instantaneously available.
- *Learning with human-like machines.* Thanks to the recorded sharp images and voice of instructors in addition to adaptable courseware, a student feels more as if they are taught directly and individually by instructors.
- *Usefulness for individualized learning.* Teachers do not have to operate the machine nor do they have to be in attendance. Results of each use are recorded and diagnosed automatically so that teachers can make the most of the students' achievement in their classroom guidance and teaching. The student can study steadily without fear of failure.

EVALUATION OF THE SYSTEM

We have been carrying out a questionnaire survey for high-school students who learn

Figure 2. *Basic appearance of the THE CAI system*

mathematics using the THE system courseware. The questionnaire items are as follows:

- The display is sharp and clear.
- The time from one display to another is appropriate.
- The THE system is user-friendly.
- My preliminary knowledge was sufficient.
- The level of the program contents was appropriate.
- It is effective to set time limits for learning.
- The time allowed for the embedded test was long enough.
- I was interested in the presentation of the program.
- The quantity of voice presentation was appropriate.
- The voice presentation is easy to understand.
- I could understand the program.
- I would like to continue to learn using the THE system.
- Compared with conventional methods of study, I found this method more exciting.
- I could learn more by using this method.
- I have got more interested in mathematics through this system.

A simple rating scale on student opinions for the THE system, as perceived by students, is used on the questionnaire:

- strongly disagree
- disagree
- uncertain
- agree
- strongly agree

The results of students' opinions of the THE system, based on the SS graph, are shown in Figure 3. From the SS graph we can find out a lot of information to evaluate the availability and effectiveness of the THE system.
Partial results are as follows:

- Ordering relationship from items one and ten to item twelve. A large majority of the students hope to continue to learn by using the THE system (Q12). It is assumed that the reason lies in the sharpness of the display (Q1) and easy understanding of voice presentation (Q10).
- Ordering relationship from item eight to item fifteen. A large number of students have got more interested in mathematics learning using this system (Q15). It is considered that the highly interesting presentation of the program (Q8) result in the awakening of their interest in mathematics.
- Equivalence relationship among items 10, 11 and 13. Simple understanding of voice presentation (Q10), high understanding of the program (Q11) and excitement of the THE system utilization (Q13) have almost similar scores and have equivalence relationships. It seems that easy understanding of voice presentation is strongly related to understanding and interest in the program contents.

As noted above, we could obtain useful information on the THE system. Observing the SS graph on the THE system, the investigation results are in agreement with features of the THE system previously mentioned under 'Multi-media CAI system'.

CONCLUSION

This paper has described an SS analysis method for rating scale data and its application to

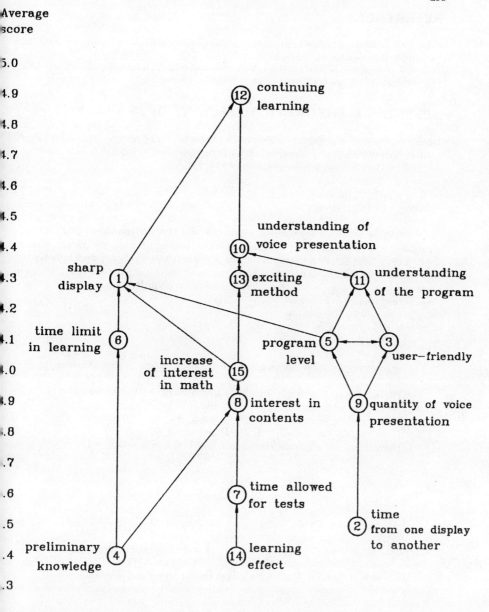

Figure 3. *An SS graph for THE CAI system evaluation*

a multi-media CAI system. More particularly, this paper has surveyed a questionnaire of the THE system from user viewpoints. As a result, we have shown the effectiveness and usability of the CAI system in addition to the utility of the SS analysis method.

REFERENCES

Takeya, M. (1987) Semantic structure analysis among questionnaire items using a rating scale method. *Behaviometrika*, **14**, 2, 10-17.
Terada, F., Hirose, K. and Ono, T. (1981) Instruction technique on using video disc systems. *IFIP Proceedings of 3rd World Conference on Computer Education*, 343-349.

APPENDIX 1: THEORETICAL ASPECTS OF SS ANALYSIS

Denote numbers of students and questionnaire items by N and n respectively. It is assumed that each of the items is scored in 1,2,...., or m. Therefore, we can express student response data in matrix representation of X as follows:

$X = [x_{ij}](i=1,2,...,N; j=1,2,...,n)$
Where $x_{ij} = 1,2,...,$ or m.

Ordering the relationship from item j to item k, it is logically considered that each student score from k is never less than the corresponding student score for any student i. In a cross-table between items j and k, let N_{qr} denote the number of students who respond q for item j and r for item k. Theoretically there exists an ordering relationship from j to k: $N_{qr} = 0(q>r)$. So the tolerance condition on ordering is expressed by the ordering coefficient as follows:

$$r_{jk} = 1- \bullet (q-r)N_{qr}/[N(m-1)]$$
$$q>r$$

Taking into consideration this situation, the following definitions are introduced:

(i)   There exists an ordering relationships $I_j \rightarrow I_k$, iff $r_{jk} > 0.93$ otherwise $I_j \rightarrow I_k$
(ii) There exists ordering $I_j \rightarrow I_k$ iff $I_j \rightarrow I_k$ and $I_k \rightarrow I_j$
(iii) There exists ordering $I_k \rightarrow I_j$ iff $I_j \rightarrow I_k$ and $I_k \rightarrow I_j$
(iv) There exists equivalence $I_j \rightarrow I_k$ iff $i_j I_k$ and $I_k \rightarrow I_j$
(v)   There exists no relationship between I_j and I_k iff $I_j \rightarrow I_k$ and $I_k \rightarrow I_j$

OXFORD
POLYTECHNIC
LIBRARY